RE:INVENTO

Expat's Guide to Reinventing Your Career and Identity

From "where do I even fit" to "this is where I belong"

Ana Denis

First Printing 2026

ISBN: 979-8-90417-077-6 (Paperback)
ISBN: 979-8-90417-075-2 (eBook)

Some names and identifying details have been changed to protect the privacy of individuals.

Cover design: Ana Denis

Dedication

To my loving husband Ivan,
You are my light. Thank you for just being there.

To my dear friend Julia,
Thank you for the deep conversations that inspired the beginning of Reinvento.

To every brave woman who opened her heart
and agreed to share her story in this book,
Thank you.

To the Female Ventures and TEDx communities, whose gatherings introduced me to so many
remarkable people,
Thank you.

To every brave, gifted woman and man across the world
who decided to pursue a new life and work that genuinely fulfills them,
Welcome to the journey.

Table of Contents

Where Do I Even Fit?

Finding a job in a new country is not what you expected, not what you prepared for, and definitely not as simple as "just apply."

Your morning starts with a glance at your phone. You've only been looking for a job for a few days, so the process still feels hopeful — that early stage where optimism is still alive. Starting a new chapter, becoming a new version of yourself — isn't that exciting?

Yesterday, you applied for a few roles. Any interview invitations? You swipe through the notifications: twelve marketing emails, five app alerts, and absolutely no interviews.

No biggie. You make breakfast for the family, pour a cup of coffee, and open LinkedIn to continue the process. And then it happens.

You stumble upon *the* job.

Every line makes your pulse quicken. You check every box — and not in the "I guess I could do this" way, but in the "this is who I am" way. It has everything: the industry you've dreamed of, a company that feels stable and human, a compensation package that makes sense, and — most importantly — a challenge that feels within reach.

You're a 200% match — even by the research-proven women's standard of applying only when we meet every requirement. Honestly, you'd still be a match if you cut your qualifications in half.

You start researching the company, and they turn out to be fantastic. Their values resonate. Their mission feels like something you once wrote in a diary. You can see yourself walking into that building. As you imagine the projects, the challenges, the person you would become by doing this work, this feels like a chance to finally become more you.

You imagine telling your friends, "I got the job at XYZ," and feeling their admiration — not for the status, but for the fit.

With shaking hands, you open your CV file. You fine-tune job titles to match the listing, add keywords to get past the AI filter, polish every bullet point. Then comes the cover letter — the one you refuse to outsource to ChatGPT because this is not an average opportunity, but a true chance to change your life. Suddenly every tiny detail feels critical. Should the cover letter be more formal or personal? How do you express your excitement without sounding desperate? And how do you finally get their attention as a standout candidate?

You decide to sleep on it. Fresh eyes always help. Except you can barely close your eyes because of how exciting this opportunity feels. By morning, you're up early, proofreading your CV and cover letter. After double-checking your contact details, you attach the updated version of both documents to the application form, review the file version and contact details one last time, and hit Apply.

"We have received your application."

It's wild how hopeful this little moment can feel. For a moment, the world is full of possibility. You start checking your email more often, already picturing the thrill of seeing that interview invitation. The "tell me about yourself" pitch gets a few practice rounds. You live in the "what if," and it feels good.

Finally, the notification you've been waiting for pops up.

"An important update on your application."

Your heart jumps as you open it.

"Thank you for applying. Your experience and personality, however, are worth nothing here. We have found another candidate who is better than you in every possible way. Please never apply again. Your skills are useless."

Of course, that's not what the email says. But that's exactly how it feels. In that moment, you feel as if a part of yourself just dies.

You've studied hard, worked hard, tried hard.

You did everything right. You have the qualifications, the experience, the recommendations. How could this be a rejection without even one interview? One chance to show who you are?

"Do not hesitate to apply again…"

An important update on my application?

Please, tell me more while I emotionally disintegrate.

When Change Arrives Uninvited

If you're an expat, you've been there.

Back home, you built a career. You earned trust, took on bigger roles, and became the person people turned to when things mattered. You were always invited because your reputation opened doors before you even walked in. You were accustomed to be one of the most qualified people in the room.

But now that you've moved, you apply for the very roles you once excelled in — and still do — and the only responses are rejections or silence. Some days you almost cry, some days you vent on LinkedIn, and some days you Google "how to monetize my existential crisis." You keep applying, adjusting, rewriting, yet the outcome barely changes.

And with every rejection, a question you've been afraid to name finally appears: *If everything I built doesn't count here, where do I even fit?*

That question is where this book began for me.

A new country changes you — including the way you see yourself. In your old life, there was a foundation beneath you — a home, a family, a job, a circle of people who know your name. These things steady us and form the inner belief that we're capable, grounded, and able to handle whatever tomorrow brings.

Then suddenly, that foundation is gone. Your university doesn't ring a bell anymore. Companies and brands once spoken with pride met with a polite, confused "sorry, could you say that again." It's not just about translating a professional life into a new culture — it's about rebuilding a professional identity and a network from zero, often in a language that isn't your first. And slowly, the job search becomes a deeper question.

Not just *What do I do?* but *Who am I here?*

Rebuilding that sense of self is already hard.

But sometimes life adds challenges you never asked for.

Some Slavic countries, for instance, have seen a lot of political and socioeconomic turbulence in recent years. In Belarus in 2020, people protested after a presidential election that independent observers widely described as rigged. As the government responded with violence and mass arrests, many people were in danger and had to flee for speaking out.

In 2022, Russia invaded Ukraine, triggering a full-scale war that forced millions of Ukrainians to leave their homes and seek safety elsewhere. And for Russians who opposed the war, expressing that openly wasn't safe, which led many of them to leave too.

I come from this part of the world, so these events weren't abstract to me. They shaped the lives of people I knew — friends, colleagues, neighbors — almost overnight. Suddenly, I was surrounded by stories of lives torn apart. They had lost much — and in some cases, everything — that once held their world together. Caught in the middle of something they never chose, they were left trying to rebuild a life from pieces.

Imagine what it feels like when the whole life you've been building is simply gone.

You lose your home, because it no longer feels like home, or because it was physically destroyed.

You lose a part of your family, because they hold different views.

You lose your social circle because you're now in another country.

You lose your social status, because even if you're highly skilled, your experience doesn't always translate across borders. And in a new language, you can end up sounding far less competent than you truly are.

You lose your income, and your savings are melting.

Worst of all, you lose the feeling of basic safety you once took for granted. You can't go back, because it's no longer safe. And you don't feel safe in the new place yet, because everything is unfamiliar.

Planning beyond today becomes impossible.

For many people, it was their daily reality.

As I watched them rebuild their lives, I became curious about reinvention. After more than 100 conversations with people from all over the world — whether their reinvention was forced by external events or chosen through a career change — what struck me was how similar the inner experience looked: the disorientation, the loss of identity, the quiet grief.

And even when reinvention isn't triggered by external events, the move is rarely the only challenge. It often arrives alongside illness, loss, a breakup, a layoff, a restructuring, or a contract that suddenly isn't renewed. One moment life feels steady; the next you're facing changes you never asked for. You didn't choose the shift — it arrived anyway. Now you're left figuring out who you are in this new chapter.

The Questions That Haunt You

If you're reading this book, chances are at least one of these turning points feels familiar:

- You moved countries and your old career doesn't fit your new reality.
- You feel stuck in a role that no longer excites you.
- You're questioning whether this is really what you want to do for the rest of your life.
- Something in your personal life shifted, and now your career needs to shift too.
- You're between jobs and wondering if this is the moment to make a complete change.
- Your profession is being outplaced by AI, and you're unsure what comes next.

Different stories, same moment: something has to change.

Deep down, you know you're capable of more than what you're currently doing. The constant questioning — *"Am I making a difference? Am I in the right place?"* — becomes a pebble in your shoe that you can't ignore.

And beneath all of it sits one persistent thought: what if a career could feel like a place you actually belong?

Mid-career, the search for a new direction becomes much more than finding a new "job." It becomes a search for purpose. You've accumulated experience, self-knowledge, and a sense of what truly matters, and when your career stops matching that inner evolution, the discomfort becomes impossible to dismiss.

Naturally, this journey brings up questions:

- Who am I now?
- What do I really want?
- Where do I even fit?

What makes these questions so unsettling is that they arrive at a moment when you thought you were supposed to have it all figured out. And suddenly, you don't.

The Stories That Started It All

Like many of you, I love a good motivational story.

But when you're in the middle of a crisis, motivation alone isn't enough.

Most motivational stories from business-book heroes don't mention losing your home country or starting over in midlife. They don't talk about the shame of sending fifty applications and getting fifty rejections. They don't talk about crying into a candle in a Dutch cellar apartment from desperation because your entire life feels like a badly timed plot twist. That's not part of the standard career narrative — but for many of us, this is what our lives look like.

Being in that crisis feels like you're standing in the middle of a life you no longer recognize, trying to hold onto pieces that don't fit anymore, wondering how everyone else makes this look so effortless — wondering if you somehow missed a manual everyone else received.

In search of answers, I turned to women who have switched careers and rebuilt their lives — women who stood in that same disorienting place — and I asked how they pieced themselves back together from there.

Women whose stories weren't linear.

Women whose journeys weren't polished into TED-talk perfection.

Women who didn't pretend to have it all figured out.

My only condition for interviewing them was simple: You don't have to tell a success story. You just have to tell the truth.

Let me give you a sense of the diversity of these stories. These women's lives span more than twenty countries and cultures, including:

- Australia
- Belarus
- Denmark
- France
- Germany
- India
- Italy
- Kazakhstan
- Kenya
- Kyrgyzstan
- the Netherlands

- Poland
- Romania
- Russia
- Saudi Arabia
- Singapore
- South Africa
- Spain
- Turkey
- Ukraine
- the United Kingdom
- the United States
- Uruguay
- Venezuela

Some are stories of success. Others are stories of survival. Many are still unfolding — as all real stories are.

But every single one of them is a real story of commitment, fear, resilience, and growth. These women weren't just expat career switchers — they were rebuilding their whole identity and life itself in a new language.

This book is for any woman who has ever looked at her career and thought, *"I've worked so hard to get here... so why does it feel like something is missing?"*

For the woman who did everything right — studying, building experience, delivering results, being reliable, being competent, being the one people count on — and now feels stuck.

For the woman who is making the bold move to switch countries so she and her children can have a better future.

For the woman who is leaving behind a whole identity — a career, a reputation, a name people recognized — and is starting from zero in a place where none of it translates.

For the woman who is rebuilding her life in a new language, learning to speak up again when even ordering coffee once felt intimidating.

For the woman who is proud of her resilience, yet exhausted by how often she has to prove it.

For the woman who knows she's capable of more, but isn't sure how to begin again without losing herself in the process.

You've tried to fix it the "usual" way: new courses, new habits, new planners, new routines, new productivity hacks, new attempts at "work–life balance." You've tried to be more confident, more visible, more strategic, more assertive, more everything. And sometimes it helps, at least for a while. Until the next time you realize you're performing a role that no longer feels like you.

The problem isn't that you're not trying. Women try all the time. We try to be excellent, agreeable, resilient, grateful, "professional." We try to stay small enough to be liked and big enough to be respected. We try to reinvent ourselves quietly, politely, without inconveniencing anyone.

Effort isn't the problem. Identity is.

The real challenge of reinvention — especially for someone switching careers and countries — is the gap between who you used to be, who you are becoming, and who the world around you expects you to be.

It's the dissonance between the life you built in one country and the life you're trying to build in another.

It's the moment you realize that the tools that once worked no longer fit the person you are now.

Reinvention isn't about trying harder. It's about learning to rebuild your sense of self in a place where nothing is familiar — and choosing a direction that finally feels like yours.

Why The Classic Path Fails

If you ask your smart friend how to switch careers, they'll usually give you the same advice — the "classic path." It's simple:

1. Revise your skills.
2. List what you enjoy.
3. Decide what you want.
4. Check if the market will pay for it.
5. Learn the new profession.
6. Get experience.
7. Find a job.

On paper, it looks beautifully logical. In real life — especially when you've moved countries — it collapses faster than a New Year's resolution. The moment you try to follow this "simple" formula, you run into barriers that stop you in your tracks. Every step that's supposed to bring clarity ends up opening a new door to existential panic. Let's see why.

1. "Revise your skills."
Sounds easy. Until you sit down and realize your skills don't fit neatly into a list.

- What if your strengths aren't valued in your new country?
- What if you're "just" the person who writes emails, connects people, or keeps projects from falling apart?
- What if your confidence is so shaken you can't tell what you're good at anymore?
- What do you do when AI overtakes the skills you've spent years perfecting?

2. "List what you enjoy."
Lovely in theory. Terrifying in practice.

- Is following your passion is viable career strategy?
- What if your passions don't pay the bills?
- What if you enjoy learning programming, but have never tried it on a real project?
- And what if — and this really is the big one — you're afraid to admit you want something you believe you're not qualified for?

3. "Decide what you want."
This is where the classic path becomes comedy.
At this point, chances are you know exactly what you *don't* want.
But what you *do* want? That's blurry.

- What if your interests keep changing?
- What if nothing feels meaningful right now?
- What if this clarity never arrives?

Besides, making a firm decision feels scary. What if you try and realize that it's not what you want? *What will everyone say?*

4. "Check if the market will pay for it."
Great idea — except the market is changing faster than your morning coff
down.

- What if AI reshapes your field?
- What if what market is ready to pay for is not what you're passionate abo
- What if you take the leap, invest years, and discover that no one is intereste
- What if the stakes feel too high and you're terrified of losing stability?

5. "Learn the new profession."
Wonderful. Except:

- What if education is too expensive or inaccessible?
- What if you can't quit your current job to study full-time?
- How do you start over when you're used to feeling capable?
- What if you spend months learning and still don't get a job?

Suddenly, "just start learning" feels like "just climb Everest."

6. "Get experience."
Ah yes, the timeless paradox:
"We can't hire you without experience."
"I can't get experience without being hired."

- What if the field you want to enter has no clear doorway in?
- What if the industry changed faster than you could keep up?
- What if the only internships available are unpaid — and you can't afford that?

7. "Find a job."
This is the big one. The one that keeps you up at night.

- How do you reinvent yourself without losing financial stability?
- How do you take a step back when you have responsibilities?

ejected all the time?

scare us more than almost anything else: *less, loss,* and
ag *less* — a slightly lower standard of living — can feel
f *loss* — losing status, influence, or the sense of being
even worse. And the whisper of *never* ("I'll never be able to
ation again if I switch careers") can be downright paralyzing.
urrent reality looks like, these fears stack on top of each other.
y're powerful enough to keep people on a career path long after
caring about it.

ve tried to follow the "classic path" and ended up overwhelmed,
, or convinced you don't have time for this, there's nothing wrong with
e simply trying to navigate a process with no clear rules.

n you want to change your life, the instinct is to look for motivation. You see
one who made it and think, *If they did it, I can do it too.* But motivation is only one
of the equation. The other part is understanding what's actually holding you back
– and gently removing it. Because if something inside you is pulling the brake while
you're trying to accelerate, you become a supercar with your foot on the gas and the
brake. All that power, all that potential, but no movement.

If you've built your identity around competence, starting over will feel threatening.
If stepping into the spotlight doesn't feel safe, you'll delay the first step. And if your
self-worth is tied to external validation, losing status can feel like losing yourself.

So we need to go deeper. To the core. To how these barriers formed in the first
place — and why. And when you bring these barriers into the light and start
dismantling them, you won't need courage to start your business or write that first
LinkedIn post announcing that you've moved into a new field. The shift will happen
naturally.

And in mid-life, switching careers is not that easy. Life is fuller. Responsibilities
feel heavier — the people who rely on you, the routines you've built, the life you've
worked hard to create. But along with the brave women reinventors I spoke with, I
truly believe that change is possible for everyone, including you. The women in this
book are living proof of that. They didn't have perfect circumstances or endless
freedom. They had real lives, real obligations, and still found a way forward.

This book is your map for the in-between — the space where uncertainty turns
into clarity, and clarity turns into a path. It won't be your guru handing you the
"right" answers. In moments of chaos, there are no universally right answers anyway.

Instead, it will remind you that you already carry what you need, helping you translate your strengths into a new direction, articulate your value with confidence, and finding a role that reflects who you are now — whether in employment or entrepreneurship.

This book is about reclaiming your voice, your value, and building a career that feels like it belongs to the person you've become — not the version shaped by old job titles, or the person you were a decade ago. It's about becoming the person who creates her own opportunities — in any country, in any industry, at any stage of life.

I applaud your courage, your commitment, and your willingness to reinvent yourself. And as an expat myself, I know firsthand how lonely these challenges can feel. That's exactly why this book emerged. My hope is that this book will sit beside you like a friend — showing you that you're not alone, sharing insights, telling stories, helping you hear your inner voice and trust it more deeply, taking you from *"Where do I even fit?"* to *"This is where I belong."*

Welcome to the journey.

Why Women's Careers Follow a Different Map

Imagine you're still looking for a job in your new country. After hours of scrolling through LinkedIn, you finally find a job that *feels* right. The company excites you. The role makes sense. The compensation is fair. And it even connects to your previous experience in a way that makes you think, *Yes, I could do this. I would be amazing at this.*

But here's the twist — the part that separates this story from the one at the beginning of this book. As you go through the job description, you realize you meet about 80% of the qualifications. Enough to be a strong candidate, but not enough to feel like the "ideal" one.

The question is: would you still apply to that dream job?

Interestingly, the research is very clear about what happens next.

A Hewlett Packard internal report — later popularized in *Lean In* — claimed that men apply for jobs when they meet about 60% of the requirements, while women wait until they meet 100%. Later research confirmed the pattern: women often hold back not from lack of confidence, but from believing they must meet every listed qualification.

Even if you push through the hesitation and decide to apply, research shows that women are far more likely to ask for less money — even when they're equally qualified. Pew Research highlights the result of this pattern: women still earn about 82 cents for every dollar earned by men.

And then there's language — the subtle, invisible layer that shapes how we present ourselves long before anyone sees our skills. Textio analyzed thousands of professional bios and found a clear pattern: women tend to use more hesitant, softening language — phrases like "I helped with…" or "I was lucky to…" — while men use more direct, agentic language like "I led," "I built," "I delivered."

And even if you get the job, the same biases that shaped the application process and the interview follow you into the workplace. For example, Harvard Business Review found that women receive far more personality-based criticism than men. When men receive feedback, they are told to "develop strategic skills" or "expand technical expertise." When women receive feedback, they are told to be "less abrasive," "more patient," "less emotional," or "more confident." In other words: men get feedback about their work; women get feedback about their character.

Put together, these findings paint a clear picture: more often than not, women hesitate, shrink, soften, and edit themselves down.

But why does this happen so consistently? To understand that, we have to look beyond job descriptions and CV templates. The real story lives in the world women grow up in — the expectations, the messages, and the invisible rules that shape how we see ourselves long before we ever write a résumé.

The Invisible Rules Women Grow Up With

Deborah Tannen, a professor at Georgetown University, has spent her career studying how conversations shape our lives. And that led her to a deeper question: why do these conversations so often go off-track? Why do we misread each other's intentions? How can one moment — one sentence — fracture a relationship that felt solid the day before?

On the surface, this has little to do with switching careers or moving to another country. But stay with me.

Deborah studied all kinds of conversations, from marriage quarrels to job interviews, noticing the subtle patterns that cause communication to break down. Her book *That's Not What I Meant* explored ten dimensions of how we speak and interpret meaning — from conversational rituals to indirectness, from power dynamics to cultural norms.

The book became a success — or, as younger people would say, it basically went viral. Deborah received dozens of interview requests and media invitations.

But there was something especially curious about these requests.

About 90% of them focused on a single chapter — the section on gendered communication. Readers wanted more. They were fascinated by the idea that men and women might be having entirely different conversations without even realizing it.

It seemed she had uncovered something worth exploring. So she decided to dive deeper into how boys and girls learn to communicate — and what she found went far beyond words.

How Childhood Scripts Become Adult Barriers

Deborah Tannen went on to highlight earlier research by anthropologists Daniel Maltz and Ruth Borker, who focused on studying how boys and girls play. They noticed that although children sometimes play together, most of their play happens in same-gender groups. And the differences were striking.

From childhood, most of us learn the "rules" of our gendered worlds long before we ever choose a career. Boys are often encouraged to operate in bigger groups where hierarchy, competition, and clear winners matter. Girls, meanwhile, are usually socialized in smaller, more intimate circles where harmony, cooperation, and shared influence are the norm. These early dynamics shape how we speak up, how we handle conflict, and how comfortable we feel taking up space.

Do you recognize any of that in your own experience? If so, you've probably felt this too: these patterns don't disappear when we grow up. They follow us into classrooms, workplaces, interviews, negotiations — and especially into career transitions.

By the time we're choosing careers, these patterns are so ingrained that they might feel like personality rather than conditioning. Someone raised to value achievement and assertiveness may gravitate toward roles where visibility and competition are rewarded. Someone taught to prioritize connection and harmony may choose paths where collaboration and relationship-building matter more.

Neither approach is better — but both can become invisible constraints. When you're trying to find your next career, these early scripts can influence everything from how boldly you advocate for yourself to how guilty you feel about wanting something different.

And those scripts run deep.

	Boys' World	**Girls' World**
Group size	Large groups	Small groups or pairs
Social structure	Clear hierarchy	Shared influence
Leadership style	Direct orders	Suggestions; "bossy" discouraged
Game style	Competitive	Cooperative
Communication	Arguing, challenging, bragging	Politeness, harmony
Status signals	Assertiveness, taking space	Maintaining relationships
Core value	Achievement	Connection

Girls learned to maintain closeness. Boys learned to establish status.

Girls learned to soften their opinions. Boys learned to assert theirs.

Girls learned to avoid conflict. Boys learned to use conflict.

Girls learned to be liked. Boys learned to be respected.

So when a talented woman looks at a job description and sees she meets 80% of the requirements, she doesn't think, *"I'll just persuade them that I'm the right fit."* She thinks, *"I'm not the one they're looking for. I don't want to waste their time. I don't want to embarrass myself. I don't want to be rejected."*

When you've spent your whole life being rewarded for being agreeable, stepping forward and advocating for yourself feels like breaking an unspoken rule. And research shows that, as women, breaking rules isn't something we've been encouraged to do.

And I would like to make something clear: I'm not saying you should suddenly start bulldozing conversations, chase status, or turn every disagreement into a battle. You are wonderful the way you are, and what you have is powerful. The ability to build closeness is a strength. The ability to be liked is a strength. The ability to read a room and understand what people need is a strength.

Yet when you spend years being praised for meeting expectations, what happens is you disconnect from yourself. You lose touch with what you need, what you want, and what actually feels right. And once that connection fades, harmony becomes something you protect at the cost of your own well-being.

You don't speak up when a partner, friend, or coworker crosses a boundary, telling yourself that "it's not worth the conflict," even though something inside you tightens every time it happens.

You agree to help a colleague, take on an extra task, or attend a family event even though you're overwhelmed — because disappointing someone feels worse than disappointing yourself.

You downplay your ambitions, avoid sharing your ideas, or staying "not ready" for far too long because you worry others might feel threatened, uncomfortable, or left behind if you grow.

Sometimes our mind convinces you that raising your prices, asking for support, or expressing a need will somehow damage the relationship.

So you swallow the need and keep the peace, holding everything together.

Until you can't.

The reason this matters now is because reinvention asks for courage. It asks you to claim opportunities instead of waiting to be chosen, and tolerate the possibility of rejection. It asks for visibility and for finding a voice that's yours — the one that's been quiet for a long time, but never gone. All of that is incredibly hard when you've spent a lifetime being rewarded for shrinking. Taking up space suddenly feels overwhelming.

That's why reconnecting with yourself — with your needs, your voice, your desires — is the foundation of everything that comes next.

And that's where we're going next.

The Mask We Learn to Wear

If reinvention requires connection with your needs, then it helps to understand how that connection erodes. And it begins earlier than most of us realize.

Jean Feldman, a social psychologist, uncovered something that helps explain this disconnection — and the surprising entry point was deception. His main question was simple: *why do men and women lie, and do they lie for different reasons?*

In one study, Feldman invited pairs of strangers into a lab and asked them to have a simple, ten-minute conversation. The interaction was recorded, and afterward each participant watched the video and marked every moment in which they had lied — even polite, or self-protective lies.

In another study, Feldman asked participants to talk to a partner while trying to appear either likable, competent, or simply "themselves." After the conversation, they again reviewed the recording and identified their lies. Turned out, people lied more when they were managing impressions — and the type of lie matched the goal.

Yet both studies, among others, revealed the same trend.

Men are statistically more likely to use deception for self-enhancement, especially in competitive or status-driven situations. These are "self-oriented" lies: exaggerating accomplishments, hiding vulnerabilities, or presenting a more impressive version of themselves. Interestingly, this tendency aligns with the social messages boys receive from early childhood — messages that reward assertiveness, independence, and achievement.

Women, on the other hand, tend to lie for prosocial reasons. Their lies are usually "other-oriented," meant to preserve harmony, protect someone's feelings, or maintain connection. You've been there: telling a friend she looks great even when she doesn't, or softening criticism at work to avoid conflict. These patterns grow out of the relational focus and empathy that girls are encouraged to develop from a young age.

It's important to remember: these patterns are just trends. They don't mean all men behave one way or all women another. There are women who speak up with ease and take the lead naturally, and there are men who value closeness, collaboration, and emotional connection. Real people are always more layered than any generalization.

But it's hard to ignore that, in general, girls grow up with a very particular set of expectations — and that the expectations placed on men and women are still far from equal. Many of us girls were raised to:

- avoid direct orders and phrase everything as a suggestion;
- look for compromise instead of establishing status;
- listen and share to create closeness;
- downplay our achievements;
- smooth over disagreements;
- invite input rather than take the lead;
- wait for a natural pause instead of interrupting;
- prioritize being liked and keeping the peace.

This is the environment many girls grow up in. And as a small girl, you carry two powerful needs inside you: the need to be yourself, and the need to be loved. When these needs align, childhood feels safe. When they don't, something inside you begins to split.

If you grow up in a healthy home, you receive support before you even know how to ask for it. Your family smiles at you, hugs you, tells you they love you. They can't accept every single thing you do, of course — but what matters most is that they accept you. They show you that your voice matters, and teach you how to understand your emotions — even the difficult ones — and how to express them.

When this happens, these two basic psychological needs — *I want to be myself* and *I want to be loved* — coexist peacefully. You grow up believing that authenticity and connection can live together.

But for many of us, childhood didn't look like this.

- Leaper and Smith analyzed over 90 studies with more than 15,000 children and found that girls received more restrictive messages about expressing anger or assertiveness. Boys were allowed more freedom to show independence or frustration. Girls were encouraged to express empathy and sadness, and discouraged from "unladylike" behavior.
- Chaplin, Cole, and Zahn-Waxler found that mothers were more likely to label their daughters' assertive or angry expressions as inappropriate. Girls learned early that certain emotions were unwelcome — and began suppressing them.
- Endendijk and colleagues analyzed 126 studies with around 44,000 children. While overall parental control wasn't dramatically different, girls faced more restrictive expectations around emotional expression, compliance, and social behavior.

Something is happening here — something that shapes how girls learn to show up in the world.

The Good Girl Training We Never Chose

How many of these messages did *you* hear growing up?

- "Be nice."
- "Don't be too loud."
- "That's not ladylike."

- "You're too bossy."
- "Don't be so emotional."
- "Let the boys handle it."
- "Girls don't do that."
- "Don't talk back."
- "Don't brag."
- "Always be kind."

These messages aren't exclusive to girls, and not everyone heard them in the same way — but if you grew up hearing none of them, that's genuinely uncommon.

I certainly heard my share. One of the most memorable was: *"I is the last letter of the alphabet."* In Russian, the pronoun "I" is a single letter — and it really is the last letter. My grandmother meant well. What she meant was that I should be considerate, thoughtful, kind. She was teaching me with the only tools she knew.

But as a quiet seven-year-old, hearing that message taught me to swallow my feelings. I was afraid that speaking up would make me seem selfish or unkind, so my interpretation of her words became something entirely different:

"Your needs come last."

"Stay silent."

"Take care of others before yourself."

And when you're a child, you learn quickly that survival — emotional survival — comes before everything else. Before authenticity. Before self-expression. Before your own needs.

You learn:

"If I want to be loved, if I want to belong, if I want to avoid pain, I need to hide "bad" parts of myself. I need to be convenient, easy, and perfect at being pleasant."

Over time, you become exceptionally skilled at wearing a good-girl mask — a protective layer that helps you move through the world without exposing the parts of you that feel too tender or too exhausted to show. You put it on when you're running on empty, when there's no emotional space to be fully present, and that's precisely what pulls you deeper into burnout. And over time, you can't imagine connecting with others without paying that price.

But the longer you wear this mask, the more you find yourself wondering, *Who am I under all this?* and secretly watching *Why Women Kill.*

The Quiet Path Toward Self-Erasure

In the final moments of *Guardians of the Galaxy 3*, Rocket the Raccoon confronts the High Evolutionary — the man who tore him apart, rebuilt him with metal and wires, and called it "improvement." After remembering every cruel experiment inflicted on him and his friends, Rocket finally faces him with a line that cuts straight through the screen:

"You didn't want to make things perfect. You just hated them the way they are."

The High Evolutionary believes he is creating a "higher" species — *"Be not as you are, but as you should be."*

But what we see is that he's torturing living creatures — innocent beings who are Rocket's friends. An otter has both arms removed and replaced with dangling metal rods, a rabbit has metal spider-like legs grafted onto her body, a walrus has his back legs amputated and replaced with wheels mutilated. And then Rocket, who is subjected to repeated surgeries and brain experiments The modifications are so brutal that even adults in the audience feel tears rising.

As humans watching other beings in pain, we wonder, *How could anyone be that cruel?* And yet — with all the kindness in the world — we rarely notice that we do a version of this to ourselves every day.

When you were born, you didn't feel ashamed for crying when you were hungry. You didn't apologize for needing comfort. You weren't striving for perfection. There was no shame attached to any of your needs.

But over time, you began to absorb the subtle cues that shape a child's sense of which needs are "acceptable" and which ones are not. Most of these lessons weren't taught directly — they were learned through tone, expression, silence, and the emotional atmosphere around you. Slowly, you came to understand all the ways a person can be seen as "not okay," and you adjusted yourself accordingly.

The teacher who praised you for being quiet when you wanted to speak up. The friend who rolled their eyes when you tried to share your excitement. The family member who told you to "stop being dramatic" when your world was falling apart.

Some of us grew up without anyone truly listening to our needs. No one made us a priority. Then there were the people who simply couldn't offer the kindness or understanding we needed. And some of us even faced people who actively tried to limit or erase us — the ones who doubted our worth, dismissed our feelings, or chipped away at our confidence.

When you needed space to be yourself, you were denied it because your emotions or actions made someone uncomfortable. Those childhood moments when you learned to behave, to be quiet, to stop wanting so much, trained you to develop a sharp instinct for what others expect. And the dangerous lesson we learn is that being yourself — wanting something, needing something, expressing something — is unsafe, creating a barrier between where you are and where you hope to go.

If you rarely experienced unconditional acceptance — if no one gave you space to be fully you — then self-erasure often becomes a survival strategy. So now, without even noticing, your first instinct is to mold yourself to fit other people's comfort.

And not being yourself is surprisingly easy. You think:

- "My mother wants me to be quiet, so I must stay silent even when I need something."
- "My teacher likes me when I'm polite, so I must never be angry."
- "My family praises me when I'm helpful, so I must never be a burden."

From Shipbuilding Engineer to Trauma Therapist (Netherlands, The United States)

Suze started her career building ships because it was the only place she felt safe. Today, she teaches doctors and therapists how to rebuild human foundations. The leap between those worlds is the story — and it's far more dramatic than you expect.
And this is how she tells her story.

My family is culturally quite different from typical Dutch families. Three of my grandparents grew up in Indonesia and were born and raised there until the Second World War, and my other grandmother was born and raised in Hungary. My grandmother met my grandfather during the Second World War in Budapest, then they moved to England, where my mother was born, and later to the Netherlands.

To give you a little bit of an example: in most Dutch families, you "act normal," right? And my father always said: I want you to think for yourself. I don't care if other people do this. You're not like other people. I want to hear what you think. But if my answer didn't meet his expectations, there were real consequences. The message was always: think for yourself — but think the right thing.

My parents had severe Second World War trauma. My mother has autism. Neither of those things are things they chose — but together, they created a home that was unpredictable and charged. Until I was seven, there was fighting every single day. Always the feeling that I was in everybody's way. We moved to the US when I was young, but the fighting came with us. I mostly remember being sent to my room, being in the way, being too much.

But on ships, our relationship was different. I had a good connection with my father. Ships were my safe space. So from a very young age, I went sailing. First with family, later with friends.

And when I had to choose what to study, all I wanted was to leave home. Shipbuilding was my escape route.

University was the first place I found a tribe — a group of like-minded weirdos who made me feel less alone. And then something happened that I didn't talk about for a long time: I was raped. After that, trusting anyone felt almost impossible. Eventually, I met a boyfriend I could trust. For the first time in a long while, I felt safe.

But halfway through the university, my boyfriend was hit by a car. Severe brain damage. A coma. I took care of him for a year and a half. But when he woke up, he didn't remember me.

That was the moment everything in my life came crashing down. I could hardly see the point of staying alive.

While I was taking care of him, I stopped my studies, and then I had to figure out how to pick things up again. But somehow I finished university anyway. I became a shipbuilder.

My first job was at a shipyard in the Bible Belt — deeply religious. I was the first woman they'd ever hired without asking about my faith. That was a mistake. Not because I object to faith — I'm deeply religious — but not in the way they were. I wasn't raised with church, and I didn't have a clue about their habits and what that meant.

Every morning you could hear a pin drop. Forty engineers working in silence. At 12:30, the grandfather clock rang, everyone stood up and went to lunch. I sat there thinking, What am I doing here? The ships were amazing — but the environment... no.

I was struggling to make sense of everything.

One night I went sailing. I was 24, maybe 25. Standing watch in the middle of the ocean, the Milky Way above me, 10,000 meters of water below, I thought, I'm just going to stay here forever.

I lifted my foot to step over the railing. And then something stopped me. Not a voice, but a deep inner knowing: This is not what you're meant to do.

And then I thought of the captain — a dear friend — having to tell my parents he didn't know where I'd gone. That was enough to pull my foot back.

So I said yes to figuring out why I am here on this planet.

My next job was TNO — a big Dutch research and development organization. I kept wondering why shipbuilding is so conservative, and why all these innovations in materials, techniques, and technology were happening outside our field while nobody in shipbuilding talked about them. I wanted to set up innovation projects for shipbuilding. And they said, 'Yeah, sure, go ahead.'

So I thought — I'll just start talking to those people. I set up large-scale innovation projects with all these people. I went to Brussels, got huge EU funding, and thought: If you just put the right people together, things will happen.

Turns out: no.

If you put the right people at one table, they don't talk to each other.

I was like — wait, what? When I speak to you guys one-on-one, everybody has brilliant ideas, but when we sit at a table together, nothing happens. This is where I thought, okay, let's figure a little bit more about people out there. And that is what set me on a journey of understanding how people work, why people don't work, and why they have these things in their heart that they want to bring to the world, but they're not doing it.

And then I got into extreme fights with my boss. Setting up all these big projects was unheard of for that company at that point. So he said: "You're only 25. You know nothing. You have no experience. We first need you to become a good employee here. Follow along. Don't start to make up your own things before you fit well here as an employee."

I thought: I didn't stay alive for this.

So I quit my permanent contract. In the middle of the 2008 economic crisis. With three months of money in the bank. Everyone said I was insane. But I thought: If I can't find work in three months, maybe I should kill myself. That was honestly my thinking.

Saying yes to finding my purpose meant giving up every idea of what other people thought I should be doing. I lived week by week. If I didn't like something, I quit. If I wanted to move, I moved. If I was interested in something, I followed it. If the world thought it was insane, fine.

But it worked out well because out of the gate I found someone who was willing to let me write a grant proposal for the European Commission, and I won those proposals, meaning that I had my entire year's revenue in the bank in three or four months.

At that point they hired me for grants — but I was not willing to do that if I couldn't also help them figure out how the project should be set up. I only did this if I believed in the project, and I would only believe in the project if the right people are on the team.

What I discovered is that innovation doesn't work in the same way as a normal project. You can't write down what you're going to do because it's innovation! And yet for the European Commission, you need to write things down, moreover, you can't change the plan halfway. If you change the plan halfway, then you won't get the money. I became a specialist in writing proposals so that even if everything changed midway, the European Commission would still stay on board. That gave me a lot of insight into people, into team dynamics, into how to structure and organize a project that isn't all that clear at the beginning — which has a lot to do with entrepreneurship actually.

I was still terrified of people. But if I could serve, I was okay. If I could help, I felt like I belonged.

In the meanwhile, I had deep conversations with people. I studied trauma. I did every trauma course I could find, but I was still mostly working on myself, and I was not really willing yet — until I was 35 or something — to work with other people.

Yet midway people started asking me deeply personal questions during lunch breaks. Then they would say, "This is the first project where I feel I matter, not just my work."

Eventually, I was asked to work with teams instead of projects. Then with leaders. Then with entrepreneurs. I realized innovation in technology and innovation in people follow the same rules: you can't plan the whole thing. You have to take the first step and let the path reveal itself.

Then I got pregnant. The father left eight weeks in. I was a single mom, running a business, still afraid of everyone. And eight months into the pregnancy, I met the man who is now my husband. He wasn't looking for a child. I wasn't looking for a partner. It just happened.

I never wanted to be a therapist. I studied trauma for myself. But people kept asking me to coach them. And eventually, I realized I could help them in ways that felt natural to me — ways that didn't follow the traditional models.

Ten years ago, I started a business academy for entrepreneurs who were still trying to do what they thought others wanted. Same pattern as the engineers — but in a different setting.

Today, I teach doctors, therapists, and coaches across the Netherlands and Belgium about trauma — not just how to fix it, but how to understand the human being inside it. Over the course of my life I have learned one thing: trauma is not a 'problem we need to solve', it is the result of our foundation not being built properly in childhood. Our system is very capable of dealing with life, with hardships, with traumatic events. Yet we need our Divine path in life to be so secure and so well built, that we will not lose it during these events. I run multi-day training programs at Hoeve de Kempe, my own venue in Voorst, where care professionals come to learn what no textbook quite covers: how their own nervous system shapes every single contact with a patient. I also study theology — because for me, the question of what it means to be human has never been just clinical. And I'm still learning to answer it.

Twenty-five years ago, I wrote a letter to God asking, "Just tell me what I'm here to do." I also described a place where people would fly in from all over the world to learn who they're meant to be and how to bring that into the world. I completely forgot about it.

On my 50th birthday, I found that journal entry again.

And I looked around at my home — the sheep in the orchard, the dirt road, the quiet — and realized I had built exactly what I wrote. To the last detail.

I don't think my story is special. I think everybody has been through their own version of hell. The question is how we can see how that entire journey sculpted us into who we are becoming. We're still developing into who we're meant to be. Humans before higher power.

> Our life is not meant to be 'ready' or 'fixed'. It is the path that is shaping us into who we are. The question is: do we dare trust it? And it makes me incredibly alive to do that.

The voices that once erased parts of you from the outside begin to settle inside, and without noticing, you start doing the erasing yourself. And just like Rocket was reshaped into something "better," you begin reshaping yourself too. You learned to be "perfect" — not being a burden, not causing discomfort, not taking up space. You adapt to every environment, switching into whatever emotion is needed, like a chameleon.

Now, you might be thinking: *but learning social norms is normal.* And you're right. Every society requires a bit of shaping. We all learn to wait our turn, to read the room, to be considerate. That's part of being human, part of living together. That's healthy.

But something different happens when the shaping becomes shrinking.

Both can look identical on the outside.

Inside, they feel completely different.

The difference isn't in what you do.

It's in why you do it and what it costs you.

On the surface, this survival strategy can look like you're thriving. As a good girl, you were praised, complimented, and "a pleasure to have in class." Because this strategy worked so well back then, you carried it with you into adulthood without ever questioning it. You keep stretching yourself to meet everyone else's needs — colleagues, managers, clients.

You stay late hoping someone will notice how hard you're trying.

You wait for your work to be seen without having to point to it.

You wish to be recognized without having to take up space.

But when you spend years being the good girl — agreeable, accommodating, self-sacrificing — the real loss is what happens *inside you.*

You adjust because you believe something bad will happen if you don't. You feel drained, resentful, invisible, or numb — because you're tired of performing the best version of yourself all day. You censor yourself everywhere — even alone — because you've internalized the rule that your needs are "too much." As a consequence:

- You lose touch with what you actually want in your career;
- You stop trusting your professional instincts and ambitions;

- You become excellent at meeting expectations but disconnected from your own direction.

I invite you to rethink whether this mechanism is serving you today. Because this pattern teaches you that if you're kind, polite, helpful, and endlessly competent, recognition will eventually come. And you learn to play that role so convincingly that, over time, you lose track of what *you* want — because you've spent years prioritizing everyone else.

It's time to face an honest question:

When you kept stretching yourself, believing that giving just a little more would finally make someone see you — was there anyone looking after *you*?

This question isn't about blaming anyone. Blame may feel justified, but it rarely helps us take the next step. People in your past may not have treated you fairly or consistently, but you can't rewrite those moments. What matters now is recognizing that your past doesn't have to dictate the rest of your life. What happened shaped you, yes, but it doesn't get to decide who you become next.

And this is not an invitation to swing to the other extreme and become self-focused or egoistic at the expense of others. Egoism is built on entitlement — the belief that your needs automatically outrank everyone else's. Healthy self-care is the opposite of that. It's the understanding that your needs carry *equal* weight. You have limits and needs like everyone else — and they matter just as much.

Yet now if you've spent years disappearing into what others needed, you might have thought: *"Okay, I admit I erased a part of myself. I performed. I was the good girl. But then... who I am underneath it all? Who is the authentic me?"*

Does being authentic mean acting out every impulse? Screaming like a toddler whenever you need something? Ignoring other people's needs? Saying whatever comes to mind without considering impact, and calling it "just being honest"? Refusing to compromise because "this is who I am, take it or leave it"?

These examples sound exaggerated — and they are.

But they expose the core issue: you can't reclaim your authentic self until you stop confusing a *good girl* with a *good person*. That's where the next chapter begins.

When Kindness Becomes a Mask

The "good girl" mask often gets mislabeled as kindness.

You may think that by accommodating others' needs — by staying small — you're being kind. But often, without realizing it, you're being unkind to yourself first. You offer everyone else patience, understanding, and flexibility, while giving yourself almost none of the same compassion.

You shrink yourself because you believe it protects others.

You silence yourself because you believe it keeps the peace.

You override your own needs because you believe it makes you kind.

That's how the "good girl" mask. Not out of deception, but out of a sincere desire to be loved. But kindness without boundaries isn't kindness — it's self-erasure. A survival strategy you learned early, not a reflection of your character.

And if a part of you feels defensive — *Are you telling me I'm not really kind?...* — that's not exactly my point. You *are* kind. Your heart is full of care, empathy, and generosity. It's just that your kindness was shaped in a way that required you to step back so others could stay comfortable.

Authentic kindness has one defining difference from the mask: it's a choice. It comes from having a full range of tools — boundaries, honesty, courage, self-respect — and choosing kindness because it aligns with who you are in that moment. You can still care, help, and make concessions, but none of it requires you to make yourself smaller.

The mask is different. It's what you use when you feel you have no choice at all. You're kind because somewhere along the way you learned you *must* be kind. Because the alternative feels dangerous, and being anything other than agreeable might cost you love, safety, or belonging.

A good girl says, *Kindness is my only option.*

A good person says, *Kindness is my choice.*

I'm inviting you to become a good person — someone who knows she is worthy of the same love, attention, and care she so generously gives to others. You deserve to have your needs met without breaking yourself to do it, without fearing conflict, without feeling like every honest word puts the relationship at risk. Your joy doesn't take anything away from anyone.

Seeing and changing this is a process. It will take time. Be kind to yourself as you unlearn the old rules. This conversation will continue throughout the book. And as you allow your own needs to matter, your kindness grows — not from sacrifice, but from wholeness. That's real kindness, not a survival strategy.

Reclaiming Your Voice

The first step to unlearning the old rules is listening to your own voice.

When you're under pressure to build a career in a new place, it's natural to reach for what feels predictable: rewriting your CV to fit the mold, trying to match what others expect from you, or holding on to your old career simply because it's the only thing that feels familiar. But safety and alignment are not the same thing.

So I invite you to pause and ask yourself — honestly:

What career do I really want to pursue?

Not what you *should* want.

Not what looks good on paper.

Not what others think is "practical."

What *you* want.

Let that be a moment of kindness toward yourself. You've spent years being thoughtful, patient, and generous with others. That pattern helped you belong, helped you cope, helped you stay steady. But it also asked you to tuck parts of yourself away.

A new beginning needs your curiosity, your energy, your longing — even if those things feel small or uncertain right now.

Following what you want doesn't make you selfish — it makes you honest. It brings you back into alignment with yourself. And when you're aligned, your connection with the people around you becomes real, not performed. You stop pretending to be fine, stop forcing a smile, stop carrying that quiet ache in your stomach that comes from living a life that doesn't fit.

When you let your true preferences and personality come forward, something shifts. Your energy changes. You move from holding your breath to actually breathing. From managing impressions to simply being present. This next chapter will encourage you to do exactly that — to stop performing and give yourself permission to choose what feels true to you.

And here's something important to remember: following the path you want — even imperfectly — will nourish you more than excelling at something that drains you. Mastery has a rhythm. Every expert you admire once stood exactly where you are — at the beginning of a learning curve. Malcolm Gladwell's "10,000-hour rule" simply reminds us that expertise grows from time, attention, and steady practice. Not talent. Not perfection. Just time, curiosity, and consistency.

So even if you start imperfectly, start with what you want.

The readiness will come later.

And let me say this gently: if you're reading a book like this, you're already someone who works hard, learns fast, and shows up fully. You've built competence over years — maybe decades. You're not starting from scratch; you're weaving the loose threads of your life into a story with shape and meaning.

As you think about your next chapter, I invite you to listen to the voice inside you that's been quiet. You are a beautiful grown woman now — a good person, steady and capable, far wiser than the girl who once believed she had to hold everything together to be loved.

It is safe to be yourself.

It is time to be yourself.

The Four Invisible Barriers to Switching Your Career

A career transition doesn't begin with applications. It begins with the stories you choose to believe about yourself.

Stories guide behavior. If you believe you're not leadership material, you'll naturally step back from chances to lead. If you believe you're not ready, you'll hesitate to pursue what you actually want. These stories are powerful — powerful enough to pull you forward or hold you in place.

Yet uncovering these stories takes time, because they never show up as dramatic breakdowns. They show up as hesitation. As overthinking. As staying "just a bit longer" in a role you've already outgrown. And that "bit longer" adds up.

It turns into years of circling the same questions.

It becomes watching others step into spaces you're capable of too.

It becomes a life that looks good but feels quietly reduced.

This chapter looks at the science behind the forces that shape these stories: the cognitive patterns and mental shortcuts that keep you exactly where you are, even when you want something different. Their danger is that they're invisible, they feel reasonable, and they influence your decisions long before you notice them.

You've probably heard versions of them in your own mind:

1) A story that reduces your entire skill set to one job title:
   "But I'm not qualified to do project management if I've always been a teacher!"
2) A story that shrinks everything you've already learned:

> *"I don't have any valuable skills. I'd need years to grow into this role… so should I even try?"*

3) A story that oversells the comfort you have achieved:
> *"Maybe my job isn't meaningful… but I like the lifestyle it gives me. Is that a good enough reason to stay?"*

4) A story that tells you your curiosity makes you look unreliable — like a jack-of-all-trades who can't commit:
> *"When it comes to my next career, I'm interested in so many things. How am I supposed to choose?"*

Once you notice these stories — and see where they came from — you can check if they're still true. And if they're not, you can replace them with stories that actually support where you want to go.

This chapter will help you do exactly that. We'll look at the forces that hold you back when you start wanting something truer to who you are now, break the patterns that no longer serve you, and build new stories that make your next step feel possible, grounded, and yours.

Nothing in this chapter is here to judge you. These barriers aren't signs of weakness or lack of ambition. They're simply the natural result of how our mind works. So you're not alone in them.

But this conversation is essential, because once you can name these forces, they lose their power. And once they lose their power, you can finally imagine — and pursue — a career that fits you, not the one you were taught to fit into. This chapter is the beginning of that shift.

1. The Single Story

One of the strongest forces shaping how we see ourselves and others is our deep, almost biological need for consistency.

Robert Cialdini, the psychologist who spent decades studying how to influence people, discovered that our brains crave neat categories. Turns out, we unconsciously and automatically sort people — and ourselves — into simple labels: *friend* or *foe*, *creative* or *analytical*, *marketer* or *engineer*.

Once a label sticks, it becomes a story. And once it becomes a story, we feel compelled to stay consistent with it — even when it no longer fits.

This is why you can spend years in a job you've outgrown, and why the sentence "I want something different" feels both exciting and terrifying. Part of the reason is that your brain is trying to protect the story it already knows, even when that story no longer fits.

Cialdini illustrated this beautifully in a now-classic study. Homeowners in a neighborhood were asked to place a tiny "safe driving" sticker in their window. Many people agreed. Weeks later, a different researcher asked them to install a massive, ugly "DRIVE CAREFULLY" billboard on their lawn. Far fewer people agreed — except one group. You can probably guess which one.

People who had said yes to the tiny sticker also said yes to the larger one. But why? Were they people-pleasers who would say yes to almost anything?

Cialdini showed that something else was at work — the principle of consistency. Once someone takes a small action, they feel an internal pull to stay aligned with it. For these homeowners, the billboard didn't feel like a new request. It felt like the next logical step in the story they had already started telling about themselves.

This is how identity works. We stay consistent with the career persona we've created — even when that persona is outdated.

Here's how it shows up in a career: for years, you introduce yourself at meetings, conferences, and on LinkedIn as "a lawyer," "a marketer," "a project manager." It feels satisfying — even better when there's a big brand behind it, when you mention a Big Four firm or a tech giant and people light up the moment you say the name.

Yet repeating the story so often becomes a kind of psychological contract. Contracts like that are hard to break. That identity becomes comfortable. Predictable. Safe. A career switch can feel like more than changing jobs — it can feel like changing who you are, and letting go of something that still matters to you. It feels *inconsistent*.

The voice inside is whispering: *"If I'm not a marketer anymore, if I'm not working for the big name, then what am I?"*

Another, louder voice piles on: *"Switching careers? You don't have experience in this field. That's not the path we've been on. You're an impostor."*

Neither of these voices represents the truth.

Your job title was never the whole story. It was just the headline.

When you repeat a label for long enough, you start to treat it as your entire identity. But I invite you to see the full story. If you've been in the same position — say, marketing — for 20 years, what does that really tell us?

In 20 years, you didn't just "do marketing."

- You navigated the shift from print to digital.
- You learned the language of platforms and algorithms.
- You adapted your strategy during a global pandemic.
- Now you're learning to work with AI.

Is that one skill? Or is that the story of someone who is, at their core, an expert learner?

The job title is just the container. The real substance — the strategic thinking, the communication, the problem-solving — belongs to you, not to any industry. Let's see what this looks like in real life.

From Journalist to Founder of a Public Speaking School (Russia → Kazakhstan)

Some people move through life with such sincerity and warmth that everything around them seems to soften. Julia is one of those people. Her story is a reminder of what happens when you follow your values with honesty, when you allow your heart to guide your choices even when the path ahead is uncertain.
And this is how she tells her story.

"I grew up in Russia. My family's mantras were clear: "Your intelligence is your wealth." "Your job must be stable." As a child, I dreamed of being an actress. I was convinced I'd end up in a sleek, high-tech office of a large international company wearing business suits. Isn't that what you're supposed to do?

I graduated with a degree in journalism. But I kept feeding and developing my inner actress. I performed in theater plays on the side. Still, the pressure for a "stable job" kept creeping in."

Julia wasn't one to conform easily. She once juggled a day internship at L'Oréal as a PR assistant. At the same time, she took extra courses in speech and diction training. She even pulled night shifts as an investigative journalist. It seemed like she was building every part of herself at once.

It was there that Julia discovered her passion for television. Being a reporter or a host on television seemed perfect as it combined a stable profession and playful spirit of an actress. The only downside this time were the night shifts. Could there be a job that combines television, leaves room for creativity but with regular hours, like in a corporation?

Turns out, it was.

Julia landed a job at Samsung, where she became the host of a small in-house video studio responsible for creating "How-to" videos for learning platforms and social media. In just three months, she was honored with the Best Employee of the Month award.

"Working in a corporation felt a lot like being in school — you do something well, you get recognized for it. At that time, I couldn't have felt more blessed and fulfilled. I'd always wanted those big brand names on my CV, so I genuinely enjoyed the journey. I also learned how to find something interesting in even the most mundane tasks. If I spotted that spark of interest, I could share it — and others would see it too."

She further continued to work in communications with leading brands across various industries, from a mining company to a popular pizza brand. With her kindness and radiating light, she was always surrounded by support and acceptance. At the pizza brand, she took on the role of morning podcast producer, inspiring and training her colleagues to talk about their work, share their stories, and even ran a few communication training sessions for one of the company's sub brands. Everyone loved working with her — except for one person: her direct manager.

He persistently frowned upon her. During one feedback session, he made a remark: "You work incredibly hard — a true 10 out of 10. It's a pity there's no talent to go with it."

"Up until then, I'd always been surrounded by support and acceptance. But now, I was faced with unconstructive and even offensive remarks. I tried to build bridges, but I failed. It was a bitter pill to swallow, but it was a lesson I needed to learn. That vulnerability ended up being a turning point. Maybe it's how I finally built my own inner sense of self-worth.

At that moment, one of my former managers invited me to join the corporate communications team at the largest banking institution in the country. Everything was perfect: my role, my salary, my colleagues.

But in 2023 our family moved to Kazakhstan. So, my next chapter began from scratch, in a new country and a new culture. I took on a lesson I learned in acting: when you as an actor are placed into a new environment, there's no time to overthink. You just start acting, improvising. I truly wanted to get to know the people and the culture.

I landed a communications position at a large bank, but it didn't work out. My work revolves around articulating values and communication. To do it well, I needed to work the top managers' attention directly — but that just didn't happen.

It became clear I needed to move on. I'd always measured my value by the brands on my CV, and now I had to face a tough question: who am I without a big brand or company name?

Someone wise said: "You have to test your dreams to see if they'll withstand." That's why, while I was still employed, I put together a course on public speaking, combining communication technology, my theater background, and years of experience. I'd work my day job, then teach a group in the evening. That gave me the sense that if I can gather one group, I could probably gather another one.

Everyone kept saying, "Are you crazy? Offline courses are the past — find a way to move it online!" But I knew my real strength was in face-to-face communication in smaller groups. I'm not afraid to work with small groups and to move slowly in the right direction. It's okay if I never become a big sensation or never hit a million followers. I'm kind of like a turtle — but it's important for me to stick to who I am.

The journey certainly comes with its challenges. I'll never forget opening my first corporate tax document — a wave of panic washed over me, and I immediately wanted to quit. If it weren't for my husband's support, I would have returned to the safety of a corporate job. That's why I'm endlessly grateful to him; he is the mastermind behind the operational side of our business, allowing me to focus on my strengths.

While there are seasons when gathering a cohort is challenging, the moment I connect with someone truly eager to learn and transform the way they communicate, I feel this is the greatest gift I could ever receive.

This is my pill against future regret. When I'm 60, I won't be looking back, thinking, 'I should have tried to build my own business when I was younger."

Julia's story illustrates that your career is not a single straight line — it's a series of evolutions. And each evolution leaves you with more tools, more insight, and more capacity than the last.

Most people know this in theory, but in practice we forget. We repeat the same label for years — *I'm a journalist, I'm a lawyer, I'm a marketer* — until it starts to feel like the only thing we're allowed to be.

This brings us to an important shift: moving from a single-story identity to a multi-story one. A single-story identity says: *I am this one thing*. It's deep, familiar, and comforting — but it can also become a cage. When you've spent years defining yourself through one role, wanting something different can feel like betraying who you are.

A multi-story identity is different. It recognizes that you're not one thing — you're several. You have more than one strength, more than one interest, more than one way of contributing. Your career becomes a collection of chapters, not a single plotline.

Even if there's one activity you've always believed defines you — work, sports, or anything else — no one is meant to fit inside a single label. You're broader, richer, and more layered than that. You hold many strengths and many ways of showing up in the world.

Yet even though this seems logical, many of us fear that changing our story will make us look inconsistent. We grow up believing that a "serious" person chooses one path and stays on it, and that shifting directions means we were wrong before or uncertain now. So instead of expanding our story, we protect it. We defend it. We cling to it even when it no longer fits, because the alternative feels like admitting we've changed — and for many people, that feels dangerously close to admitting we don't fully know who we are.

But let's pause to consider this.

When our parents were growing up, staying in one field for decades was normal and safe. The world rewarded stability. Companies rewarded loyalty. Careers moved in straight lines.

Today, that world is gone. According to the U.S. Bureau of Labor Statistics, the average person changes jobs every 2.8 years, and Gen Z professionals switch even faster — sometimes every 18 to 24 months. A recent LinkedIn analysis found that people entering the workforce today will hold 12 to 15 different jobs in their lifetime. And chances are, this will include a few switches too. The number of job changes — including lateral moves, promotions, and side gigs — can easily reach or exceed 12–15 over a working life.

And the pace is only accelerating. Considering that 50% of all employees will need significant reskilling within the next three years, and that up to one-third of today's jobs may disappear within a decade, how can anyone expect to stay on the same track forever?

Our parents grew up in a world where change was suspicious.

We're growing up in a world where reinvention is a survival skill.

In other words, the idea of choosing one field in your 20s and staying there until retirement is no longer an option. As you move through life, you reinvent yourself and grow. In your twenties, your interests might orbit around exploration — trying new cities, new hobbies, new hairstyles you later pretend never happened. Maybe you're obsessed with travel, brunch, self-discovery, or figuring out who you are through a series of questionable jobs and even more questionable dating choices.

By forty, your priorities shift. Suddenly, sleep is a hobby. Stability is sexy. You care about things like health insurance, peace and quiet, and chairs that don't hurt your back. What matters expands, deepens, or changes entirely. That's what makes life interesting — you're not meant to stay the same.

So if you've ever felt guilty for wanting something new, or worried that switching paths makes you inconsistent, remember this: in today's job market, staying in the same role for too long doesn't make you look stable — it makes recruiters wonder if you've been trapped in a basement.

And this brings us to the second part: you don't need to destroy your old story. You just need to expand it. The same psychological mechanism that kept you stuck — the consistency principle — can help you to expand your identity instead of limiting it. Your brain wants your actions and identity to match, so give it new evidence.

You do this by consciously applying your transferable skills in a new context that points toward your desired future.

Problem-solving.

Communication.

Analytical thinking.

Your ability to coordinate, plan, mediate, organize, or lead.

All these skills are not tied to one industry.

- The analyst who volunteers to write the narrative for their team's final report is gathering evidence that they are "a person who translates data into compelling stories."
- The operations manager who mentors a junior colleague is gathering evidence that they are "a person who develops talent."
- The administrator who organizes a community event is gathering evidence that they are "a person who has good people skills."

Each small project, each new learning, each tiny step is another sign placed in the window — a quiet but powerful signal to your brain: *"This is who I am becoming."*

Over time, these small proofs accumulate. Your brain, craving a neat and consistent self-narrative, begins to integrate this new evidence. And the shift doesn't happen in a single, dramatic leap. To logically rewrite the story from the inside, you'll need a series of consistent actions.

And when you change your actions, your identity follows.

2. The Invisible Toolbox

The second hurdle in any career transition is this: many of us struggle to claim our skills and achievements, and therefore the ways we can develop our careers. We were never taught to see these things clearly.

As your career unfolds, you meet countless people. Every new person becomes a mirror reflecting back something about you — "You're so organized," "You're great with people," "You always know how to fix things." Over time, these reflections become part of your identity. But are they fragments or the full picture?

The truth is, we rarely see the full map of our own capabilities. We get so focused on the narrow path in front of us — the tasks of our current role — that we forget how many skills we've accumulated along the way.

Earlier in the book, we explored where that habit comes from. Women, in particular, are experts at overlooking their own abilities. We often downplay our strengths. And sometimes, we don't describe them at all — we erase them.

Do these sound familiar?

- "I just managed the budget."
- "I just coordinated the weekly meetings."
- "I just write emails."

We use the word *just* as if these were small, simple tasks anyone could do — instead of complex acts of foresight, organization, diplomacy, and leadership that you've quietly mastered. (And yes, describing them this way might feel exaggerated or boastful right now — we'll work on that.)

In addition, some kinds of work are more visible and more "countable" than others. And that matters — both in how others see your work, and in how *you* own it.

Take event organizing. The result of your work is right there in front of people. Every time, there's a clear finish line — a moment where everyone can see what you pulled off. Even if you don't think your skills are special, at least you can point to something and say, "I made that happen." It helps you recognize and own your own strengths — organization, communication, coordination.

Owning your skills is harder when your role is all about process, like customer success, where the wins aren't always visible. The list of customers keeps growing, the work never really ends, and almost nothing you do has a neat, ta-da moment. Your work lives in meetings, emails, spreadsheets, and conversations. So what's your masterpiece?

It's a hard question to answer because your masterpiece is often invisible. It's the conflict that never erupted because you sensed the tension early and steered the meeting in a better direction. It's the team that stayed aligned because you explained the plan clearly enough that no one had to guess. It's the risk you spotted early on. These accomplishments don't sit on a pedestal, but they are your achievements.

Another challenge in recognizing your skills is that most of us in corporate are surrounded by people from the same field. When you sit next to twenty colleagues who do similar work, your perspective shifts. Whatever you're good at starts to feel ordinary. You begin to believe everyone can do what you do. You stop seeing yourself from the outside, and your expertise becomes invisible to you.

Repetition in the same environment makes the extraordinary feel ordinary. In your pond, running a complex project might be a standard Tuesday. You might think, "Well, of course anyone could do this."

But step outside your pond for a moment. Ask someone who has never had to align different personalities, manage a tight budget, or keep a team moving toward a deadline whether they could do it. That little experiment would reveal a lot — and it's a shame we rarely get the chance to see ourselves through that lens. What you're good at isn't universal. And when you finally acknowledge the abilities you've been carrying for years, you reclaim the power to choose your career instead of waiting for someone else to recognize you.

From Lawyer to Head of Project Management (Russia → Turkey → Netherlands)

If you met Anna today, you might assume her career had always been steady: a clear trajectory, a disciplined mind, a woman who always knew where she was going. But her real story is far more layered. It's a story of starting over — twice. Of losing a profession, a country, a language, and rebuilding all three. Of discovering strengths she didn't know she had until life pushed her into places she never planned to go.

Anna graduated with honors as a lawyer in Russia. In her first roles, she worked as a real estate attorney, helping clients with purchase and sale contracts. It was there that she met a guy who worked in tech at an international company.

They started dating, and their relationship continued for a few years. Then, he received a six-month assignment in Turkey. After careful consideration, they decided to embrace the opportunity and relocated together.

This was pre-COVID time. Remote work typically required being a freelancer or entrepreneur. Anna managed to negotiate a temporary remote arrangement with her real estate agency employer and continued working for them.

When her partner's contract got extended, Anna focused on language courses, improving her English and learning Turkish. Around that time, Russian real estate law changed — all transactions now required notarization, effectively eliminating 70% of her responsibilities. Practicing law in Turkey wasn't feasible either, due to legal differences and language barriers.

"I've always valued my independence, both professionally and financially," *Anna explained.* "Suddenly I'd lost both. I was looking for a new career and new life in a country that is completely different from my own. When discussing next steps with my partner — who'd been in tech for years — he suggested, "Why not try pivoting careers to IT, and try something that you could easily learn, like QA?"

QA (Quality Assurance) involves testing software products to ensure functionality. When software products are created, someone has to make sure that you don't get a blank page when you click Buy. It's considered an entry-level tech role since it doesn't require programming knowledge.

My approach was straightforward: to prove your skills to a potential employer, get certified. When I learned about an internationally recognized certification for QA engineers (ISTQB), I began preparing. Since the materials were in English, this also improved my language comprehension."

After I received the certificate, I started to apply for jobs. This was my first time looking for a job in Turkey. I faced constant rejection. A Turkish friend explained then that employers here typically want graduates from specific prestigious Turkish universities or candidates with exceptional experience and referrals. I had neither.

There were moments of real despair. I knew I would be amazing at this job, I just needed a chance. I doubted anyone would ever give me that chance though.

Seeing my tantrums, my partner stepped in. He asked around at his company whether they were looking for a junior QA engineer. His team wasn't hiring, but it turned out that the adjacent team was looking for a support engineer.

I prepared my self-presentation and walked in with shaking hands. The interview went well. I even agreed to work the first month for free — and they hired me. It wasn't the position I had imagined for myself, but it got me into tech from scratch. I should've been happy at that point. And yet, it felt like the challenges just kept piling up.

At first, communication was a huge challenge for me. While all my colleagues were fluent in both Turkish and English, I lacked confidence in my own English. I had a few certifications, but this was my first real immersion in an English-speaking workplace. And even though I had passed a Turkish exam at the C1 level, I still felt unable to speak — my mind would go blank in conversations, and I struggled to form sentences without hesitation.

My new role required me to work closely with four local colleagues. Luckily, they turned out to be amazing, pushing me to move past the awkwardness and learn the language on the spot.

After some time, the company opened a position for a quality assurance engineer. I applied and transitioned into the role. This was what I truly wanted, and working with that team felt deeply rewarding. For the first time in a long while, I was genuinely happy.

The story could have ended at this point. Yet it seems that after you switch countries once, you develop an extraordinary sense of adaptability that makes every next transition easier."

After a few years in Turkey, due to social and political instability both of them admitted they would welcome changes. They were thinking about switching countries again.

"We had a close friend in The Netherlands, we visited him a few times and we liked the country. At the same time, we knew that it would be much harder to find a job in the Netherlands, because Dutch managers consider that all of your experience outside Europe or, more precisely, outside the Netherlands is a different story. That's what I just heard from one of the Dutch managers — not really my opinion.

This friend of ours shared a role in their company that was a great fit for my partner. The interview process started. At some point, they invited him to a face-to-face interview. We had to get from Istanbul to the Netherlands to make it to the in-person interview. When the company confirmed they were prepared to make him an offer, he casually asked:

"You wouldn't happen to have an open QA engineer position, would you?"

"Actually, we do," they replied.

When we returned to Istanbul to pack, I already had an interview lined up too. The first interview went well. The second one was on-site since we'd already moved by then. During the final interview with the senior manager, he expressed doubts about having both me and my partner work at the same company. But then my Ukrainian colleague — bless her — stepped in. "Actually, it's an advantage," she told him. "When a product issue arises, she'll be our bridge to the engineering team." I'll always be grateful for her support.

I've been with my current company ever since, and I couldn't be happier. My career has progressed from QA manager to release manager, then delivery manager, project manager, and now I lead a team of project managers. Remembering how others helped me when I needed it most, I now actively help people join our company too.

While working at her current company, Anna referred eight other professionals, many for their first tech role. "I make sure their career transitions are smoother than mine was," *she says with a smile.*

I'm happy I found my dream job. There's only one downside: when your core skill is spotting risks early on, it spills over into everything, including your personal life. For example, when my partner or friends get excited about wild ideas, I can't help but play devil's advocate and point out why they might not work. But my friends and family already know I mean well. Plus, this same critical thinking is exactly what makes me good at my job, so I eventually see it as a blessing."

Stories like Anna's — and perhaps parts of your own — reveal that you are far more capable, adaptable, and resourceful than the narrow label of your past job title ever captured.

As you begin to examine your invisible toolbox, you'll start connecting dots you've never connected before. You'll see how your talent for organizing information in your admin role is directly related to data management. You'll recognize that coordinating volunteers for a community event is, in fact, project management and stakeholder engagement. You'll realize that the conflict you prevented, the process you streamlined, the team you aligned — these were not "just part of the job." They were demonstrations of leadership, foresight, and strategic thinking.

Bringing your identity into words is a very important part of this process. Therefore, pay attention to the language you use when you talk about yourself. Sometimes, without meaning to, the way you describe yourself makes you smaller. You might think you're "just being honest" or "keeping it simple," but simplicity can backfire. When your language stays too humble or too junior, it doesn't reflect the real depth of what you do — and it can quietly limit how others see you (and how you see yourself), especially in corporate environments.

You might say, *"I help the team stay organized."*

A senior leader would describe the exact same work as: *"I drive alignment across teams and ensure execution stays on track."*

Same skill. Same person. Completely different signal.

If this feels artificial at first, I invite you to try slowly. Reinventing the way you refer to your career journey can feel uncomfortable, even a bit fake at first. But naming your skills with stronger, clearer language isn't about pretending to be someone else — it's about finally giving an accurate description of who you already are.

In this chapter, we are moving the narrative from:

"I don't have the experience for my new career."

to a far truer, more empowering understanding:

"I already have a strong, relevant foundation. I am a good candidate — and with focused learning, I can quickly get better."

By the end of this reinvention, you'll be able to look at a job description for your desired new role, point to specific experiences in your past, and say with grounded confidence:

"Yes, I can do that. Here is my proof."

Not because you're pretending.

Not because you're stretching the truth.

But because you finally see who you are clearly.

3. The Golden Cage

Let's name the number one reason so many people hesitate to make a change in midlife: the golden cage.

It's the version of life where you worked hard, and your hard work paid off. And that's exactly why so many people stay in roles they've outgrown — because status, ego, self-worth, financial security, and being good at something get tangled together until they form their own kind of prison. You stay because you've invested years into becoming someone others rely on, admire, or expect you to be. There's too much at stake — both out in the world and inside your own identity. And walking away from that version of yourself can feel almost impossible.

First, something needs to be made clear: chasing status doesn't mean you're shallow. In many cultures, status simply means respect — and respect matters. When you have status, people listen to you. They recognize your expertise. Your title sounds impressive at family gatherings, making you parents proud.

Status also brings power — and that matters more than most people admit. Power gives you influence. You get used to being the one who makes decisions, sets direction, and shapes outcomes. You've earned your place in the hierarchy, and it feels good to be the person others rely on. You get used to being the person others turn to for answers. Confidence becomes part of your identity, and starting over feels like an unnecessary — and a painful — step backward.

Then there's material success — also deeply valued in many cultures. And if you grew up poor, the material side matters even more. When your role comes with real, tangible benefits — the company car, the five-star hotels, the admiration, the mortgage for a home you genuinely like in a luxury neighborhood — it feels like proof that all your effort paid off.

Why would you walk away from that? Because even golden cages shrink over time. The work that once energized you now drains you. You've mastered the role so completely that there's nothing left to learn. And sometimes staying starts to cost more — emotionally, mentally, sometimes physically — than leaving ever could.

Yet so many capable, ambitious people stay in roles that no longer fulfill them. On the surface, the reasons sound practical:

The mortgage.
The market.
The children.
The stability.

But if you keep asking yourself carefully, you'll find out that the true reason is deeper. Researchers once asked Harvard students a simple question: would you rather earn $50,000 while everyone else earns $25,000, or earn $100,000 while everyone else earns $200,000?

What would *you* go with?

In this experiment, more than half chose… the lower salary. It made no financial sense — but emotionally, it did. They preferred the version of themselves who *felt* successful in comparison, even if they were objectively earning less.

If you've ever discovered that your title matched your colleagues' while your salary sat at half of theirs, the outcome of that study probably doesn't surprise you. You know that quiet sting — it's a very human reaction. Status isn't just about money; it's about belonging. Psychologists Roy Baumeister and Mark Leary argue that humans have a deep need to belong, so deep that it shapes our behavior without us even noticing. So when we fear losing status, what we're really afraid of is losing our place in the group.

We all want to feel valued, and it's easy for that need to get projected onto the symbols of our professional lives — the title, the recognition, the place we hold in the group. Status also feeds the ego —   the sense of importance — and many people mistake ego for identity.

But that same ego becomes your biggest hindrance to growth. It assumes it already knows the answers. It clings to what's familiar. And to grow, you have to shift into a different mode — the *"I have no idea, but I'm going to figure it out"* mode. That's the mindset of reinvention, and it's the exact opposite of what ego is comfortable with.

The same ego that keeps you safe can also keep you small, especially when you're standing at the edge of change. And when your ego becomes intertwined with your role, it starts shaping your decisions about the future long before you realize it.

When you make compensation or status the primary lens for choosing your next career step, your options shrink dramatically. You begin to ask:

"Where can I go without losing what I have?"

instead of

"Where can I grow into who I want to become?"

And that first question is the one that keeps people stuck for years. Because the truth is, mid-career transitions often involve a temporary dip in status or income. Not always, but too often. And when you're in your late 30s or beyond, with responsibilities, mortgages, children, or aging parents, that dip can feel terrifying —

and sometimes completely unsustainable. So if you've ever blamed yourself for not being able to walk away from the status you've built — even when you know it's time — you're not alone.

But here's something worth considering.

Psychologist Mihaly Csikszentmihalyi, who studied creativity, flow, and what makes life feel meaningful — and who interviewed thousands of people across professions, from artists and surgeons to athletes and factory workers — found that humans experience the deepest satisfaction when a task is just slightly more challenging than their current ability. Not too easy, not too hard. Just enough to stretch you.

The problem is that many mid-career professionals are no longer stretched. They're overqualified and bored.

They're stuck in roles that once felt exciting but now exist mostly to maintain a certain standard of living.

Externally, a prestigious job looks like success.

Internally, it feels like stagnation.

It's a strange kind of trap: you're comfortable, but not fulfilled. You're respected, but not growing. You're stable, but not alive in your work anymore. And the longer you stay, the harder it becomes to imagine anything different —because the cost of change feels too high.

You want to grow, but you don't want to fall.

You want change, but you don't want loss.

You want meaning, but you don't want uncertainty.

You're a supercar driver who presses the gas pedal with the brakes on.

How do you pivot then?

From Head of Innovation to Empathy Coach (France → Netherlands)

Marjolein never imagined that a career built in pharmaceutical sales, marketing, and corporate innovation would one day lead her to become an empathy coach and trainer. For eighteen years, she climbed the ladder in France and the Netherlands, collecting promotions, responsibility, and constant achievement — until burnout, motherhood, and a deep value clash forced her to question everything. Losing her best friend to cancer cracked her open even further, pushing her to leave her golden cage, and rebuild her life around freedom, kindness, and human connection. And this is how she tells her story.

I guess in terms of career, I was building my CV in a good way.

For the first 18 years of my life, I lived and studied in France. I studied biomedical sciences because I was fascinated by the human body.

When I was choosing my first career, as I had had experience losing a dear family friend to cancer, I had this utopian dream of finding the cure for cancer. I was following the path to become a researcher. Along the way, I realized that I'm more of a people person, with a need for a dynamic working environment so I also did an MBA specializing in the pharmaceutical industry. It turned out to be the perfect shift, leading me into an 18-year career in the pharmaceutical world.

I began my career as a sales representative. In that role, you go out in the field and visit doctors — sometimes general practitioners, sometimes hospital specialists, nurses, and others.

I hated it.

I hated every minute of it.

Because in reality it was all about sales, not really building equal relationships.

Besides, it's a solo job. You get in your car in the morning and get home at night, and once every month you have a team meeting. That's it.

So I really wanted to make a transition from sales to marketing because all the materials you use as a sales representative and all the topics you discuss are being developed by someone in the office. After some time, I got this position. And then I really started to enjoy the work I was doing.

I did that for quite a few years. I was also a perfectionist, and I think I was a lot of a people pleaser in my job, and life. At some point, I was managing a team of 30 people. My manager also asked me to take on an additional role in another therapeutic area. As a true people pleaser, I was saying yes to everything.

As I had two positions and a daughter, who had some medical issues at birth...

I felt like I was a bad mom because I was working quite a lot, and our daughter was going to daycare.

I felt like I was a bad employee because I felt I was not delivering on the job.

And I felt like I was a bad wife because I was very stressed at home and not running the household as I had wanted to.

Back then, I had a massive burnout. And I learned a lot about myself in that time. Until that point, I think I was always like:

What do my parents expect of me?

What does my manager expect of me?

What does the company expect of me?

And there's this culture in corporate of "the only way is up."

What's the next promotion? What's the next step?

So I came back from that, and that's when I said, okay, you know what?

I don't want to lead a team anymore.

They really wanted to keep me, so they said, "Well, if you want, we can develop a staff position. You'll be part of the management team without the staff."

People around me said "Brilliant. You're going to be on the management team, you're going to get a more important role, a bigger car and a higher salary." And they were like, "This is your chance."

We all want to be successful in a certain way. Back then, to me success meant how much money I made, how big my car was, and how often and how far I traveled. Today, my definition of success is very different. But in the corporate world, walking away from that standard of living was a crazy idea.

I'm not sure whether what happened next was a result of personal development or a reconnection with my values, but…

I said, no.

Which is kind of weird because "no" is not really an answer when you get a promotion.

But they wanted to keep me, so we created this new role, a Head of Innovation. That implied not innovating the medicines, but innovating on the programs to help doctors and nurses in patient care. My role was to embed a culture innovation within the whole company and I could start facilitating workshops and training people.

I enjoyed every minute of it, for several years. I had discovered a new passion of mine. But even though it was fun and meaningful to me, my motivation started to decrease. It became quite repetitive, and the space I was given by my manager to be creative and innovative began to shrink significantly. We didn't share the same vision for my role and the outcomes I needed to achieve. It became clear that our values were miles apart.

That's when my best friend discovered that she had breast cancer. We didn't know it was going to get so bad, but there was this sense of, wait — if I'm not fulfilled in the work that I do anymore, am I really spending my life the way I want to spend it?

And since I was already getting a little bored, so to speak, I took it as a sign to explore new options, and maybe leave corporate. Leave my golden cage.

A lot of people told me, "Gosh, go and start your own business." No way. I didn't want that. I was convinced I didn't have an entrepreneurial mindset. I was looking for a way to do what I love doing, which was helping people grow by building new skills, through training and workshops. So I looked at all the training bureaus — you know, there are so many of them that train corporations. But those agencies don't hire trainers; they work with freelancers.

Around that time, an agency reached out to me when I was still Head of Innovation — they wanted to run a project with me, within the company I was working for, basically within my cage.

So I had a conversation with them, and halfway through that conversation, I told the director, "I think we need to switch the conversation. I think I need to take off my corporate hat and put on my entrepreneurial hat, because I want to come and work for you."

That moment made me realize I could actually work with them. There was zero guarantee they would have jobs or assignments for me, but that's where it all began. I quit my corporate job and spread my wings, finally flying out of the cage. I left everything behind — my salary, my pension scheme, my car, some dear colleagues — everything that had once felt secure.

I had three or four months of zero income. That was tough.

But then the assignments started rolling in. And so, suddenly, within half a year, I was making more money than I made in the corporate job!

I didn't want to be a freelancer, but once I was a freelancer, I was like, there's the word "free" in freelancer. So I discovered something I didn't know was important to me — freedom.

I embraced the freedom to develop myself, and trained to become a coach.

Meanwhile, my best friend's health was deteriorating. It slowly became clear that she wasn't going to win the battle against cancer. This felt insurmountable to me. I couldn't be with that thought. I needed help. I've been through therapy. I studied positive psychology. After she passed away, I was heartbroken and depressed. I did a lot of soul searching. That is also when I started working with a coach who taught me how to live by myself, for the first time in my life. And I found my purpose — to spread my best friend's kindness in this world by empowering women to become their own best friend first.

The hardest part in this is that I strongly believe in my skills as a coach. I see the results in the women I've coached... but I will say I'm not such a good marketeer for myself. Working in corporate, I was never active on LinkedIn, let alone Instagram — I didn't need to. I had this allergy to promoting myself.

Yet with time, I've learned to reframe it.

It's about giving people — women, mostly women — the opportunity to work on themselves, potentially with me. If I don't show up, if I'm not visible on social media, I am taking away their chances to get someone to help them. It's about their needs, not my insecurity.

Now I truly feel that I'm living on purpose, authentically. I think previously there was one part of me at work, the professional side and then me personally, the other side. And I think these two are much more blended together now, because I bring in so much of myself in my work.

Because now it's me as a human being.

Breaking Free from the Golden Cage

So what could possibly give you the courage to leave the golden cage when everything in your life looks comfortable and complete?

Happiness — and the research behind it — offers a clue.

Research on happiness consistently shows that while income increases life satisfaction at lower levels, the effect plateaus once basic needs and a sense of stability are met. Nobel laureates Daniel Kahneman and Angus Deaton found that emotional well-being levels off around a certain income threshold. Beyond that point, more money doesn't make daily life feel better — it only increases your perceived status.

If I ask you how much money you need to be happy, the optimists among us will provide a ridiculously large number — enough to cover every possible expense until they're 100. That's just how the brain works.

But if you answered realistically, research already gives a pretty good idea of how your number compares to what you earn now.

Sonja Lyubomirsky's work on happiness shows that regardless of what you earn, you tend to believe you need about 40% more to be happy. And once you reach that number, it quickly becomes the new baseline. The cycle repeats endlessly, and you might get stuck in this loop.

It's not that money doesn't matter — it does. But when money becomes the primary goal in a career transition, it tricks you into thinking you're chasing happiness, when in reality you're just chasing a number. And like any external reward — status, praise, compensation — it comes from outside you, so it rarely leads to genuine fulfillment.

So perhaps the more helpful question isn't: *"How do I switch careers without losing status?"* but rather: *"What kind of work would make me feel alive, even if the status came later?"*

Becoming a beginner in your 40s can feel daunting — and it's not exactly flattering for the ego. It's uncomfortable because it asks you to trade certainty for possibility, and we as humans don't like risk.

Ego isn't bad; we all have one. Every human being carries a lifetime of experiences, lessons, and interpretations that shape how they see themselves. Ego is simply the part of you that wants to feel competent, respected, and safe. At this stage of life, you've already built competence, credibility, and a certain rhythm in your work. You're used to being the person others come to for answers, not the one raising your hand with basic questions. Starting over means stepping out of the identity you've spent years building and into a space where nothing is guaranteed — not recognition, not confidence, not status.

But your ego isn't the only part of you that gets a vote.

There's another part — the part that's curious, alive, hungry for something meaningful. The part that lights up when you talk about what you actually care about.

The part that remembers what it feels like to be energized by your work, not drained by it.

That part is your foundation for any career transition.

When you're doing something you truly adore — something that sparks your curiosity, stretches your mind, or reconnects you with your sense of possibility — the discomfort of being a beginner becomes bearable. Even exciting. Passion gives you the courage to be clumsy for a while. Curiosity gives you the patience to learn. Together, they soften the ego's fear and make space for growth.

You don't overcome the beginner stage by pretending it's easy.

You overcome it by caring enough that the difficulty feels worth it.

And that's where reinvention really begins. Not with a perfect plan, but with the quiet pull toward something that feels more like you.

Status can be rebuilt. Skills can be learned. Income can grow again.

But time — and meaning — don't wait.

4. The Fog Of Too Many Options

How many different roles have you held so far in your career?

If you're like most midlife professionals, it's at least three or four — enough to prove you've already reinvented yourself a few times. You'd think that after doing it once or twice, the next shift would feel easy — you've stepped into new roles before, adapted, and succeeded.

But strangely, it doesn't get easier.

Even applying for roles that sit squarely within your professional background can feel like a small identity crisis. You rewrite your CV for the fifteenth time. You adjust your headline. You tweak your summary. You try to anticipate the keywords this particular hiring manager wants to find. Every application becomes a negotiation between who you've been and who you're allowed to be next.

If that's what happens when you're applying for something familiar, what happens when you step into a completely new field?

The moment you enter a world of *infinite* possibilities — when you realize you could do many things, not just one — the ground shifts beneath you. Suddenly the problem isn't a lack of options. It's the opposite.

This is the paradox of possibility: the more options you have, the harder it becomes to move toward any of them. You scroll through job boards, and every listing sparks a different version of your future. You imagine yourself in ten different roles, ten different industries, ten different lives. And instead of clarity, you get fog.

And there's a reason for that — a biological one. Neuroscientists have found that when we're faced with an overwhelming number of choices, the brain shifts into cognitive overload. The prefrontal cortex — the part responsible for planning, decision-making, and long-term thinking — becomes strained.

Barry Schwartz's research on the Paradox of Choice shows that more options don't create more freedom; they create more anxiety. When the brain is overloaded, it defaults to:

- avoidance (doing nothing)
- rumination (thinking endlessly without acting)
- risk aversion (choosing the safest, not the truest option)
- self-doubt ("What if I choose wrong?")

Functional MRI studies show that too many choices activate the anterior cingulate cortex — the region associated with conflict and error detection. In other words, your brain interprets "too many possibilities" as a threat, not an opportunity.

This is why you can stare at a job board for an hour and walk away feeling more confused than when you started. That's what neuroscience says. And when you're multi-passionate, it gets even louder.

> **From Political Science to Sound Researcher & Attention Strategist (Italy →
> Netherlands)**
>
> *Concetta grew up dreaming of comics and music, not careers or titles. Years later, she would reinvent herself again and again — from political science to job-market research, from sound engineering to corporate tech, and finally into the work that feels most like home: helping people reclaim their focus and attention.*
> *And this is how she tells her story.*
> I never really saw my life as a career. When I look back, I see a long experiment — a continuous process of learning, testing, and discovering who I am. As a child, I wanted to create comics. I wrote, I drew, I imagined entire worlds. Music was the other constant in my life. But when it came time to choose a degree, my father suggested political science. I didn't have a rigid plan, so I followed the suggestion.
> Political science ended up shaping me more than I expected. It taught me to look at everything from 360 degrees, to understand that nothing has a single cause, that every

situation has multiple perspectives. At the time, I thought I'd never use this. Now it's the foundation of how I think.

After university, I spent eight years researching employment disruptions, managing projects, and lecturing. It was interesting, but it lacked creativity. And worst of all, I didn't see any impact. So much paperwork, and nothing changed. I felt like I was pouring energy into a system that didn't move.

So I turned back to my passions. I chose music. I had been singing and playing piano, but I wanted to understand the sound itself. I studied sound engineering, worked at concerts and studios, and eventually completed both a bachelor's and a master's in sound studies. That's where everything started to connect. I became fascinated by how sound shapes perception, behavior, and emotion — how it changes us without us noticing.

Then life forced me to pause.

At 30, just before moving to the Netherlands, I had major surgery. The surgery wasn't the hardest part. What came after was. Doctors told me I had a short window to decide whether I wanted children. At the same time, I was in a difficult relationship. Everything stopped. I needed to understand myself before making any other decisions. That period — almost four years — became one of the most important of my life. It was the first time I stopped thinking about "career" and started thinking about myself.

When I moved to the Netherlands, I arrived with a research grant from Italy, but the funding wasn't enough to live on. I needed a job. I found one in corporate, at a company whose technology aligned beautifully with my sound research. It was a fresh start. Again.

In Italy, the culture is very formal and very hierarchical. Everything you achieve, you achieve late in life — you can become a professor at 60 or 65. At the same time, if you are 45, you're already in that part of the job market where the government is expected to take care of you, because it's considered "too late." You also need far more certified skills — the right degree, the right path — and once you're on a path, it's very difficult to leave it. Everything is structured and rigid.

Here in the Netherlands, if you are 35, you don't have to worry that you are 35. You can always find a new place, even in corporate.

So I stayed in the corporate for eight years. And then one morning, I woke up with a clear thought: I want to work by myself. To build something of my own. To bring my research to people, not just to papers. So I made the decision the same day — and then I "burned the ships." No backup plan. No "I can always go back." I cut off the old path so I could fully build the new one.

I tested ideas constantly: workshops, conversations with strangers, masterclasses, informal interviews. I learned that people don't describe their problems the way experts do. I learned that a workshop should have one point, not ten. I learned that transformation requires simplicity, not academic overload. Entrepreneurship required new skills — marketing, business, market analysis — so I learned everything. I took an MBA. I studied digital tools.

Along the way, I learned a few things about the world — things that shaped every decision I made.

I learned that my identity is not my career. This is why switching paths never felt like failure. If you detach who you *are* from what you *do*, you stop fearing rejection, status loss, or starting over. You make decisions based on alignment, not fear.

I learned that money is never the reason to choose a path. Money can be adjusted. But choosing something that isn't aligned with you — that's much harder to fix.

I learned that decisions don't need perfect clarity. The hardest decisions are when two options look equally possible. In those moments, I choose — intentionally, quickly — and only afterward do I evaluate whether it was right. Staying stuck is worse than choosing.

Today, I'm an attention strategist and independent researcher. I work one-on-one with clients — senior professionals, entrepreneurs — helping them improve focus, manage information overload, and reconnect with their internal compass. I'm also building an AI assistant that guides people through focus sessions, manages their environment, handles notifications, and helps them work with clarity.

My journey isn't linear. It's cumulative. Every step — political science, job-market research, sound engineering, corporate work, academic research — became a building block. Nothing was wasted. Nothing was irrelevant.

If you take a snapshot ten years ago, you see one thing.

If you take a snapshot today, you see something else.

But it's not because I changed.

It's because I added more pieces.

Ironically, the people with the broadest, richest skill sets — the ones who could thrive in many environments — are the ones who get stuck the longest, because their brain keeps whispering, "You could be anyone... so who do you want to be?"

Take someone who has worked in marketing, managed a team, dabbled in product strategy, and picked up some data skills along the way. When they open a job board, they can picture themselves as:

- a marketing lead;
- a brand strategist;
- a product manager;
- a content director;
- a communications manager;
- a growth strategist;

- a consultant;
- or even a founder.

And because they can imagine themselves doing all of these roles, their brain starts running simulations:

"If I go into product, I'll need to upskill. But if I stay in marketing, I'll be pigeonholed. Consulting sounds exciting, but what if I hate the lifestyle? Maybe I should freelance. Or maybe I should go in-house. Or maybe I should switch industries entirely."

Each imagined future triggers a new comparison.

Each comparison triggers a new doubt.

Each doubt triggers a new round of research.

By the time they've scrolled through the first page of listings, they've lived six alternate lives and committed to none of them.

If this is you, there's nothing wrong with you. In fact, I invite you to see yourself as a multipassionate person in a new light. What if this isn't inconsistency at all, but a sign of how many different ways you're capable of contributing?

There's a few names for this way of being. They come from psychology and creativity research:

- **Divergent thinking**: the ability to generate many ideas.
- **Multipotentiality**: having multiple aptitudes and interests.
- **Scanner personality**: people who learn fast, love variety, and move on once they've mastered something.
- **High openness to experience**: a personality trait linked to creativity, curiosity, and reinvention.

Notice what all these theories have in common: none of them describe a flaw. They describe a temperament — one that's curious, expansive, and deeply adaptive. A temperament that doesn't want one life, but a life big enough to hold many interests.

There are entire careers where a mind like yours is a huge advantage. Fields like journalism, product management, consulting, UX, marketing, research, creative direction, entrepreneurship, and operations don't want someone who stays in one lane. These roles reward curiosity, range, and the ability to shift gears quickly. Specialists go deep, but generalists see the whole landscape — and in these environments, that wide-angle view is exactly what makes you stand out.

The reason you see so many possible paths is because you *have* so many. Instead of forcing yourself into a single lane, try designing a career that lets you move. Let your curiosity be data. Let your range be an asset. Let your mind work the way it naturally wants to.

You're not inconsistent.

You're multi-dimensional.

And your career can be, too.

The Conversation With Yourself

A career change often begins with an honest admission: *this no longer feels like me.* You feel the misalignment long before you can articulate it, sensing that something in your work no longer fits. The meaning has faded, the energy has shifted, and the version of you who once belonged there feels increasingly distant.

But when all you have is the feeling that "this isn't it," clarity about what comes next rarely arrives on command. Instead, you're under pressure to choose something sensible, something you're already a "good fit" for, something that won't require you to stretch too far. Meanwhile, the paths you'd truly love to explore feel unrealistic, too bold, or reserved for someone braver, someone with fewer doubts and more certainty.

From the outside, many directions look appealing, which only makes the question *"What should I do next"* feel heavier. It's not a lack of options that keeps you stuck — it's the absence of a clear yes. So you hover between possibilities, circling ideas without landing on any of them, unsure whether you're hesitating out of fear or simply waiting for something to feel true.

And when you're standing at the edge of a career change, there's a moment when everything feels unsteady. The old role is losing its shape, the new one isn't solid yet, and you're caught in that in-between space where nothing feels fully true anymore.

So what do you stand on to reinvent yourself?

Why Identity Matters

A mid-life career change isn't just about choosing a new job — it's about choosing a new version of yourself to grow into. And that's why it can feel so disorienting.

Most of us try to find clarity by scanning job boards, comparing ourselves to other people's paths, or jumping from one "maybe this" profession to another. It's like riding a follower-coaster: exciting for a moment, dizzying the next.

If this feels familiar, I want to invite you to pause for a moment.

First, it's completely normal to feel lost in a moment like this. We all go through seasons when the old answers stop working. Feeling unsure doesn't mean you've lost yourself — it simply means you're in a transition, moving from one version of your life into another. It's a phase of reinvention. Something in you is growing, stretching, rearranging itself, and your mind hasn't caught up yet.

When you're searching for your next step, it can feel like walking through a landscape covered in fog. You keep looking ahead, hoping the path will reveal itself, but the more you strain your eyes, the less you see. The world outside stays blurry.

But the truth is, you don't need the fog to lift — you need your compass. Because clarity doesn't come from the path becoming visible. It comes from knowing the direction that feels true to you.

As long as you're chasing someone else's approval, or someone else's definition of success, it's almost impossible to feel that quiet, grounded sense of *this is who I am*.

When your identity feels unclear, you naturally reach for whatever is closest — old labels, past strengths, former passions — even if they no longer match the person you're becoming. You might still hear yourself say "I'm not creative," "I'm not a leader," or "I'm not technical," even though those beliefs were shaped by earlier chapters, not by the one you're in now.

This is why identity matters. It's your foundation.

Exploring identity gives you something steady to stand on. It helps you see which parts of you are truly yours, which parts you inherited without choosing, which parts have outgrown their usefulness, and which parts are ready to evolve. It brings clarity without pressure, and compassion without confusion, revealing:

- who you used to be
- who you've been told you are
- who you actually are today
- and who you're becoming

When you understand these layers, the career transition stops feeling like a free fall. You're not guessing anymore — you're building from the inside out.

You discover clarity in conversations.

First, a conversation with yourself.

Then, a conversation with someone you trust.

And only then, a conversation with the world.

This is the structure of the book: inner clarity → trusted circle → outer world. Because meaningful change doesn't start with job boards or LinkedIn searches. It starts with understanding what matters to you now, what you value, what energizes you, and what you're no longer willing to carry. That inner conversation is where your priorities take shape, where your needs become visible, and where your next chapter begins to form.

Once you have that foundation, the next step is to bring other people into the process — not to outsource your decision, but to let your world support your transition. These conversations aren't about asking for permission. They're about gathering information, expanding your perspective, and letting yourself be seen in your becoming.

Only after those two layers — the inner clarity and the trusted circle — does it make sense to speak to the wider world. By the time you get there, you're not guessing anymore. You're moving with intention.

The desire to switch careers is rarely random. It's a signal that who you were and who you are now are no longer the same person. Reinvention begins in that space — the space where your old identity stops fitting, and your new one hasn't fully formed yet.

This chapter is the beginning of that reinvention. It's the conversation with yourself, exploring what identity really is — and how to connect the old version of you to the version of you that's ready to emerge.

Who Are You?

In Greek mythology, Theseus was the hero who defeated the Minotaur and saved Athens. His ship became a symbol of courage and identity, so the Athenians kept it in the harbor as a monument. As the years passed and the wood began to rot, they replaced each plank with a new one. Slowly, piece by piece, the entire ship was rebuilt. Not a single original plank remained.

That's when the philosophers asked their famous question:

If every part has been replaced, is it still the Ship of Theseus?

And if you gathered all the discarded planks and rebuilt a second ship, which one would be the "real" one?

It's a clever puzzle — until you realize it's actually about you. Your beliefs shift. Your habits evolve. Your skills change. Your body renews itself cell by cell. The person you were at twenty is not the person you are now — and not the person you'll be ten years from today.

And this matters, especially now, because a career change isn't just a professional decision. It's an identity decision.

When you imagine a new path, you might feel a quiet resistance:

That's not who I am.

That's not me.

I don't fit in there yet.

That resistance isn't about the job. It's about identity — the version of you you've been carrying, and the version of you you're becoming.

The hardest part of reinvention is the identity shift. Most of us were never taught how to move from one version of ourselves to the next. But when you see the structure of identity clearly, something shifts. You stop trying to drag your old self into a new life. You start merging who you were with who you're becoming. And the inner transition — the one that usually takes the longest — becomes faster, smoother, and less painful.

So here are the questions that really matter:

What makes you *you*?

What is identity, really?

What's the *you* that stays while everything else changes?

Identity becomes especially important when you're standing at the edge of change. Imagine someone who has spent ten years in finance. They're good at it. Competent. Reliable. Their skills are solid, their résumé looks impressive — but inside, something feels off. They're drawn to design, or psychology, or writing, but every time they consider it, a voice says, *"That's not who I am."*

So what do they rely on?

If they rely only on their skills, they'll stay where they are, because their skills point backward, not forward.

If they rely only on their passions, they might chase something exciting but unsustainable, because passion without identity can be impulsive.

If they rely only on their past, they'll repeat old patterns, even if those patterns no longer fit.

If they rely only on their future fantasies, they'll feel overwhelmed, because imagining a new life is easier than stepping into it.

But if they understand their identity — the deeper layers of who they are, who they've been, and who they're becoming — the decision becomes clearer. They can see which parts of them are stable, which parts are inherited, which parts are outdated, and which parts are asking to grow.

Identity becomes the compass. Not a single, fixed point, but something layered — more like four pieces of wood laminated together than one solid block. Each layer has its own history, its own influence, its own way of shaping how you see yourself and what you believe is possible. They're always there, guiding you, even when you're not aware of them.

Before we go deeper, it helps to see the outline. Let's look at each layer briefly, and then we'll explore them more fully.

1. The Physical Identity

This identity is the part of who you are that's shaped by your body — how it moves, appears, reacts, and is read by others. It's the layer of identity that crosses every border with you, influencing how you see yourself and how the world responds before you even speak.

2. The Inherited Identity

This is the layer you didn't choose — the one that was handed to you long before you had the language to question it. It's the cultural script, the family expectations, the "this is how life works" messages you absorbed simply by existing in your environment. It shapes things like:

- what "success" is supposed to look like;
- how much space you're allowed to take;;
- what emotions are acceptable
- what people "like you" should or shouldn't do.

It's subtle. It doesn't shout. It whispers.
"Be humble. Don't make a fuss. Work hard and don't complain."
This layer becomes your default operating system — the background code that runs your decisions even when you think you're being completely rational. And because it feels familiar, it often feels *true*, even when it's outdated or limiting.

Again, understanding this layer isn't about blaming your upbringing. It's about seeing the invisible rules you've been following so you can decide which ones still serve you — and which ones you're ready to rewrite.

3. The Reflected Identity

This is the version of you that exists in other people's minds — the identity shaped by how others see you, describe you, and respond to you. It shows up in:

- the labels people gave you;
- the expectations others project onto you;
- the stories people tell about you.

This layer can be warm and affirming — like when someone sees your potential before you do. But it can also be limiting, because no one sees the full picture. People see you through their own filters, their own needs, their own history with you.

The reflected identity is one of the mirrors — useful, but incomplete. It can show you something true, but it can never show you everything. Part of becoming yourself again is learning to distinguish between who you are and who others have decided you are.

4. The Remembered Identity

This is the identity built from everything that has ever happened to you — the moments that shaped you, the stories you tell about yourself, the memories you carry like evidence. It includes:

- the achievements that made you proud;
- the failures that made you cautious;
- the heartbreaks that made you guarded;
- the criticisms you never forgot.

This layer is powerful because it's your lived experience. But it can also become a trap. A single moment from ten years ago can still define what you believe you're capable of today. A mistake you made once can convince you that you're "not good at that," even if it's no longer true.

The remembered identity is like a scrapbook — full of meaning, but heavy to carry. And sometimes, you need to put it down long enough to ask: *Is this still who I am, or just who I used to be?*

5. The Chosen Identity

This is the layer most people forget they have access to — the identity you are actively shaping through your choices, your desires, your values, and the future you're moving toward. It's the part of you that says:

- "I'm ready to grow."
- "I'm not defined by who I used to be."
- "I get to choose what comes next."

This identity isn't bound by your past or your programming. It's not limited by what others expect from you. It's the part of you that can look at all the other layers and say:

"Thank you for everything you taught me. But I'm writing the next chapter."

This is the version of you that is capable of reinvention, direction, and agency. And this is the layer that becomes essential when you're changing careers, changing countries, and changing the story you've been living.

The Physical Identity

We often talk about identity as if it lives only in the mind — in our thoughts, memories, values, and ambitions. But there's another layer that shapes everything we believe about ourselves: the body we live in. Unlike culture, relationships, or careers, your body is the one part of you that crosses every border. It arrives first, speaks before you do, and sometimes reveals more than you intend.

Most of us treat our bodies as a given. We assume our legs will carry us, our eyes will see, our lungs will expand, and our hands will reach — until something interrupts that freedom and reminds us how much we rely on a body that works.

And even when everything functions, the body is never a neutral part of who you are. It shapes you, marks you, and claims a part of your identity. It's part of how we move through the world, how we're read by others, and how we read ourselves.

That's why our physical identity — our height, posture, expressions, energy, health — quietly shapes how we see ourselves and how others see us. And for expats, this becomes even more visible. Your body becomes a kind of passport — the one people read before you say a word.

Think about the first months in a new country. You walk into a room and suddenly become aware of your body and its language in a way you haven't felt in years. You notice your accent, your gestures, your clothes, your pace. You notice how tall or short you are compared to everyone else. You notice how tired you look after translating your thoughts all day.

And because identity is always tied to what we believe we can or cannot do, our physical self becomes part of that story. If you've ever avoided speaking up because your accent felt "too much," or hesitated to apply for a job because you feared looking "too old," or felt smaller because you didn't understand the cultural cues — that's physical identity shaping your sense of possibility.

Through public speaking, I learned that the body is always a mirror of what happens inside. But the influence works both ways. You can strengthen your confidence by working on your mind — and you can also strengthen your mind by working with your body. When you don't feel sure of yourself, even a small shift in posture, taking a bit more space, can change how you feel.

Through physical change — even small ones — we often rediscover parts of ourselves we thought we lost. A daily walk that clears your mind. A posture that makes you feel grounded again. A voice that grows steadier with practice. A face that softens when you finally feel safe. These shifts are not superficial; they are psychological. When your body feels supported, your identity has room to expand.

Your body is telling the story before your mind can put words to it. Whether you are happy with the body you were given, or see it as a limitation, this is the only body you will live in — and science, unfortunately, isn't offering upgrades yet. So take care of it. Treat it with respect. Offer it love. Start gently and slowly — with simple steps.

- Notice where your body holds tension — the shoulders that have been living up by your ears for months.
- Pay attention to your breath, and how shallow it becomes after a rejection or a difficult conversation.
- Observe your physical reactions to events: the tight jaw, the clenched stomach, the sudden heaviness.

- Notice what you eat and how it makes you feel — energized, foggy, restless, grounded.
- Build small routines that keep your body well: movement, rest, hydration, sunlight, stillness.

Your physical identity is part of your story — not separate from it. You can't rewrite your height, your bone structure, or the way your face naturally settles when you're tired. Many things about the body are fixed, or at least very hard to change. But what isn't fixed is how you care for it, how you inhabit it, and how you let it support you.

When your body is in pain, everything else fades into the background. Goals, dreams, reinvention — they all shrink.

But when your body feels strong — even in small, ordinary ways — your sense of self expands. You stand differently. You speak differently. You make decisions from a steadier place. A healthy body doesn't solve your problems, but it gives you the capacity to face them.

From Strategic Communicator to Intentional Founder (Germany → Netherlands)

Kristin's story is about choosing yourself and the courage to outgrow your own surroundings. After 15 years in communications in Germany, she moved to the Netherlands and created the space to confront the truth about her marriage, her unhappiness, and the person she truly is. A daily 15-minute walk sparked a total reinvention of her life and career. Today, she is the Founder of her own consultancy, building communication "operating systems" for companies and leading a national team at Female Ventures, living a life defined by freedom and integrity rather than obligation.

I always say my story isn't really about changing careers — it's about changing *myself*. The career pivot came later, almost as a side effect. The real shift happened inside.

I grew up in Germany, and at fifteen I already felt restless, curious, ready to see the world. I spent a year in the U.S. on a high-school exchange, and it was one of the happiest times of my life. When I came back and finished school, I had no idea what I wanted to do with my life. I didn't feel prepared for any job. The only thing I knew was that I loved English. So I studied English literature and Catholic theology — not because I was religious, but because interpreting texts, understanding how people make sense of the world, felt natural to me.

After my master's, I still had no idea what to do with an English degree. I ended up in a temporary placement at a leading global automotive supplier and applied for a junior role in corporate communications. I remember the moment they hired me — I hung up the phone and did a happy dance. It was my first real job.

I stayed for seven years, moving from junior to mid-level roles, writing standards, managing media relations, building processes and communities, and working with inspiring colleagues, even winning an award for our work. But as I grew professionally, something inside me whispered, *This can't be it.* I was married, working nine to five, coming home, eating, sleeping, repeating. I felt stressed, tired, irritated, and I didn't know why. I gained weight because food was the only thing that made me feel good. I kept thinking: *Is this really my life?*

When my husband was offered a job in the Netherlands, we moved. I left my employer, and my former manager — who was now leading a communications agency — offered me a remote job. It gave me breathing space. I told him I would work only 30 hours a week because I needed time for myself. That decision changed everything.

With that extra time, I looked inward. I walked more. I tried aerobics with a new friend I made. I lost weight. But the unhappiness didn't go away. One night, watching a rom-com, I saw a couple laughing on a date and thought, *I wish that were me.* And then I realized — *but that is supposed to be me. I'm married.* Why didn't my reality match my emotions?

It took me three years to admit that the life we had built together was no longer aligned with who I was becoming. We had been together since I was seventeen. You don't just walk away from that. I tried to bridge the gap, to see if there was a version of "us" that could accommodate this new version of "me." But we were growing in different directions, wanting different things from our future. In the end, I realized that staying meant staying the person I used to be — and I had already outgrown that skin.

So we divorced. It was one of the hardest experiences of my life. I didn't just lose a partner — I lost his entire family, people I had loved for almost two decades. I moved out during the first COVID lockdown, built furniture alone in my new apartment, and tried to survive. My job became my anchor. My manager, who over the years had become my friend, supported me, raised my salary, and helped me land on my feet. A kindness that will stay with me forever.

But emotionally, I fell apart. I had dark thoughts. I needed help. I started therapy — first online, then group therapy for two years. I was rebuilding myself from the inside out, anchored by honesty and vulnerability.

My whole reinvention started with a 15-minute walk. That's it. Just a walk.

And then I realized: I needed a community. I had one friend in the Netherlands. That wasn't enough. So I pushed my introverted self to join a Meetup group for introverts. I lurked in the WhatsApp chat for months before finally replying to someone asking for breakfast recommendations. That tiny message led to my first meetup, which led to a friend, which led to another friend, which led to a housewarming, which led to a vegan dinner, which led to meeting one of my now best friends… and eventually to Female Ventures.

Female Ventures became home. I volunteered, became Marketing Manager, then City Director, and now National Marketing Director. It's a full day of work each week — event management, partnerships, community building, leadership — but 85% of it doesn't feel like work. It feels like belonging. It's the first place where I could show up exactly as I am, without masks, without corporate politics, without pretending. In this community, we share a beautiful space of being vulnerable and authentic.

And so, my life slowly became the life I had imagined: I lost weight, built friendships, found a supportive partner, adopted a dog, created a community, and finally felt settled. I wanted my job to reflect that same sense of "local" belonging, so I applied for one role — just one — and got it. External Communications Specialist. Two interviews. Hired. It felt like everything had finally aligned. In hindsight, I can see that I was trying to buy a sense of security that I already possessed. I traded my freedom for a seat in a corporate office, only to realize that the "perfect" local job was actually a step backward for the person I had become.

But luckily, life — as it does — shifted again.

Following a company-wide restructure, the strategic landscape of my role shifted. The communications function, which I had always led as a core business driver, was repositioned as a marketing support function. After fifteen years of building high-level strategies, I recognized that this new direction no longer utilized what I had to offer — nor did it align with the impact I want to make.

But it was the first time I had ever been pushed out of a job. I was shocked. Hurt. Angry. But I wasn't alone. I reached out to my Female Ventures network, to people who had been through this, to a psychologist, to a lawyer. And I realized something important: this time, I wasn't falling apart. I was standing up for myself.

Now I'm in a new phase — intentionality. I'm asking myself deeper questions: *What do I actually want? What aligns with my values?*

I founded my company in 2022, originally to help solopreneurs with branding and design. But that wasn't fully me. So I rebranded. Now I build the strategic communications operating system for NGOs, B-Corps, and female-led businesses — process optimization, AI enablement, strategic communications, everything I've learned across fifteen years. It finally feels aligned.

If the version of me who took that walk could see me now — making intentional career decisions, leading a national team, building a business rooted in freedom, integrity, and curiosity, living a life aligned with my values — she wouldn't be surprised. She would cheer on the woman she was always fighting to become.

Your body is the house you live in. It doesn't define you entirely, but it frames the space where your identity unfolds. When you maintain it, even gently, you give yourself more room to think, to feel, to grow, and to reinvent.

Today you are the youngest you will ever be. You are beautiful, and your body deserves attention, respect, and care — because the way you treat it shapes the way you believe in who you can become.

So ask yourself gently:

1. What is your relationship with your body right now? Do you treat it as a partner or as a machine you push until it breaks? Is it a body that feels cared for, or a body waiting for permission to rest?
2. What does your body need to feel good?
3. What patterns do you notice in your body when you're stressed, excited, lonely, or hopeful? How do you release the tension?

The Inherited Identity

Japan has one of the most distinctive work cultures in the world. Even if you've never lived there, you've probably heard about the tradition of long-term employment. And as you might commit to one company, in many traditional companies — especially the large ones — it's still common for the organization, not the individual, to map out an employee's entire career path.

Imagine sitting with a document that quietly tells you who you'll be at 40, 50, 60. Not your decision — the company's decision for your future.

At one of our Reinvento Club gatherings, I met a brave, soft-spoken woman who had left Japan mid-life. She was working in Japan, and one day she sat down with that whole plan of her career until retirement — the one her company expected her to follow — and she felt a stillness inside.

She realized, "I don't want this journey."

So she moved to the Netherlands to build her business, making a choice most of us struggle to make: stepping away from the traditions she inherited. Very few people ever do.

And that's the thing about identity — so much of it is shaped long before we ever get to choose. It's the layer shaped by culture, family, and the norms you grew up inside — your inherited identity. It's the starting point you didn't choose, but it influences how you see yourself until you learn to see more clearly.

The Cultural Blueprint You Didn't Choose

Culture isn't just food, language, or traditions.

It's the invisible operating system running quietly in the background of your mind — shaping what you think is "normal," and even what you believe a *good life* looks like.

If your identity is a house, your inherited identity is the land it sits on and the foundation beneath it. You didn't choose the land — your culture, your family, your early environment. You didn't pour the foundation — the values, fears, and expectations you absorbed before you even had language for them.

Inherited identity is the deepest layer because it forms in early childhood and sinks into the unconscious. This layer sets the boundaries of what feels "normal," "acceptable," or "possible. And it is incredibly powerful in defining what "success," "ambition," and a "dream career" are supposed to look like for you.

Before we go further, two important notes:

- **These are broad cultural patterns, not personal labels**

You might not see yourself — or even your culture — in every description, and that's completely normal. Hofstede's work describes tendencies across societies, not fixed traits in individuals. Think of these dimensions as broad cultural climates, not personal verdicts. Some parts may feel familiar, others may feel completely foreign. Both reactions are valid. They simply show that you are more than the environment you grew up in — and that you've been shaped by many influences, not just one.

- **Think of this as early influence, not programming**

These cultural forces don't determine who you are. They simply create the environment you grew up in — the air you breathed before you even had words for it. Most importantly, cultural theory is not stereotyping: it relies on researched patterns rather than on guesses about people.

And here's something important:
You're allowed to feel good about the culture you come from.
You're allowed to feel proud of it, connected to it, shaped by it.
You're also allowed to be nothing like it.

Some people grow up deeply aligned with their cultural roots.

Others grow up feeling like they were born facing a different direction entirely.

Both are normal. If our inherited identity is the land where your house is standing, the purpose of this chapter is to examine it and see if you still want to live at this address. If that's a part of who you are today, that's absolutely fine. But if some parts of it don't feel right anymore, you have the right to let them go. It's not a failure or a betrayal. It's simply a sign that something in you has shifted — that you're growing, evolving, and beginning to see yourself with new clarity.

How Cultural Dimensions Define Your Career

Let's take a closer look at what shaped you before you ever realized it — and the beliefs your culture handed you about what a "good" career is supposed to look like.

Geert Hofstede, a Dutch social psychologist who studied how cultures shape human behavior, analyzed a massive global dataset of workplace values and identified six dimensions that consistently explain how societies differ. You don't need to memorize them. What matters is recognizing how deeply culture imprints itself on you — shaping what you believe is "success," what you think is possible, and how you define a good life — often without you noticing.

1.Individualism vs. Collectivism

This dimension is interesting because your idea of a "good career" may come from this dimension alone.

Individualistic cultures — like the US, UK, Australia, and the Netherlands — teach you to:

- "Find your passion."
- Make choices based on personal fulfillment.
- Build a career that expresses *you*.

If you grew up here, you might feel guilty for choosing stability over passion — as if you're "settling." For example, turning down a startup job for a steady corporate role might feel like you're betraying your "potential." And wanting a quiet, simple life might feel like you're doing life "wrong" because the culture celebrates ambition and self-expression.

Collectivist cultures — like China, India, Japan, Mexico, and many African countries — teach you to:

- Consider the family first.
- Choose a path that brings honor or stability.
- Avoid disappointing others.

If you grew up here, you might feel ashamed of wanting something different — as if you're being selfish. For example, choosing a creative career over medicine or engineering might feel like you're letting your parents down, and wanting a job that makes you happy — instead of one that looks respectable — might feel irresponsible.

2. Power Distance

This dimension shapes how you relate to authority, and whether taking risks feels natural or dangerous.

High power-distance cultures — like China, Malaysia, Russia, and many Middle Eastern countries — teach you to:

- Respect hierarchy.
- Follow the rules.
- Avoid challenging your boss.

If this is your background, changing careers can feel like breaking a sacred order. You might hesitate to ask for a promotion because it feels disrespectful, wait for permission instead of taking initiative, or assume your manager "knows best" even when you disagree. You might even stay in a job longer than you want to because leaving feels like disloyalty.

Low power-distance cultures — like the Netherlands, Denmark, Sweden, and New Zealand — encourage you to:

- Speak up.
- Question decisions.

- Treat your boss like a colleague.

If you grew up in a low power-distance culture, the opposite can be true: you may expect open discussion, equal input, and the freedom to question decisions. You might openly disagree with your manager and be surprised when it's seen as disrespectful, assume decisions will be collaborative, or feel frustrated when hierarchy overrides logic. You may even interpret silence as agreement, not obedience, and feel confused when others defer to authority without question.

3. Uncertainty Avoidance
This is about how comfortable you are with the unknown.

High uncertainty-avoidance cultures — like Japan, Greece, France, and South Korea — value:

- Stability.
- Planning.
- Predictable paths.

A career change may feel terrifying not because you're weak or indecisive, but because you grew up with the message that uncertainty is unsafe. You might find yourself over-researching every option, delaying decisions until you feel "100% sure," or sticking with a job long after it stops fitting simply because it's familiar.

Low uncertainty-avoidance cultures — like Singapore, Sweden, and the UK — tolerate:

- Ambiguity.
- Experimentation.
- Trial and error.

If you grew up in a low uncertainty-avoidance culture, experimentation, and trial-and-error feel more natural. You might get restless in rigid systems, feel energized by change, or be confused when others fear taking a risk. You may even assume that "figuring it out as you go" is normal, and feel surprised when others see that as irresponsible or dangerous.

4. Masculinity vs. Femininity

This dimension is about what a culture rewards — not about gender. It has nothing to do with men or women, and everything to do with the values a society elevates.

Masculine cultures — like the US, Japan, Germany, and Mexico — value:

- Achievement.
- Competition.
- Status.
- Visible success.

If you grew up in a more masculine culture, you were taught to value achievement, competition, status, and visible success. You may feel constant pressure to "climb," even when you're exhausted, because the culture frames ambition as the default and rest as something you have to earn. You might judge yourself harshly for wanting a slower pace, feel guilty for choosing balance over advancement, or assume that success must always look big and impressive.

Feminine cultures — like the Netherlands, Sweden, and Norway — value:

- Balance.
- Well-being.
- Equality.
- Quality of life.

In a feminine culture, success is measured in free time, autonomy, and the quality of your Tuesday afternoons. You might prioritize harmony over competition, feel uncomfortable with aggressive career paths, or be puzzled by environments where people constantly push for more. Your definition of success may be inherited from this dimension — not consciously chosen — which means part of your work now is deciding whether it still fits you.

5. Long-Term vs. Short-Term Orientation
This dimension shapes how you think about time.

Long-term cultures — like China, Japan, and South Korea — value:

- Perseverance.
- Gradual progress.
- Future rewards.

If this is your background, wanting a career change "too soon" can trigger guilt, not because you're impatient, but because you absorbed the belief that good things take time and that stability is earned through endurance. You might feel pressure to stay the course, or "not waste" what you've already invested, even when something no longer fits.

Short-term cultures — like the US, Canada, and many African countries — value:

- Quick results.
- Immediate outcomes.
- Fast decisions.

If you grew up here, you might feel impatient during reinvention — as if you're "behind" if things don't change quickly. You might get impatient with slow progress, expect clarity early, or feel frustrated when change takes longer than you hoped. In these cultures, momentum is rewarded, and waiting can feel like failure.

6. Indulgence vs Restraint
This dimension shapes how you relate to pleasure, rest, and giving yourself permission to want things.

Indulgent cultures — like the US, Australia, Mexico, and many Latin American countries — value:

- Enjoyment
- Freedom

- Self-expression
- Personal happiness

If this is your background, pursuing what feels good may come naturally, because you were taught that desire is a valid reason to act. You might feel comfortable changing direction when something no longer fits, taking breaks without guilt, or choosing a career for lifestyle reasons. You may also feel confused when others treat rest as indulgent or believe joy must be earned through sacrifice.

Restraint-oriented cultures — like China, Russia, India, and many Middle Eastern countries — value:

- Self-control
- Discipline
- Duty
- Delayed gratification

If you grew up here, you might feel guilty for wanting something "just because," or worry that choosing a path that brings joy is irresponsible. You may push yourself harder than necessary, dismiss your own needs, or struggle to rest without feeling like you're falling behind. In these cultures, pleasure is often seen as something to justify.

Clara's story — like so many others — shows how deeply these early messages shape what we believe is possible.

From Engineering to Digital Transformation Consultancy — and Into Sustainability Research (China → Netherlands)

Clara grew up in China, where a woman's life was expected to follow a narrow script: a respectable job, a stable path, marriage, children. Years later, in the Netherlands, Clara found herself questioning every expectation she had inherited — and every definition of success she once believed in.
And this is how she tells her story.

"I am not successful. I am still struggling."
That's how Clara began.
"I grew up in China," *she continued.* "My parents always wanted me to be a teacher or a government worker. 'Good status for a woman,' they'd say. 'Stable. Safe.' They also wanted

me to get married and have kids. In the culture I grew up in, women who are older, single, and childless are often judged.

When it comes to careers, a single exam score can shape the direction of your entire life. Mine was just high enough to keep certain doors open, but only barely. My choices were narrow.

Back then, I thought I was a technical person. So I chose an engineering track. The idea of building things that would last felt powerful. Exciting. Never mind that I had no real idea what it meant.

Around me, more and more people were pursuing Master's degrees, even PhDs, just to meet rising expectations. I went straight through for a combined master's and doctoral track. On paper, I was doing well. Inside, I was not happy.

The academic path I followed was demanding in ways I hadn't anticipated. Guidance often felt like obligation, and responsibility extended far beyond my own research. My days filled up quickly. My own work had to happen whenever there was space left, usually late at night. Somewhere along the way, studying stopped feeling like learning. After some time, I decided to finish my master's degree only.

I always had an idea of living in another country. A doctorate abroad became my most realistic way out. I researched programs and focused on highly ranked universities in Europe. Then I heard one of the professors would be attending a conference in my city.

I went. I found him afterward. We talked.

I applied and I got in.

So I moved to the Netherlands.

As I was doing my doctorate in a new country, it took me a long time to see myself differently.

One of my first lessons was realizing that my doctorate was, in fact, a job. Still, I approached it with a student mindset. In my background, doctoral training was framed more as studying than as professional work, and that perception stayed with me. Only later did I gradually understand that this experience counted as professional work: managing projects, handling pressure, and coordinating with supervisors and stakeholders.

It took a long time to adjust to that perspective. You simply don't see yourself through that lens.

After my PhD, I did what only some academics do: I left academia. I joined an engineering firm. I wanted to touch real projects, to see how things actually got built, not just how they looked in textbooks.

I worked in an engineering role for a while. But during the pandemic, sitting alone in my apartment, one thing became clear: I didn't want to do purely technical work forever. I set my sights on project management and consultancy

I had carried a fantasy about consultancy for a long time. In my mind, it was a glamorous job, travelling, talking to people, solving big problems.

I started to look for this job.

Then one company replied. They were looking for a consultant to support digital transformation, working with data, emerging technologies, and innovation.

That was me!

When the application deadline passed and I hadn't heard anything, I decided not to wait. I called their HR department, and we had a great conversation. Looking back, I think that decision made a difference.

My doctoral background from a well-regarded university also helped, as did my engineering foundation and my early experiments and knowledge with data and systems. I even conducted part of the interview in Dutch.

In the end, I got the job.

At first, I was genuinely excited. It was a brand-new field, but it was still connected to my background. That first year, I wanted to do everything. I talked to almost everyone around me. I threw myself into any project that would help me grow. It felt like I was building something. That energy carried me through the first year. And then… something shifted.

The team had started strong. The projects were good. There was momentum. But then the market tightened. Uncertainty crept in. At higher levels, pressure started to build, and it had consequences.

My manager started to question my expertise and visibility. My portfolio was broad - I had worked on many different things - and suddenly that breadth was framed as a weakness.

I internalized it. I thought, He's right. I'm not skilled enough. That's why I'm not getting good projects.

So I slipped into an exhausting loop: trying to prove myself, asking for work, taking on whatever I could to justify my place. The heaviness settled slowly. Then all at once. I burned out. My head felt constantly cloudy.

At that point in my life, I struggled to even get out of bed. Mornings felt hopeless. That dull, gray feeling lasted for months.

I spoke to my supervisor. He suggested I talk to the company doctor.

The doctor told me I might be experiencing burnout. This created a conflict I couldn't resolve. Where I grew up, burnout isn't something you're supposed to have. When you feel bad, you endure. You push through. That idea is deeply ingrained. I was struggling with the notion of taking sick leave for something happening in your mind, at least for myself. Asking for help felt too costly. In my head, it meant risking my credibility, my career, my place. I believed I would be replaced without hesitation.

So every morning, even while feeling desperate, I got up. I went to work.

Then something happened.

Someone I knew sent me a vacancy for a research position at a university, in a different faculty than my own background. The topic was sustainability and systems change. It sounded interesting. At that moment, I had no intention of returning to academia, but I applied anyway. I passed the interviews.

Then, I talked with the professor who would become my supervisor. He was really open—the kind of person who gives you space and trusts you to find your own way.

A position is temporary, with a limited contract. But then again, I realized that's exactly what I needed. The role allowed me to focus on projects, without office politics, without teaching obligations. For the first time in a long while, I felt I could breathe.

For a long time, I had equated success with status. And what status means is climbing up the ladder and being the boss. I had chased that image. I evaluated my choices through the eyes of others.

Last year, I often woke up feeling hopeless, without fully understanding why. I started seeing a psychologist. Slowly, I learned that I had become disconnected from myself.

My psychologist asked me to start noticing small things in my life that I appreciate and to write them down. At first, that felt almost impossible. My focus had always been on "big" things, titles, credentials, achievements. But over time, I began to notice smaller moments. Little by little, I started to feel lighter and happier.

I used to feel intense anxiety about the expectation of having children. Now, I accept that it's okay if I don't want that. I talked to my parents about it, and that conversation felt unexpectedly liberating.

I started to sense who I am beyond my thoughts. I'm glad I chose this research position. I met people who gave me room to grow and the freedom to shape my own work.

I'm still trying to define what success means to me.

I want to do something I feel connected to.

I don't want to be trapped.

I don't want to look back one day with regret.

I have one year left in this role. I don't know what comes after. But I've learned to trust myself more. Whatever happens next, I know I can handle it.

Certain beliefs have a way of defining us. And when I interviewed women for this book, the same phrase surfaced again and again.

- "I'm not successful."
- "I'm not really there yet."
- "I haven't made it."

It wasn't just Clara — who was, of course, a talented and remarkable woman. It was almost every woman I spoke to. These were women with degrees, careers, families, responsibilities, and resilience. Women like Clara — who crossed continents, changed fields, rebuilt her life more than once — and still whispered, "I'm not successful."

So let me ask you something right here:

What's your idea of "making it"?

What's the moment when you'll finally feel complete — when you can stop proving anything to anyone and make choices that make you happy?

It's okay if you don't have a clear answer. Most people don't. That's honest. But before you can figure out what you want, it's important to see that the definition of success isn't universal. It varies wildly across cultures, families, and generations. And your culture — the one you grew up in, the one you breathed like air — plays a leading role in writing that definition for you, often without you realizing it.

Clara's story is a perfect example. She grew up in a world where stability, status, and respectability were the pillars of a "good life." Even after she moved across the world, even after she built a new identity, those early messages still echoed inside her. That's how deep these influences run.

One of the smartest women I know — a strategist who has built bridges between continents — shared how surprised she was when she applied for a job in Germany for the first time: *"When I was interviewing from Australia for a role with a German company, I was shocked. In Australia, interviews are structured to avoid bias During a job interview we talk about experiences, figures, and results. In Europe, I was asked personal questions: "What's your name? How old are you? Do you have a boyfriend?" I thought, Why are we talking about this? What about my professional experience?*

In some cultures, talking about your private life during a job interview would feel irrelevant. This is why switching careers — and especially switching countries — can feel existentially terrifying. You're not just changing jobs. You're stepping into a new world with no rank, no borrowed respect, no familiar markers of success.

The rules you trusted — be modest, wait your turn, display your ambition, hide your ambition — are suddenly labeled wrong, strange, or simply ineffective. You're told, subtly and repeatedly, that your instincts are off. Which makes you wonder if *you* are off.

When the rules you grew up with stop working, your ego steps in to keep you safe. It nudges you toward roles that look impressive, even when they don't feel right. It pushes you to chase the kind of success you were taught to admire, even if it no longer fits the person you're becoming.

Clara lived this. Many of us do.

And that leads us to the terrifying, and ultimately liberating question that forms in the cracks between these worlds: If not status, and if not the social norms we were born into, what should guide us then?

When the rules you grew up with stop making sense, you need a different kind of compass — one that comes from within rather than from the world around you.

Your cultural blueprint is a part of your identity. What it's not is a sentence. You are free to choose. For some, the finish line is wisdom. For others, it's community respect, or inner peace, or meaningful contribution. In some cultures, success isn't about standing alone at the top — it's about being the keystone in an arch, valued for the way you hold everything together. So before we can see what you want, we have to spot the filter you've been looking through. That feeling — "I'm not successful yet" — might not even be your own voice. It might be someone else's definition, comparing your life to a finish line you didn't choose.

Let's start to see it clearly.

Your Action Plan

Grab a notebook. Find a quiet moment, and answer these questions.

1. Bring into the light some patterns

Finish these sentences exactly as they come out. Don't judge it. Just write whatever comes first, before you start editing yourself:

- In my life, I pursue...
- In my life, I should...
- In my life, I must...

You might end up with something like this:

- "I should be more successful."
- "I must buy a house before I'm 30/40."
- "I should always fight for myself."

Whatever it is, now ask two gentle question:

- Why should you follow that?
- Whose voice is that?

Was it your decision to pursue those things? Or was it a quiet voice from a parent, a teacher, a friend, the air you grew up breathing? Don't be angry with the voice. It often means well. But it might not be what you need right now.

2. Rewrite the rule

You have full permission to drop the "should" and the "must." Those words carry obligation — like a rule from the outside. Take the sentences you wrote and rewrite them in a new way:

- Instead of *"In my life, I should…"*, write *"In my life, I want…"*
- Then write *"In my life, I choose…"*
- And finally, *"In my life, I value…*

See how it changes.

"I should build a life that feels secure." → *"I want to make time for my family."* It moves the idea from an external rule to an internal choice.

Sit with that for a moment.

3. Redefine success — or choose a different word

What is your definition of success — not the one you inherited, but the one that feels unapologetically yours? And maybe "success" isn't even the right word for what you're seeking in your career. The word itself might belong to an older script.

Sometimes we chase the idea only to discover it doesn't fill us the way we hoped. If success isn't the main goal, what is? What are you truly longing for in this season of your life — freedom, connection, peace, growth?

Then take it one step deeper:

What does that actually look like in real life?

What does "freedom" look like on a random Tuesday?

What does "peace" feel like in your chest?

It might seem like just language, but it's not. We use thousands of words a day without ever asking what they mean to us personally. And when you define the parts of life that matter — in your own words, on your own terms — you gain something quiet but steady.

Integrity.

You gain authorship over your next chapter, because the definitions finally belong to you.

4. Keep what supports you. Release what doesn't.

Your culture and family have given you a rich foundation — values, strengths, ways of seeing the world. You don't have to turn away from all of it. The point is to filter what aligns with who you are *right now*.

It's okay to keep this foundation.

It's okay to expand it or build a new one.

It's okay to search for a place that feels like home.

The choice is always yours.

The Reflected Identity

You might believe your life decisions — and even your identity — are entirely your own. Most of us do. But what if even the simplest things you *see* can be reshaped by the people around you?

Imagine you're sitting with six other people at the table.

All of you are shown two cards:

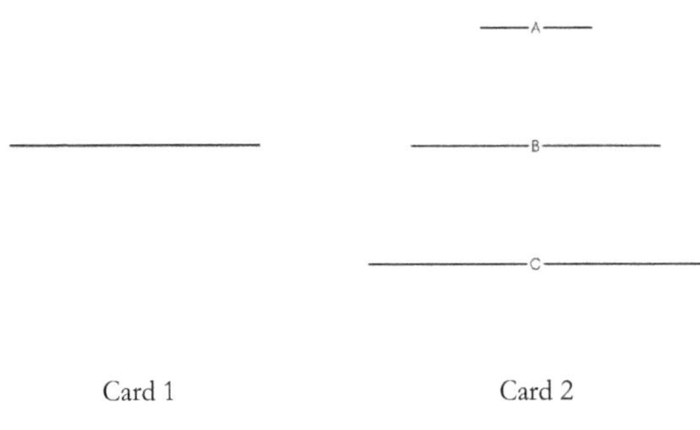

Card 1   Card 2

You are all asked a question:

Which line — A, B, or C — is the same length as the line on Card 1?

The answer is obvious.

Line A is too short.

Line C is too long.

Line B is the match.

But then the experiment begins. The experimenter asks each person, one by one, to say their answer out loud.

Confederate 1: "C."

Confederate 2: "C."

Confederate 3: "C."

Confederate 4: "C."

Confederate 5: "C."

Confederate 6: "C."

Now it's your turn. What do you say?

You'd like to believe you'll choose "B." B is correct, it's the one you *want* to imagine yourself giving. But that's not what happens — not for most of us.

We might believe our adult decisions are independent. But in reality humans are wired for belonging so deeply that sometimes we'll deny what our own eyes see just to avoid standing out. In a classic experiment, when the group unanimously gave the wrong answer first, about one-third of participants followed along — and 74% conformed at least once. That's how powerful the pull of the group can be.

If culture shapes the first layer of who you think you are, the second layer comes from the people who think they know you. A reflected identity is the version of you that lives in other people's minds: the "you" your parents describe to relatives, the "you" your old classmates still picture, the "you" your former boss imagines when your name comes up. And whether you like it or not, those reflections influence how you see yourself far more than you might expect.

If your identity is a house, your reflected identity are the photographs of what the house looks like from the outside. It's the paint color you chose because others admired it. The garden you keep tidy because it makes you "a good neighbor." The lights you leave on in certain rooms because that's where people expect you to be.

Reflected identity is shaped by how others see you — or how you *think* they see you. It's the version of your house that faces the street, the one you maintain so you'll belong, be accepted, or avoid standing out.

The Multiverse of You

Think about the last time you met someone from your "old life." Maybe it was a childhood friend, a former colleague, or a cousin you adore but haven't seen in years. Without even noticing, your voice shifts, your posture softens, you laugh at jokes you haven't heard since you were twenty. For a moment, you feel younger, smaller, or simply different from who you are today.

And it happens fast.

Perhaps you were once "the shy one" in your family. Since then, you've since led teams, spoken at conferences, and built a life that requires courage and visibility. Yet when you go home for the holidays, someone inevitably says, "Oh, don't ask her to speak, she's always been so shy," and suddenly you feel yourself shrinking. Not because you *are* shy, but because you're being reflected that way.

There's an episode of *How I Met Your Mother* where Lily — one of the main characters, a woman in her early thirties — has a high-school friend visit her in New York. The moment this friend arrives, Lily's entire personality shifts. Her voice changes, her clothes change, even her posture changes. As she slips straight back into her teenage self, her current friends watch in disbelief.

It's exaggerated for comedy, but it captures something real. Psychologists call this associative regression — the automatic return to an earlier version of yourself when you're around someone who knew that version well. We all have people who pull us back into old versions of ourselves.

Every person in your life remembers you in different ways. And when your current identity collides with the identity they still hold of you, there's friction. You feel the tug between who you are now and who you used to be, and for a moment, the past wins.

From childhood, we start collecting labels:

- "You're so smart."
- "You're not very athletic."
- "You're the creative one."
- "You're the troublemaker."
- "You're the quiet one."
- "You're the leader."

These labels stick — not because they're accurate, but because they were repeated, and repetition has a way of becoming truth in the minds of others. They become shortcuts for other people — and eventually, for us. And once a label is repeated enough, people begin to treat you through that lens — which is where things get interesting.

Labels are powerful, and here's how they can lift you or limit you. In the famous Rosenthal and Jacobson study, a group of teachers were told that certain students were "intellectual bloomers." In fact, the researchers selected a group of students randomly, and told the teachers that these particular students were expected to show unusual academic growth that year.

What happened next surprised everyone.

Because the teachers *believed* these students were special, they unconsciously treated them differently — with more encouragement, more patience, more opportunities, more positive attention. And by the end of the year, those students actually performed better.

It's simple. High expectations lift us. Low expectations shrink us.

From Lawyer to System Analyst (Russia)

Irina never expected to end up in IT. For most of her life, she was a lawyer — a profession she entered not out of passion, but because her parents insisted she choose something "normal" and practical. She built a solid career, tried small businesses, and kept going even as the legal market around her changed. But somewhere underneath all of that, she always felt she wanted something more — something she couldn't name yet.

And this is how she tells her story.

I always had an interest in computers. Even as a child, before we had one at home, I had a book about IBM machines. I didn't understand much, but I kept flipping through it. It was this abstract fascination that never developed into anything concrete.

In my teenage years, I wanted political science. It was the early nineties — the era of new freedoms, new ideas. I loved social studies, politics. But my parents were authoritarian and very pragmatic. For my mother, the idea that her child would go to the philosophy faculty was a tragedy. She told me: first you get a normal profession, then you can think about your soul.

A "normal profession" meant law. So I became a lawyer.

I wasn't a star, but I was good — a solid, reliable specialist. I built a career, grew to senior roles, even tried small businesses with friends. But I always felt like I wanted to realize myself in something else. I just didn't know what.

Then the legal market started collapsing. Digitalization took away routine tasks. Competition in litigation became absurd — clients would come after losing two court instances, with no money left and no realistic chance to win. The market was sinking.

At the same time, my husband — a developer — had been working from home long before COVID. I dreamed of working remotely too. I tried to move my clients online, but back then it was not an option. And no one wanted to pay me in any other role. I was too senior as a lawyer, and any other job meant a huge pay cut.

We took out a mortgage. We moved into a house with both our mothers. And I found myself constantly away at work, earning far less than my husband, while the household needed me present.

One day he said: "Listen, enough. Let me help you switch into technology."

He was working on a government project — full of requirements based on legal regulations. His team struggled to interpret the normative documents. "To read those documents, you need a legal background," he told me.

So he started asking me for help. I became a volunteer on the project without even realizing it. We would walk the dog in the evenings, and he would talk through problems — using me as the "rubber duck." He'd ask: how do we translate this bureaucratic text into logic? Into code? And I would explain what the author of the regulation actually meant.

Eventually he said: "Why aren't you working with us as an analyst?"

I was 40+. The managers were in their early thirties. For them, a woman over forty with zero IT experience was… frightening. They didn't understand why they needed me. But two people believed in me: my husband and the project lead. They fought for me, explaining my value and pushing until the company agreed.

That period was emotionally brutal for me. I cried a lot. I felt like if they didn't take me, something terrible would happen — like my whole life depended on this chance.

I always had high self-esteem. I always believed: if I want something, I can do it. And suddenly I was facing a wall. I wanted a new life, and they were basically saying: "Who are you?" It was the first time in my life I felt truly unwanted professionally. I couldn't understand why they didn't want me. I felt like I was bringing value, and yet I had to fight for the right to even try.

But I got in as a junior analyst.

Later, the managers admitted they had put me through the toughest tests. Young people with a certificate would get a green light immediately. And I — I had to prove myself twice as hard.

Yet I was so happy.

My job was to read normative documents, interpret them, and translate them into requirements. In technical terms, I was at zero. User stories, use cases — it was all a dark forest. I learned everything myself: articles, books, YouTube.

The team accepted me warmly. At first they thought I was imposed on them, but as they realized I'm asking questions and eager to learn, they taught me everything. My project lead was incredibly supportive.

After a year and a half, I realized I had evolved — but my image in the company hadn't. I was still "the woman over forty who never worked in IT." My salary was low, even for a junior specialist.

So I started to look for another job. Within a month, I got an offer from the IT arm of the Russian postal service — as an analyst for their mobile app.

I asked the manager: "Why me? I really don't know anything about mobile apps." And he said: "A person who changes careers at forty and succeeds — that's the kind of person I want."

I worked there for a year and a half. Then the company went through a brutal restructuring. My manager — the one who believed in me — was fired. The team collapsed. I told him, "I'll follow you anywhere." And he said, "Okay, let's go."

The next project was… unexpected. Tracking satellite signals of maritime and river vessels. Ships, ports, cartography, space. I didn't understand anything. There were no clear requirements, no market feedback. I was the only analyst, in a domain I didn't understand, with no one to ask.

The team bullied me kindly. Overall, they didn't mean harm. But the attitude was: "Well, Irina doesn't understand this anyway." The worst part was when I tried to discuss something with the team. I would ask a complex question, trying to understand how something should work. And they would say: "Well, you're the analyst. You should tell us how it works."

It crushed me.

I cried. I felt like my self-esteem was being erased. I thought: maybe I'm not an analyst at all. Maybe I made a mistake. Maybe I should leave the profession entirely.

Then the project stalled. That same day, I opened a job search platform, and I saw a vacancy: analyst with a legal background. It was my dream company — the one that had revolutionized legal work in Russia. I had used their products for years. I was their fan.

I applied. Every interview ended with: "You passed. Next step." Within a week, I had an offer. It felt like everything in my life finally aligned.

Now I work at the intersection of my two worlds: law and IT. My legal expertise makes me invaluable. My analytical skills are stronger than ever. I want to do great things. And for the first time in my life, I feel like everything I've ever done — law, analysis, even the crises — finally makes sense.

I've found my place.

This expectation effect shows up everywhere in adult life.

You've felt this too. Think of a time someone genuinely believed in you and immediately you wanted to be the best version of yourself — for them. And think of a time someone doubted you, dismissed you, or underestimated you, and you felt yourself shrink. Sometimes that shrinking becomes the reason you want to switch careers altogether, because reflected identity doesn't just shape how others see you; it shapes how you see yourself.

This is the power of reflected identity. It's the version of you that lives in other people's eyes — and the version you sometimes unconsciously perform. But here's the real question: do you want to give these people the power to define who you are and how you live your life?

Reflected identity is only one layer. It isn't the truth, and it isn't the whole story. It's a snapshot of who you *were* in someone else's eyes — a kind of movie about your past self, not an accurate picture of who you are today. You get to decide which reflections you keep, and which ones you finally put down.

From Classical Musician to Teacher to Life Coach (Denmark → France)

Katrine left Denmark to become a classical harpist in London. She moved to France to become a teacher. And somewhere between those two careers, Katrine realized that the labels she worked so hard to earn were the very things keeping her from becoming who she truly was — and who she would eventually help others become.

After little Katrine visited the Swan Lake ballet with her parents, as everyone's eyes followed the ballerinas, she couldn't help but focus on the sound coming from the orchestra pit. The magical sound of the harp.

Katrine was so fascinated that she decided to pursue a career as a classical musician. She went from Denmark to London to attend music college — a wild move, unheard of at the time. Moreover, it turned out she was eligible for a scholarship.

She became a classical musician who played the harp. A good one.

"I enjoyed the journey for many years, I really did. Aside from playing the instrument, being a musician meant you fit in everywhere. As soon as I'd introduce myself as a classical harpist, people would react with, 'Wow. When did you learn to play the harp? Can I come to listen to you? By the way, my friend is single.' Everyone just glowed with admiration, enjoying the company of an artist.

But there was a downside, too. An average harpist's day is this: you get up, eat breakfast, and then you play for four to six hours to stay at the top of your abilities. No one reaches out to you. I felt very lonely.

Besides, playing classical music feels like reaching for an ideal you're never able to achieve. Classical music is perfect. It's a standard you can never quite meet. Even when I was complimented on my playing, deep down I felt I wasn't good enough.

So I decided I wanted to become a teacher, and I enrolled in a Master's degree in teaching. I had this idea that I would teach at a university. But in France, when you're a government worker, you don't get a say. You just go wherever you're sent. And I was sent to teach thirteen-year-olds.

My whole world—where I was polished, poised, and perfect — turned upside down. You can't be polished and perfect in a room full of thirteen-year-olds.

But that wasn't the only challenge. Remember the delight I got when I introduced myself as a classical musician? In my teacher's role, I'd introduce myself and get a reaction closer to a flat "Nice." I hadn't changed. Only my label had. Why did the same people react in a different way?

At the root of trying to hide behind a label is the thought that we're not good enough as we are. We think we need to be much bigger than ourselves to be worthy of attention.

I went home thinking, 'Why don't they like me?' I was terrified that if someone could catch a glimpse of who I really was beyond polished, poised, and perfect, they would reject me. In reality, I had gotten used to rejecting a whole part of myself: the raw, the flawed, the imperfect me.

It was only there that I realized only when I dropped my labels and allowed myself to be vulnerable could a real encounter take place between my students and me.

Being a teacher changed me forever. It was a challenge to adapt to how differently people saw me. But I realized that by clinging to their old view of who I was, I was letting other people control my identity.

At the same time, I'm grateful for that experience because it taught me to accept the real, imperfect me.

I taught a Career Development program at the university, and what I saw was that it's not the opportunities that the students miss. It's something in their head that should be changed. But I didn't have the time to work one-on-one with every student. So I became a life coach.

Now, as a life coach, when my clients tell me they don't know who they are beyond their labels, I say, 'Great, let's find out. Why don't you allow yourself to be sometimes extremely hard-working and at other times deliciously lazy? Once you stop limiting yourself to a label, you can start exploring the full richness of your personality without judgment. Like the harp. The point is not to play just one of the chords, but rather to play them all. Sometimes being subtle and restrained, at other times wild and creative, but always expressing who you are.

As a life coach, I see many people adopting the label "failure." But the real problem with many journeys is that we approach them half-heartedly. You try something — like being an entrepreneur — and you feel it just didn't work. It's easier to say "that didn't work" than to admit, "I did my best, and it wasn't enough."

But how do you drop the label without really knowing where you're going?

"This understanding comes from who you are and who you want to be. For example, when I'm looking for a job, I can't control the job interview. I can't control the questions they ask me. But I can see how much of a leader I am today. It all comes down to this question: what kind of person do you want to be? That is what changes everything. Eventually the right opportunity will come your way. It always does."

When Your Job Becomes a Label

Katrine touched on something important: professions carry emotional labels, and those labels can vary wildly depending on culture, upbringing, and personal aspirations. Sometimes the hesitation around a career change isn't about the change itself — it's about how we imagine others will interpret it. A job title can feel like a social signal, a shorthand for status, ambition, or worth. And when those signals clash with the identity you're trying to grow into, the fear of being misunderstood can be stronger than the fear of starting over.

Switching careers is hard. It becomes even harder when other people's reactions start to feel like the deciding factor — when the imagined look on someone's face carries more weight than your own sense of direction. Maybe you're leaving a well-paid corporate job to become a masseuse. It might be the path that brings you real fulfillment, yet part of the stress comes from rehearsing other people's reactions in your mind.

How often have you felt anxious not about the change itself, but about explaining it? How often have you worried about how colleagues or friends will respond when you tell them you're leaving project management to become a coach?

Because you already know how it looks from the outside.

In a few places in the world, the social structure is flat. A plumber and a professor can have coffee as equals. You choose a career because it fits you, not because it shines for others. The labels — "prestigious," "not prestigious" — don't stick. They don't matter.

Most places aren't like that. In fact, in much of the world, social hierarchies are strong. In many cultures, your career becomes a label — a heavy one. *Prestigious* is the doctor, the lawyer, the executive — the titles that make parents nod with quiet pride. *Not prestigious* is the barista, the delivery driver, the sales assistant — work that may be skilled and vital for the society, but more often described as "it pays the bills" or "I'm just figuring things out."

In many cultures, these labels stick. One role makes you feel like a luxury item; the other makes you feel like something placed on the discount shelf — not because of your true value, but because of how people in this culture have learned to categorize it.

When you choose a job, you choose a social script — how people see you before you speak. So when you think about changing careers, you're choosing a new label. The world will read you differently. It might feel like stepping onto a different tier of an invisible ladder.

But pause for a moment. Here's what most people forget — and what can quietly trap you.

A label only exists on the outside.

It's a tag someone else sticks on your professional "jar" to tell the world what's inside. On LinkedIn, it shows up as *Engineer, Artist, Manager, Maker, Strategist, Founder.* But the headline isn't the person. The label isn't the work. It's not the substance — the way your mind clicks into place when you solve a problem, the flow you enter when you're creating, or the quiet satisfaction of doing something that feels deeply true to you.

A prestigious label might get you a better seat at a dinner party, but it won't sit with you at your desk on a Tuesday afternoon when you need the will to keep going. A "non-prestigious" label might make someone's glance slide past you, but it can't touch the internal scorecard that tells you you're finally building something that feels like your own.

If you find purpose in your work — if you feel that small flicker of joy or that joyful sense of rightness while you're doing it — then the label on the outside starts to matter a lot less.

A label is just the sticker on the outside, not the contents. Not the texture of your actual day-to-day experience. It's not the real you.

You have the power to rewrite any label.

Your Action Plan

Find a quiet moment. Bring a notebook. This exercise works best when you give yourself permission to be honest, unfiltered, and a little curious about the person you've been — and the person you're becoming.

1. The Labels You've Collected

List the labels you've carried at different stages of your life — roles, traits, reputations, expectations. A simple way to surface them is to answer: "Who are you?" Here are some examples to spark your memory: "the introvert," "the gifted one," "the creative thinker," "the smart one," "not leadership material," "the strong one." Write down whatever comes to mind — both positive and negative definitions. Don't judge them.

Then ask yourself: Which of these did I choose, and which were handed to me?

2. The "Good" and the "Bad" Labels

Now let's look closely at the restrictions each of these labels places on who you are. With negative labels, it's quite straightforward: if you're "not leadership material," the invisible rule behind it says you can't be a leader — which, of course, isn't true at all.

But the "good" labels can be just as limiting. You might think it's helpful to have been called "the smart one," yet that label can stop you from trying and failing. You might believe that being "the strong one" is admirable, but it can keep you from asking for help. When you look at all your labels — the flattering ones and the painful ones — you bring the invisible rules you've been following into the light and can finally decide whether you still need them.

Here are a few more examples:

- "Perfectionist" might block experimentation.
- "High achiever" might make you fear starting at the beginning.
- "Corporate professional" might make you doubt a creative path.

Write down the labels that feel incompatible with who you're becoming. These are the ones to release.

3. Other Reflections That Hold You Back

Reflected identity isn't only about labels — it's also the emotional imprint people leave on you. Think about who, or which kinds of people, make you feel small; who pull you back into an old version of yourself; who still see you as who you were ten years ago; who expect you not to change.

Write down the names or initials of people whose perception still shapes your behavior.

4. Rewriting the Reflection

Choose one limiting label or reflection and rewrite it in a way that supports your future. Examples:

- "I'm the shy one" → "I speak when it matters."
- "I'm the achiever" → "I can explore without proving anything."
- "I'm the stable one" → "I'm capable of change."

This isn't pretending. It's just nothing in life is black and white. We're more complex than this. Even shyness includes the ability to speak when something truly matters. Rewriting these labels is reclaiming the right to define yourself.

The Remembered Identity

So far, we've looked at how identity is shaped from the outside — by society, culture, and the expectations of the people around us. But sometimes the most limiting barrier to reinvention isn't external at all. It's internal.

It's the way we keep seeing ourselves through an old lens, through our own outdated labels, long after life has moved on.

Some labels become so powerful that they turn into pillars of your identity. You might get used to introducing yourself through your profession — *"I'm a marketer," "I'm a product manager," "I'm a lawyer," "I'm a designer."* There's nothing wrong with that. It's natural to take pride in what you've built. But it becomes hard to let go of that label when you move past that chapter of your life. The identity stays even when the job doesn't.

The single-story trap you read about earlier is the external version of the same internal pattern. We don't just let other people reduce us to one story — we do it to ourselves. Once a narrative forms, the mind clings to it because familiarity feels safe. Even when life has changed, even when you've grown, your brain keeps returning to the old storyline simply because it's the one it knows best. That's how we're wired: we mistake repetition for truth. And so we keep living inside an outdated version of ourselves long after it has stopped being accurate.

If your identity is a house, your remembered identity is what the house feels like on the inside. It's the atmosphere you carry, the history in the walls, the way you instinctively know when something is off. You know when the pipes are leaking, when a window doesn't close properly, when a floorboard creaks in a way it never used to.

Your remembered identity works the same way. It's the rooms you return to again and again: the childhood moments that shaped you, the labels you were given, the roles you learned to play, the stories you repeat until they feel like the truth. It's the internal knowledge of what feels right, what feels wrong, and what needs attention.

Remembered identity isn't about how others see you. It's about how *you* see yourself, based on everything you've lived through.

From Teacher to Doula (South Africa → Netherlands)

Madi never expected to become a doula. For most of her adult life, she was a high-school biology teacher in South Africa — the kind of teacher who loved her subject, traveled the world through international schools, and always carried a sense that something else might be waiting for her. When she moved to the Netherlands in 2018, she arrived as a teacher. But over the next few years, between lockdowns, loneliness, and a growing fascination with women's bodies and hormones, she found herself pulled into a completely different world: birth work.
And this is how she tells her story.

I used to be a full-time high-school teacher. I studied biology, got my degree, and then realized I couldn't do much with it unless I wanted to sit in a lab — which I knew wasn't me. So I thought, okay, I'll do a year of teaching. My mom's a teacher, I know a lot of teachers, it'll be fine. It'll be my backup.

I did the one-year teaching qualification, and because there's always a shortage of teachers, I got a job quickly. After that, I traveled — I even worked on a cruise ship for six months. The day I landed back home, my mom picked me up from the airport and said, "There's a school that needs a teacher. You have an interview tomorrow." I had no idea what was happening, but I took the job.

Fifteen years later, I was still teaching.

Teaching abroad became my way of traveling. I taught in international schools, met my Dutch boyfriend in China, and eventually found a school in the Netherlands that could sponsor my visa. I came here as a teacher in 2018. I taught for two or three years… and then COVID happened.

Somewhere in that period, a fellow teacher mentioned she had done a doula course. I didn't even know what a doula was. When she explained it — someone who supports women emotionally and physically during birth — something clicked. It was biology, it was education, it was people. It was everything I loved, but in a completely different context.

I decided to take a chance.

I signed up for doula training through an American company. It was supposed to be in person, but then COVID hit, so it became an online course. I actually really enjoyed it. But the problem was: I was stuck in the Netherlands during the lockdown. Doulas weren't allowed at birth. I didn't speak Dutch well. I had no experience. And I didn't know anyone.

So I kept teaching. I registered a business — but not even as a doula. I thought maybe I'd do something as a teacher on the side. I didn't know how anything worked. I just wanted to start something small while everything was slow. Also teaching four days a week was exhausting. Working with kids drains your emotional battery. I had no energy left for anything else.

A year or two later, I realized I needed to start saying out loud: *I am a doula.* Even if I had no clients. Even if no one knew I existed.

My Dutch had improved by then, so I reached out to a doula academy here. They offered a course on how the Dutch healthcare system works — hospitals, midwives, protocols. The course was entirely in Dutch. I could understand enough, and the instructor let me speak English. That course was a turning point. Not because clients suddenly appeared — they didn't — but because I finally connected with other doulas. I wasn't alone anymore. I was in a WhatsApp group. I saw how people worked. It made me feel like I belonged.

But I still wasn't getting clients.

I'm not a business person. I'm not a marketing person. I spent hours on Instagram, following all the rules about posting and hashtags and engagement. I built a website I didn't enjoy building. I sat behind my laptop, not talking to anyone. None of it worked.

In two and a half years, I had one client.

I wanted to give up so many times. I kept thinking, What are you doing? You have so much to give — why doesn't anyone know that?

Then something shifted.

I started offering birth photography. Before teaching, I had worked as a photographer on a cruise ship, so I had some background. I didn't even know birth photography was a thing until I started talking to people. But I liked taking photos. I liked attending births. So I thought, maybe I can combine them.

Within a year, I had six clients.

The first two came from Facebook groups — women who had complicated pregnancies and wanted something special but couldn't afford full prices. I was still building my portfolio, so I reached out. Others came through word of mouth. One woman found me because months earlier I had answered her question about visas in a South African expat group. I didn't even remember telling her I was a doula. It was all random. But it was finally taking off.

Honestly, I don't think I would have made this jump if I had stayed in South Africa. The Dutch system makes it easier to transition gradually. Here, I can teach part-time and build my doula work slowly. In other countries, you're either a full-time teacher or you quit completely. There's no in-between.

The identity struggle has been real.

Who am I?

A teacher?

A doula?

A photographer?

Someone who wants to become something else entirely?

But then I realized this switch isn't as big as it looks. I'm still working with biology. I'm still working with people. I'm still educating — just teenagers in one world and mothers in another.

What drew me to doula work was the biology of it — hormones, physiology, the incredible intelligence of the human body. I struggled with my own hormonal cycle in the past, so I knew how powerful hormones are. Pregnancy hormones are another universe. I love explaining that to women. I love helping them understand what's happening in their bodies.

Before my first birth, I was terrified. But when it happened, I went home and told my partner, "It feels like I've always been doing this." That feeling is what kept me going through the two years of almost no clients. Every time I attend a birth, I think, *I can't stop. This is too amazing.*

My work now is a mix of education, emotional support, and practical preparation. I spend hours with couples before the birth — explaining physiology, interventions, breathing, positions, postpartum realities. I want them to have as much information as possible so they can make decisions under pressure. I want to reduce trauma. I want them to connect with their babies. I want them to feel supported.

People sometimes ask if I have children. I don't. And yes, I worried about that in the beginning. Am I qualified to be a doula without going through giving birth myself?

I do have the answer to this question now. Yes, I'm qualified. I've seen more births than most mothers. I know the physiology. I know the system. I know the emotional landscape. And what about the fact that many gynecologists are men? They weren't giving birth to children either, still they have expert knowledge and are able to help a lot of women.

My long-term dream is to build a community — a team of birth workers who complement each other. Prenatal yoga, postpartum meals, lactation consultants, chiropractors, aromatherapy, education — a place where women can find everything in one space. I want teamwork. I want mothers to know they're supported from every angle.

I'd love to be a full-time doula and birth photographer. But it's hard. You're on call for weeks. You can't go far. You can't turn off your phone. You can't plan holidays. Most doulas have additional services — yoga, massage, postpartum care — because it's nearly impossible to make a full living from births alone. I wish I had known that earlier.

People say you have to be obsessed to make something work. That the ones who don't give up are the ones who succeed. And I'll be honest: there were moments when I thought about quitting almost every week. But after three years, when I still had only a handful of clients, I kept asking myself: *At what point do I say I've tried? At what point do I admit it's not working?*

Your new career is not just about passion.

It's about rent.

It's about debt.

It's about the pressure on your relationship.

It's about how much sacrifice is too much.

There were moments when I wondered if life was telling me this wasn't my path. But I held on. Maybe out of stubbornness. Maybe out of hope. Maybe because every time I went to a birth, I felt like I was exactly where I was supposed to be. And now — finally — things are moving. I feel like I can dream again.

There was never a guarantee it would turn around. There still isn't. But even the hardest days of building this business have felt more meaningful than going back to something I didn't love.

Madi highlighted something important: for many of us, it's difficult to start using a new label as if nothing happened. You can't just step into a new identity when you're still carrying the old one inside you.

So what makes it feel so slow, so heavy — and how do you make stepping into the new identity feel lighter?

When you hold a small, private picture of your next career — a director, a comedian, a founder, a writer — it feels like a dream. Something bigger, truer, or more meaningful than what you're doing now. A role you admire, but don't yet feel ready to claim.

And that hesitation has a simple, human reason. You know the parts of yourself no one else fully sees. The doubts. The missteps. The failures. You remember every version of you who felt small, uncertain, or not enough. And that remembered identity doesn't update just because you've chosen a new direction.

You've lived through your own shortcomings. The promises you made to yourself and others and then didn't keep. The seasons when you hid, avoided, or numbed instead of facing what mattered. The times you swallowed your voice, or spoke from fear instead of clarity. These memories linger.

This is your remembered identity — the old story your mind still carries, even when your life has moved far beyond it. And that remembered identity can make your dream feel too bright, too bold, too "not for someone like me." When you imagine stepping into a new career, it can feel as if it demands a flawless version of you that has never existed.

So here are some real struggles:

- How do you face the raw feeling of "I'm not good enough" that freezes you when you start something new?
- How do you forgive your mistakes and move forward?
- How do you overcome the shame that keeps you stuck?
- How do you accept the worst parts of yourself?

Answering these questions is what reinvention is truly about. You can have the perfect plan, the right network, a polished résumé — and none of it will bring you closer to the next version of yourself if the person carrying the plan forward is still tangled in an old story about who they are and what they're allowed to be.

The work is learning how to bring all of your pieces — not only the ones you love but also the ones that are harder to love — into a mosaic that is unmistakably you.

Befriend Your Inner Critic

A few years ago, while preparing for one of my workshops, I was intrigued by a question that sounds simple: *What does it mean to love yourself?*

People who carry that kind of inner love always project a certain light. You can sense their calm, their authenticity, and the way they're rooted in themselves long before they speak. I wanted to understand how someone arrives at that place. At the time, I was in the middle of my own reinvention, and instead of moving forward, I kept tightening the net around myself with questions I couldn't escape: *Am I good enough? Am I allowed to take space?*

As I dug deeper, something kept resurfacing: the biggest barrier to feeling loved — by others or by ourselves — is negative self-talk.

It wasn't the world holding me back. It was me, dragging myself down.

Interestingly, none of us were born with that voice. When you arrived in the world, you didn't question your worth or your place. You didn't wonder whether you were "enough." Those doubts came later. Over time, you absorbed what you heard, what you saw, and what you made sense of — and those impressions slowly shaped a voice that sounds like yours.

We all know our shortcomings. Some of them we're lucky enough to forget, but many of them — we don't. They stay with us. They follow us into new chapters, new relationships, new attempts at change.

And when you're reinventing your life, the temptation is strong to shove those parts of yourself into a closet, slam the door, and throw away the key. Maybe then, you think, the voice that keeps pointing at your imperfect pieces — the one that holds you in the same place and drags you back to who you used to be — will finally lose its grip.

But that's not how it works. It keeps finding its way back.

So instead of running from it, let's turn toward it for a moment. I want to invite you into a question that's uncomfortable, but necessary — a question that brings this inner voice into the light where you can finally see it clearly.

Do you actually like yourself?

Not the polished version of you.

Not the "on a good day" you.

Not the edited you.

I mean *you* — the real, imperfect human you.

Let me guess. There is no resounding "yes." You probably don't wake up in the morning thinking, "I adore myself exactly as I am." Most of us don't. It feels weird and self-absorbed.

What happens much more often in the morning is this: you look in the mirror and immediately that voice spots something that's not right about you. It starts with the external — your skin, your weight, your hair (honestly, why do we always want to change our hair?) — and then it slides straight into your career and your story. Every woman in the world has a lineup of internal comments on how she could improve.

"Ugh... look at those dark circles."

"You keep saying you'll change, but you never do."
"You're such a mess."

And it's hard to love yourself when a part of you rebels against it. And because you're human, you will *always* feel imperfect, especially at the time of a new reinvention. That's just part of being alive.

So is it even possible to love yourself — truly, not theoretically, not as a slogan, but as a lived experience?

In one of the previous chapters, we looked at how from a young age, girls are encouraged to be "good." Good girls who don't take up too much space, don't speak too loudly, don't make mistakes, don't disappoint. And every time someone said, "Be careful," "Don't brag," "Try harder," "You can do better," or "Why can't you be more like…," a tiny seed was planted. Not out of malice — often out of love, or worry, or habit. But still, the message landed: there's a bar you're supposed to reach, and if you can reach it, people will approve of you.

You were young, and young minds absorb everything. So you took those messages in, trying to be good, better, and perfect.

Slowly, those seeds grew into a voice.

A voice that wanted you to be liked.

A voice that wanted to protect you from embarrassment.

A voice that believed perfection was the safest place to achieve both.

By the time you reached adulthood, that voice felt so familiar you assumed it was you. It's the voice we all are familiar with. A voice that says you should have done better, tried harder, known more, draining the joy from moments that should feel good.

And since it sounds familiar, you take it as fact.

Yet that voice doesn't belong to you. It was shaped by years of expectations, warnings, and comparisons — messages we all absorbed long before we had the power to question them. And this voice is powerful, because it was practiced for so long it feels familiar. Each time you do something, it has a remark or correction, keeping you stuck in one place.

So what do you do about this voice?

Some people push back. They argue with that voice, try to outsmart it, try to prove it wrong. But the moment you start proving anything, you're already treating its opinion like it might be true.

Others turn that voice into fuel. They call it motivation — the idea that if you're hard enough on yourself, you'll finally become the person you're supposed to be. The harsher the critique, the better the performance. At least that's the story we tell ourselves.

I invite you to choose a different way.

Your inner critic isn't an enemy you need to defeat. It's a part of you that once tried very hard to protect you — from rejection, from failure, from disappointment. For years, it kept you alert, pushed you to prepare, and helped you navigate environments where being perfect felt safer than being human. In many ways, this voice genuinely made you better.

But now, it's overworking. It's trying to protect you from things that you can handle — like an overprotective friend who keeps grabbing the steering wheel even though you're perfectly capable of driving. And that's why the goal isn't to silence it or fight it. It's to befriend it, beginning with seeing this part of yourself through loving, compassionate eyes.

Loving eyes see the *intention* of this voice behind the specific words. They see the child in you who once believed that being perfect was the only way to stay safe. They see the teenager who tried to avoid embarrassment. They see the young adult who thought she had to earn her worth.

Loving eyes don't excuse the critic — they understand it.

And understanding softens everything.

When you look at your inner critic with loving eyes, it starts to feel like looking at someone you care about who's simply scared and doing the best they can. Imagine a small child tugging on your sleeve saying, "Be careful, don't mess up, don't embarrass yourself." You wouldn't yell at her. You'd kneel down, meet her eyes, and say:

"I know you're scared. I know you're trying to protect me. But I'm grown now. I can handle this. You can rest."

That's what it means to see your inner critic with loving eyes. It's you stepping into the role of the adult in the room — the one who can hold all your parts with steadiness and compassion.

You might tell your inner critic:

"Thank you for everything you've done for me.
Thanks to you, I've worked hard, stayed responsible, and achieved so much.
You'll always have a seat at the table.
I will listen to you — but I won't obey you.
Because there are other parts of me that also deserve a voice."

This is how you shift the relationship.

Not by silencing your inner critic, but by putting them in the right role — just one voice among many. And when you do that, something shifts. You start to feel like you can finally breathe again. You stop feeling like you're at war with yourself. Instead of pouring energy into fighting your own mind, you begin to feel supported from the inside out. When you learn to lead that inner voice with warmth and steadiness, reinvention stops being a struggle and starts becoming possible.

Of course, this doesn't happen in a day. Trust takes time. Be calm with yourself. Be patient. Just notice the voice the next time it shows up. Talk to it. Ask it questions. And remember: you're the one steering the wheel.

Meet the "Worst" Parts of Yourself

While growing up, you were encouraged to be kind, patient, grateful, agreeable. But when you're raised to be a "good girl," what do you do with the emotions that don't fit that script?

Where do you put your shame?

Where do you put your resentment?

Where do you put the moments when you're not grateful at all?

Our right to have these feelings and express them is often denied from the very childhood. So many of us learned to tuck those feelings away, pretending they don't exist. We learned to smile through pain, to stay composed, to pretend we were fine. Moreover, we started believing that having these emotions made us unworthy. That something must be wrong with us for feeling anger, guilt, envy or shame.

In fact, having these emotions is completely human. We don't talk about them in daily conversations, but no one gets through life without feeling this way. Having these emotions doesn't make you a bad person; it simply means you're going through a hard moment or facing a challenging situation or person in your life.

But finding your identity — becoming *you* — means putting everything in your inner house in order. And that includes the emotions we'd rather avoid. We can't build a new version of ourselves while pretending the uncomfortable parts don't exist.

So let's look at the emotions that tend to make us shrink, hide, or feel "wrong," and how to soften them instead of fighting them.

Shame

Shame is the voice that tells you *you* are "bad." It's the moment you stop seeing a behavior or a mistake as separate from who you are — and start believing that you are unworthy, either because of something you were born with or something you did.

Shame insists that something about you makes you less deserving — less deserving of opportunities, of belonging, of being chosen. It attaches itself to the parts of your story you were taught to hide. And when that belief settles in, you begin to unconsciously avoid anything that puts you in the spotlight. You shrink a little. You hesitate. You hold back. And in that quiet retreat, shame grows quietly.

Over time, it spreads. It starts clinging to other parts of your life — the choices you made, the chapters you lived through, the relationships you wish had gone differently. Suddenly it's not just *"I shouldn't feel this way,"* but *"I shouldn't have this story."*

Shame is not an emotion you're born with. It's a learned, social response — something we absorb from the environments and people around us. And unfortunately, along the way, many of us encounter individuals who teach us to feel ashamed of the most human, ordinary aspects of ourselves — and even of the qualities that make us special.

- the country you come from, or the accent that reveals it;
- your age — being "too young to be taken seriously" or "too old to start over";
- the color of your skin or the way you look compared to beauty standards;
- not speaking perfect English, or searching for words in a second language;
- being laid off, fired, or stuck in a job that doesn't match your potential;
- a burnout that forced you to stop when everyone else seemed to keep going;
- not having children, having children "too early," or "too late," or struggling with motherhood;
- financial mistakes, debt, or not being where you thought you'd be by now;
- your body changing — weight gain, weight loss, illness, aging;
- not fitting into the culture of the country you moved to;
- feeling like an outsider in your own family or community.

Which of these do you find yourself tucking away during job interviews — and in social interactions — because you worry they'll make others see you as someone they wouldn't choose or welcome?

I want to say this with all the love I have: none of these things are shameful. What *is* shameful is that someone, somewhere, made you believe they were.

People who teach you to feel small are speaking from their own fear, their own limitations, their own unexamined stories. Their judgments say everything about them — and nothing about your worth.

Yet shame is there — so instead of trying to erase it, let's look at how you can work with it. Shame matters because it disrupts your connection with others. When you're ashamed — whether it's shame for not living up to your own promise, shame for your background, or shame for a chapter of your life you wish had gone differently — something in you pulls back. You stop reaching out. You stop letting people see you. You hide the parts of yourself you've decided are "too much," "not enough," or "unacceptable." And in those moments, you don't just disconnect from others — you disconnect from yourself.

Shame convinces you that you're safer alone, when in reality, isolation is the very thing that keeps the shame alive. That's why it's so important to understand shame for what it truly is: not evidence that you're inherently worse than anyone else, but a story someone once told you — intentionally or unintentionally — that stayed with you for reasons that had nothing to do with your worth. Where you see something unforgivable or embarrassing, others often see nothing at all. And when you're finally strong enough to bring your shame into the light, you'll be surprised by how much support, understanding, and even admiration you receive.

Shame grows in darkness. And because no one taught you how to hold these parts with compassion, you learned to hide them. But hiding doesn't heal. Hiding only reinforces the belief that something is wrong with you and must never be seen.

The work isn't to eliminate shame — that's not realistic, and it's not necessary. Healing begins not by silencing shame, but by speaking to it with the same kindness you would offer someone you love.

Meeting Your Shame

Shame: "I'm ashamed of being fired."

You: "What part of it feels the heaviest?"

Shame: "What if someone finds out? What if they think I wasn't good enough? What if they assume I messed everything up? People don't get fired unless they fail… right?"

You: "Being fired doesn't mean you failed. It means something wasn't working. It might've been the role, the environment, the timing, the support you had. But it doesn't define your talent or your worth."

Shame: "But it feels like a stain. Like something I need to hide."

You: "Many people get fired at least once in their career. Some of the most successful people you know have been fired. It's just a turning point. A moment that pushed you toward something better."

Shame: "Still… what if employers judge me?"

You: "Some might. The right ones won't. People lose jobs for countless reasons — restructuring, burnout, misalignment, toxic leadership, moving countries, life happening. Being fired is not a moral failure. It's a human experience."

Shame: "So it doesn't make me look irresponsible?"

You: "No. It shows you've lived through something hard and kept going. It shows resilience, honesty, and the courage to start again. That's not irresponsibility — that's strength."

Shame: "…I never thought of it that way."

You: "You don't have to hide this anymore. We can tell this story with dignity and truth. Look at who you've become since then."

Guilt

Guilt is one of the quietest emotions, but also one of the heaviest. It doesn't shout. It doesn't demand attention. It just sits inside you, tugging gently at your confidence, whispering that you should have done more, been more, tried harder, chosen differently.

And because you're a woman, you've learned to feel guilty about almost everything. As Marjolein, one of the reinventors, said in her story: *"I felt like I was a bad mom because I was working quite a lot and our daughter was going to daycare. I felt like I was a bad employee because I wasn't delivering on the job. And I felt like I was a bad wife because I was very stressed at home and not running the household the way I wanted to."*

Work too much, and guilt says you're failing your family.

Rest for a moment, and guilt says you're failing your work.

Choose yourself, and guilt calls you selfish.

Ignore yourself, and guilt insists you're giving too much away.

It's exhausting.

And yet, guilt often feels like the "responsible" emotion — the one that proves you care, the one that keeps you in line, the one that stops you from being "selfish." But guilt often becomes a barrier. It can keep you tied to an identity you've outgrown. It can make you hesitate when you're ready to move forward. It can convince you that you don't deserve a fresh start because of something you did — or didn't do — in the past.

Guilt is the voice that says,

"You don't get to move on yet. You haven't earned it."

I invite you to see what guilt really is. It's not a moral compass, it's a voice. A scared, protective voice that believes holding you back is the safest option. Guilt often forms when you look at your past with the knowledge you have now. You judge your younger self for not knowing what you know today. You forget the circumstances, the pressure, the fear, the lack of support, the limited options you had at the time. You forget that you were doing the best you could with the tools you had.

And when you forget that, guilt fills the space.

So what do you do with guilt?

How do you forgive yourself for the past mistakes?

You talk to guilt the way you would talk to someone you care about — gently, honestly, without rushing. You ask it what it's afraid of. You listen. You respond with compassion. You remind it that you're allowed to grow and move on. Remember that forgiving yourself isn't about erasing the past. It's about releasing the belief that something from your past disqualifies you from the future.

So go talk to guilt the way you'd speak to someone you love.

Meeting Your Guilt

Guilt: "I feel guilty about leaving that job after only six months."

You: "What feels heavy about it?"

Guilt: "A responsible person would have stayed. People were counting on me."

You: "You cared, and that's why it hurts. But staying in a place that drained you wouldn't have helped anyone. You were exhausted. You needed space."

Guilt: "But I disappointed people."

You: "You protected your well-being. That isn't selfish — it's human. The people who truly care want you to be well."

Guilt: "I still feel like I should have handled it better."

You: "You did the best you could with the clarity you had then. And your best was enough. Now you're allowed to move on, to grow, to forgive yourself."

Envy/Jealousy/Resentment

Envy is one of the most painful emotions we experience. It shows up when you see someone living a version of the life you secretly want, and instead of inspiring you, it presses on the bruise of what you still don't have.

Sometimes it shows up as irritation toward the person who has what you want. Sometimes it feels like resentment. But underneath those sharper emotions is usually something much softer: longing, grief, or a dream you haven't given yourself permission to pursue yet.

It might sting when someone posts their book launch and you haven't written a page in months. It might sting when someone finds their "people" while you're still searching for belonging. It might even sting when your friends announce their big life changes — buying a home, getting promoted, moving forward — while you're still trying to catch your breath.

In those moments, you often don't just see someone else's success — you interpret it as evidence of your own failure. Their progress becomes your stagnation. Their beauty becomes your flaw.

What makes it even worse is the guilt that rises with it, telling you that feeling envy makes you a bad person. You might catch yourself thinking, *"What a horrible human being am I if I can't be happy for my friend?"* You don't want to be that person, so you try to push the feeling down, pretend it's not there, act as if you're above it.

But there's actually a good part about envy — a reason it's precious.

Envy is an honest compass. It points to a need you weren't ready to reveal even to yourself, long before you consciously recognize it. It's a longing wearing a painful mask, but if you listen to it instead of judging it, envy becomes guidance. It shows you what truly matters and reveals the direction your life wants to grow toward.

Feeling envy doesn't make you a bad person, because our brain is wired for automatic comparison. It's simply how it works. It scans, it measures, it ranks, all without your permission.

In a famous study, researchers asked women to rank their appearance. Then they showed them photos of models and asked them to rank themselves again. Their self-evaluation dropped by more than 12.3% — in just a few minutes. And what's worth noticing is that, for many of them, this wasn't even the most important thing in their lives. It wasn't their deepest value or their biggest priority. Yet comparison still had the power to shake how they saw themselves.

In a minute, we'll see what you can do about comparison. But right now, remember this: envy is a natural response from a mind built to compare.

When someone reminds you of a version of yourself you're secretly mourning, your instinct is often to pull away. It might be too painful. You assume the person is the threat — that if you avoid them, the discomfort will disappear. But the discomfort isn't about them; it's about the part of you that still longs for what they represent.

Instead of distancing yourself, I invite you to try the opposite: find a way to genuinely like that person. Look at them with loving eyes and ask yourself, *"What is it that's beautiful about them?"* Bring them closer. Get curious. Ask how they did it. Let their story show you what's possible. Their presence can become a bridge toward your own becoming.

And something beautiful happens when you do this. Not only does the envy fade — you may even find yourself loving the person you once felt threatened by.

Judging yourself for a natural human response like envy only keeps you stuck. When you shame yourself for feeling envy, you're adding a second layer of pain on top of the first. So instead of judging yourself for it, ask what envy is trying to reveal: *"What is this feeling pointing toward, and what could I do today to move in that direction?"*

So go talk to envy the way you'd speak to someone you love.

Meeting Your Envy

Envy: "I feel awful every time I see someone announce their book. It stings."

You: "What hurts about it?"

Envy: "They're doing what I want to do. They're writing. They're finishing things. They're putting their work into the world. And I'm… not. It makes me feel behind. Like I missed my chance."

You: "So you're not angry at them. You're hurting for yourself."

Envy: "Yes. I want that life too. I want to write. I want to have something I'm proud of. I want to be seen. And every time someone else does it, it reminds me that I'm still not there."

You: "That longing makes sense. It means writing matters to you. But what if you see it as a direction?"

Envy: "But it feels so ugly. I don't want to be the person who gets jealous of other people's success."

You: "You're not jealous of *them*. You're grieving the version of you who hasn't had the chance yet. And there's a part of you that refuses to give up on this dream."

Envy: "…I never thought of it that way."

You: "Now look at you — you've found a new direction. What if you make the first step toward this life today?'"

Letting Go of Comparison

When you're switching careers, it can feel like you have nothing real to offer in a new field. Your experience feels limited — or nonexistent. You feel like you're "just a person," just you. Motivation seems like the only thing you can put on the table.

If any of this feels familiar, keep reading.

For most of your life, you relied on an internal sense of worth — your own sense of how well you were doing. But with social media and constant visibility into other people's lives, not comparing yourself has become harder. You see how your peers seem to be progressing — or at least how they choose to appear — and without noticing, your sense of value begins to shift. Your worth becomes as unstable as spring weather — bright one moment when you feel ahead, overcast the next when you feel behind.

You read about a 20-year-old who built a multimillion-dollar company, and suddenly your own path feels like a failure. You see a celebrity who's 60 but looks 35, and instantly you feel inadequate. Nothing about you changed in that moment — only the comparison did.

Then you hear about someone who lost their job or their home, and — not because you're happy about it — but something in you softens. You feel compassion for them, and at the same time, you're grateful and this perspective helps you cherish what you already have.

There *is* a name for this phenomenon: reference dependence — the idea that your brain doesn't evaluate your life in absolute terms, but in comparison to the people around you. The mind is, at its core, a social organ. It doesn't ask, "How am I doing?" It asks, "How am I doing compared to *them*?"

Your friends, colleagues, and the group you want to belong to — psychologists call this your reference group — become the yardstick you measure yourself against.

And whenever you're not matching the majority, your brain interprets it as danger. As failure. As *"something is wrong with me."*

- If everyone around you is thriving in their careers and you're job searching, you'll feel behind.
- If they own homes and you're renting, you'll feel inadequate.
- If they're moving forward and you're standing still, you'll feel stuck — even if, objectively, you're doing fine.

And this is where comparison completely messes us up, because your reference points are rarely objective. They're just close. And closeness tricks your brain into thinking "this is normal," even when it's not.

Let's use a simple example related to your income — not because money is the most important thing, but because it's easily measurable and the easiest way to illustrate the point.

Looking back at your earnings from the past year, how do you feel about them — would you say they were low, acceptable, or genuinely good?

Now that you've picked an answer, ask yourself this: what do you think the global top 10% earns — and how close do you think you are?

According to the World Bank, the global top 10% income threshold is around $13,000–$15,000 per year (PPP)[1]. To be in the top 5% earners in the world, your income has to be $69,000 per year. Objectively, on a global scale, you might be doing extremely well. But if you live in San Francisco, and you're drowning with income like this, this "objective" information doesn't make your life easier.

This comparison mechanism shows up in every part of life — it spills into everything: beauty, education, homes, children, careers, relationships. In every area, you measure yourself against the people closest to you, not against any objective reality. And because you never chose those reference points consciously, they end up shaping your self-worth without your permission. But once you *see* what's happening, you can start to manage it.

---

[1] **PPP (Purchasing Power Parity)** adjusts income for differences in cost of living across countries. It doesn't measure your salary after tax — it measures how much *real life* your income can buy where you live compared to someone in another country. So when we say that earning above $13,000–$15,000 (PPP) per year places you in the global top 10%, it means your *purchasing power* is higher than 90% of the world's population, even if that amount wouldn't feel like much in a high-cost place. In other words, the global comparison reflects what your income can buy on average worldwide, not what it feels like in your specific city or economy.

People say, "Only compare yourself to yourself." And yes, that's ideal — but it's not how our minds are wired. What *is* possible is to separate yourself from the people around you long enough to remember that they have different needs, different paths, different timing — and that yours doesn't have to match theirs to be valid.

So here's how you destroy the power of comparison.

Comparison works a lot like envy, because that's the mechanism behind it. It only has power when you reduce someone to a single metric. The moment you learn their story, it loses its grip. So here's a small antidote: whenever you catch yourself comparing yourself to someone and feeling inferior, get curious. Get to know them. Ask about their path. You'll quickly realize it's not as effortless or perfect as it looked, and the comparison will lose its charm.

In the end, we're all just people with stories — complicated, messy, beautiful stories. And once you stop measuring yourself against the wrong things, you start seeing your own story more clearly.

Your Action Plan

Here are a few ways to begin reflecting on your remembered identity, especially if you tend to see your past through a harsh or unforgiving lens.

1. Look at Your Past as Data, Not Destiny

A past failure might feel as a story about who you are: *"I was naïve," "I gave up," "I'm not cut out for this."* Try stripping the emotion away. Look at it like a scientist. What were the conditions? How old were you? What did you know then? What actually happened? What worked, and what didn't?

Then ask yourself: if my best friend made this mistake, how would I speak to them — and why don't I offer myself the same compassion?

2. Instead of Judging Your Shame, Guilt, or Envy — Ask What They're Trying to Tell You

Emotions aren't moral verdicts. They're signals.

Shame often points to a place where you feel disconnected from your values. Guilt highlights something you care about deeply. Envy reveals a desire you haven't yet allowed yourself to claim.

Instead of collapsing into *"I am the problem,"* try shifting to: *"This feeling is a message. What is this emotion trying to show me?"* It shifts the entire experience from self-attack to self-understanding.

The Chosen Identity

Up until now, you've explored the identities you didn't consciously choose. They become the invisible baggage you carry into every transition — the beliefs, fears, expectations, and old stories that shape what feels possible long before you take a single step:

- Physical Identity — your body and its limitations and possibilities;
- Inherited Identity — the one you absorbed from the world you grew up in;
- Reflected Identity — the one reflected back to you by the people around you;
- Remembered Identity — the one you still carry from earlier chapters of your life.

Seeing how much of your story was shaped before you ever had a say can bring a sense of relief. *Finally. Now I get to create the new me.* It's a hopeful thought — the promise of a fresh start.

When those identities start to feel tight or outdated, it's natural to feel the urge to wipe the slate clean. To start over somewhere new. To step into a life where no one knows who you used to be or what you were once expected to carry.

Many of us sense a fuller version of ourselves — confident, visible, fulfilled, that whispers possibilities like: *What if I finally trusted my intuition, stopped shrinking and let myself be seen?*

And yet, the moment that perspective appears, something tightens. The dream feels too far from the woman you are today — imperfect, insecure, still carrying old promises.

If we're honest, this isn't your first attempt at reinvention. You've tried to start fresh before:

A new job.

A new team.

A new city.
New people who don't know your past.
New expectations.
Sometimes even a new country.
And still, after a while, the same familiar feeling returns — that something is off. Often, it feels like an internal tug-of-war:

One part says, *"I deserve a chance."*
Another part answers, *"But what if they discover I'm not that qualified?"*

One part says, *"I'm ready for something new."*
Another whispers, *"But what if I fail again, like that time?"*

One part says, *"I want to be visible."*
Another part of you whispers, *"Please don't notice the parts of me I'm still ashamed of."*

Trying to fully embrace yourself can feel like wearing a dress while knowing there's a stain on the back. You become hyper-aware of the parts of your story you'd rather keep tucked away — the regrets, the awkward moments, the choices you wish you could redo. You move carefully, angling your body just so. A surprising amount of your energy goes into keeping the stain out of other people's sight, hoping no one turns you to the side you're still self-conscious about.

But what if the stain didn't need to be managed at all? What if the place where you see a stain is, to everyone else, nothing at all? What if it could simply… stop being a stain?

Not by putting on another dress.
Not by pretending it was never there.
And not by trying to "start from scratch" — because life doesn't work that way. Instead, it begins with approaching yourself differently: understanding what the stain is made of, where it came from, and finding the right chemicals to either wipe it away or weave it into your costume.

So when we talk about chosen identity, the real question is *How do I tame the voices that keep dragging me back to who I used to be?*

In the previous chapters, you learned how to acknowledge the hardest parts of yourself — not as stains to hide, but as valuable parts of you that formed for a reason, parts that once protected you, parts that still want to keep you safe.

Now it's time to strengthen the other voice inside you — the one that steadies you, backs you, and remembers who you are when you forget. Because even if you switch countries or industries, even if you walk into a room where no one knows your history, you don't arrive as a blank slate. You arrive with everything you've lived through — your strengths, your fears, your habits, your brilliance, your insecurities, your resilience.

Reinvention isn't about erasing any of that. It's about learning how to carry it with more kindness, more clarity, and more direction. Reinvention isn't a change of scenery. It's a change of relationship with yourself, and as a consequence with others.

That includes these unhealed pieces. The unhealed pieces don't just disappear. They travel with you. They ask to be seen. And until you turn toward them with honesty and care, they'll keep pulling you back to the same familiar place.

From Project Management to C-level Executive (Venezuela → Australia → Netherlands)

Estela has reinvented herself more times than most people dare to imagine. She grew up poor in Caracas, migrated alone to Australia with a toddler and no English, rebuilt her life from scratch, and then — when most people would have settled — she uprooted everything again to start over in Europe to become a leader at one of the top technology companies. Her story is not linear. It's not neat. It's a story of courage, stubbornness, and the kind of resilience you only develop when you've had no other choice.

And this is how she tells her story.

I was born in Caracas, Venezuela, into a poor family. We didn't have much. I decided early that I wanted to go to university, but to afford it I had to work during the day and study at night. I studied computer science.

I didn't want just any job. I wanted a job in a company where I could grow. And I found one — an energy company. I started as a personal assistant and grew into a project-manager-type role. It was a great learning experience. I did my thesis there. I built a human-resource management system — a full system — and it won a prize at an engineering congress.

That system changed my life. The company was bought, and they gave me a payout. And at the same time, I had just had my daughter. I was 23.

When I was doing my thesis, my boss had to ask the CTO for permission for me to work on the system because it required an engineering profile. The CTO looked at me and said, "She won't be able to do it. She's too young and she's a woman."

My boss ignored him. He had three kids; he understood potential. He let me do the project. When we presented it to the CPO, the guy asked, "Who did you hire to build this?" And my boss said, "Estela did it." The man said, "My apologies. I was wrong." That moment stayed with me.

But after my daughter was born, I realized I didn't want to raise her in Venezuela. You are afraid for your life every day. There is no safety. I was always scratching for money. So I researched the best countries in the world. Australia came first.

I decided to migrate as a skilled independent immigrant. I didn't speak English. I had never been to Australia. I arrived with my daughter and my daughter's dad in my arms and nothing but two suitcases. I left him shortly after 2 years after we arrived in Australia.

My first job in Australia was cleaning houses. That was the only job I was genuinely terrible at. Then I started doing websites — for a programmer, that was at least decent.

I barely spoke English, so I needed to learn the language. I needed a job. I needed to raise my daughter. All at the same time.

The advantage of Australia is that they help immigrants. They understand how hard it is. They gave me 500 hours of English lessons. They gave integration training — not just language, but culture, customs, how the society works. It made a huge difference.

Then I had a job interview. I came home and my friend asked, "How did it go?" I said, "I don't know. I barely understood what they were saying." She said, "Call them. Put them on speaker."

So I called and said, "Thank you for the interview." They replied with something in English I didn't understand at all. I hung up thinking nothing had happened. My friend looked at me — absolutely glowing — and said, "They hired you! They said it was great to see you and they'll see you on Monday."

I worked 12 years for that newspaper. They became like a family to me. They helped me raise my kid. The editor-in-chief was my emergency contact. I learned everything from scratch — a new programming language, integration systems, all the backend technology. My job was always changing, and I loved that. By the end, I became a team leader. I discovered I loved helping teams, building teams, and bringing people along.

Australia also taught me trust. Once, I left my wallet and passport on a bench. Someone called me: "I found it. I don't want you to be without your papers." On farms, people leave apples outside with a money box. You take what you need and leave the money. Nobody takes advantage. I loved that.

Then my daughter grew up and left home at 18. Suddenly I thought, *What am I going to do now?* So we took a trip to Europe with her — no plans, just two tickets. Every day we decided where to go next. It awakened something in me, and I decided to move to Europe.

My first choice was Switzerland. Then Germany. Everyone told me I was crazy. "Why leave Australia? You have a good life." But I wanted something else.

So I applied for jobs with intention. I didn't want to repeat the same roles, I wanted something new. But after enough rejections, you start doubting everything — your CV, your name, your experience, your direction.

In the end, my Spanish helped. My curiosity helped. My willingness to learn helped. I have a pattern: every job I've gotten, I started unqualified on paper. I learn fast. I bring people with me. I think strategically. That's what people hire me for.

I got a job in Germany. I didn't speak German. They gave me a tutor. They taught me the culture — what to say, what not to say, how things work. I found warm people. I had a relocation agent who helped me with everything — hairdresser, supermarket, public transport, housing. It made a huge difference.

But my daughter stayed in Australia. She was not coming to terms with me for leaving. She stopped talking to me. That was hard.

I went back to Australia for a while to think, mend my relationship with my daughter and take my old dog with me to Germany. Then one night, I applied for jobs again — randomly. One was my dream job at a bank in Germany. Another was as a CTO. Another was with a tech giant in the Netherlands.

I got interviews with all of them. I told the tech giant: "I have never worked with this technology. I have never worked in this industry. You need to make an informed decision about hiring me." They hired me anyway.

When I moved to the Netherlands, I struggled more than I expected. The culture was different. People were colder at first. Everyone minds their own business. My first Christmas here was miserable. No decorations. No warmth. I felt alone. I couldn't find friends. I didn't understand what people were saying. I didn't understand the job. I felt incompetent. I cried a lot.

But I held on.

My manager believed in me. In one of our first one-on-one business meetings I broke down in tears. He said, "Let go of the noise. Stop double darting yourself. You go for something and you get it done. That's why I hired you". Not because I had the experience — I didn't — but because I brought people along into the journey. I get things done. If he asks me for lunch I bring him a five course gourmet meal.

And that's the thread through my whole life.

I've reinvented myself again and again — not because I wanted to, but because I had to. Because staying where I was would have been worse. Because I wanted a better life for my daughter. Because I wanted a better life for myself.

And every time, I started from zero. Every time, I learned a new language. Every time, I built a new career. Every time, I found a new path forward.

I might not be the most qualified candidate on paper.

But I am the one who will figure it out.

The Power of Choice

Before we move into creating this new identity, there's something important I want you to consider: even though you have a history, you are free to choose what's next in your career and in your life.

Take a moment with that. Notice how it lands in your body.

Sometimes it might not feel liberating at all, bringing up irritation or sadness — because right now, you may not feel free. You may feel stuck in a career that no longer fits, but it's not as if you can simply change it.

As Madi, one of the reinventors, said: *"Your new career isn't just about passion. It's about rent. It's about debt. It's about the pressure on your relationship. It's about how much sacrifice is too much."*

When there are real-life factors pressing in on you from all sides, you might feel trapped. One woman in the Reinvento Club described it perfectly: *"It feels like a prison."* And when life feels that tight, it becomes very hard to see yourself as someone with choices.

Yet what the science says is this: before anything can shift on the outside, you need to reclaim the sense of autonomy on the inside — the sense that you have a say, that your choices matter, that you're not just an audience member in your own life but an active presence on the stage.

Having said that, let's face the elephant in the room: none of us are completely free. Life comes with constraints — financial, emotional, relational, practical. So how do you reclaim your agency when challenges keep coming from all sides?

I invite you to use the power of choice, starting with baby steps. Agency doesn't begin with big decisions. It begins with the smallest choices — the ones that are always available to you, no matter your circumstances.

Your breath.

The way you soften your shoulders.

The way you place your feet on the ground.

The moment you pause before reacting.

The choice to speak one sentence more honestly than you did yesterday.

These tiny acts are the first proof your nervous system receives that you are not helpless. When you can influence your breath, you can influence your state. When you can influence your state, you can influence your choices. And when you can influence your choices — even in small ways — you begin to trust that you can influence your life.

From that place, real change becomes possible.

From Make Up Artist to Cook (Belarus → Uruguay)

Tatiana spent her life in Belarus, made it through the harsh nineties, raised a daughter, built a career in film, and never imagined that at 55 she would have to start over. But the political reality and her inability to stay silent made her life unbearable. She left for Uruguay — a country she knew only from family legends. There she lost everything familiar: her language, her profession, her status. But she found something she had never had before: a slower rhythm, human warmth, the ocean, and the ability to live the way she needs.
And this is how she tells her story.

I had lived a long, full life: I danced, taught aerobics, survived the harsh nineties, worked as a makeup artist in film, raised my daughter, and cared for my mother after her stroke.

In the 1980s, I danced in a troupe called "Charovnitsy" — first it was amateur, then professional. We toured all over the Soviet Union. Then I taught aerobics. Then came the nineties. It was a difficult time when the country we had fell apart. It wasn't about career, it was about survival. We would sell butter or hats — whatever we could to survive.

I had been doing makeup since I was young — for performances, concerts, photoshoots. It was something I loved. And at some point, I got into the film industry — almost by accident.

A director needed a first-floor apartment to film a scene of someone being thrown out of a window. They liked our apartment's location, rang our apartment's bell, and my mother answered. During the conversation, she mentioned that I was a makeup artist. The next day I was at the film studio, and two days later I was on a work trip. I was 34 then.

Then came years of being a make up artist, my mother's stroke, work in a theater, a return to the film industry, more shoots, more travel. I worked a lot, honestly, with love. But in the last few years everything changed. I felt the country sliding toward something from which there would be no return.

In 2020, Belarus held a presidential election. Most opposition candidates were arrested beforehand, and peaceful mass protests erupted across the country. The demonstrations were suppressed, and the results were widely reported as falsified. Sviatlana Tsikhanouskaya, who won the vote according to the independent observers, was forced to leave the country. And in 2022, Russia launched a full-scale invasion of Ukraine, escalating the regional crisis.

At some point it became impossible to live in that reality. I'm the kind of person who cannot stay silent when something unjust is happening around me. It literally made me shake to pretend nothing was happening. The last film I worked on, in August 2022 —

another war film — became the point of no return. I realized: I can't work anymore, I can't live, I can't breathe in this. I felt: if I stay, I simply won't be able to live.

And then our family story resurfaced. My father was born in Montevideo, Uruguay. His parents were Belarusians who left for Latin America in the 1920s. My grandmother was illiterate, my grandfather a handsome man who worked as a trick rider in a circus.

In 2014 my daughter Masha went to a carnival in Brazil, stopped by Uruguay, and in five days — during carnival, without speaking the language — found my father's birth certificate in the archives and the address of the house where he lived.

This family legend suddenly became our lifeline. In 2021 we received Uruguayan passports. And in 2022 it became clear: the time has come.

I was 58 when I finally decided to leave. In Belarus I would already have been retired, but life had other plans. I sold the apartment after the very first viewing. And I left through Vilnius — because Belarusians weren't being allowed into Poland. I traveled through fear, through uncertainty, through borders where they could have turned me back. But I made it.

When I arrived in Uruguay, I saw the ocean — and for the first time in a long time, I could breathe.

I started from scratch. Here no one knows I worked in film. No one cares about my achievements, my films, my years of experience. To work in the film industry, you need Spanish — which I'm not exactly fluent in yet.

I work with my hands — cutting hair, coloring, doing makeup, cooking. It turned out I can cook so well that people come back. Dumplings, pies, draniki — all of that became my new profession. I watch a recipe on YouTube and make it. Pies? Sure. Pilaf? Easy. Chocolate-covered curd bars? No problem. I'm thinking about opening a small café.

People here are different. They live slowly. They smile. They ask how you are — and actually listen. On the bus you must say "hello" and "thank you" to the driver. On the street strangers smile at you. If you get lost, they'll walk you to the right place, find a translator, put you on the right bus. I had never experienced anything like this in Belarus.

I miss Minsk — not the place it became, but the fact that I can't return. It's a special kind of pain only those who lost their home country understand. I understand the most important thing: if I had stayed, I wouldn't know how to live. I simply couldn't.

But here I have the ocean.

When I feel bad, I just go to listen to the water. Sit. Look. And everything inside settles. I understand why people who live by the ocean are so calm.

I don't know what will happen next. But I know that here I can breathe.

Here I can live. And sometimes that's enough.

Whether you're working a job that no longer feels like yours, recovering from the sting of being let go, or leaving the country that became dangerous to stay in, the starting point is always the same: you still have a place inside you that you can choose.

You may not control everything — circumstances, timing, the economy, the decisions of others — but you do have influence over how you meet what happens next.

Viktor Frankl, who endured the unimaginable after losing his entire family in a concentration camp, wrote that everything can be taken from a person except the freedom to choose their attitude and their response to life. He learned, in the harshest conditions possible, that even when the world strips away almost everything, there remains a small inner space that still belongs to you.

If someone living through suffering that profound could hold on to that tiny space of choice, then your ability to choose who you become is something you already carry.

But what does it mean to build an identity that isn't inherited, assigned, or expected — but chosen?

Your New Supportive Voice

By now, you've met several of the voices that live inside you.

- You've met the critic, the part of you that scans for danger and tries to keep you safe by pointing out everything that could go wrong.
- You've met shame, who worries that certain parts of you are too messy or too complicated to be seen, and tries to protect you by keeping them hidden.
- You've met guilt, who holds tightly to the past because it's terrified you might repeat it.
- You've met envy, who quietly mourns the version of you that you haven't stepped into yet — the one you sense you could be.

And you've learned something important: these voices might speak loudly, but they don't always speak the truth. They're part of you, but they're not the whole of you.

Once you begin hearing them as voices — not as facts, not as verdicts, not as your identity — something shifts. You stop fighting them. You stop assuming every anxious thought is a prophecy. You start seeing that each of these voices is trying to protect you in its own clumsy way. And when you see that, you can finally make space for a voice that has been too soft for a very long time.

When you imagine a new path, the fearful voices tend to show up first. They're quick, familiar, and very convincing. They say things like, *"Switching jobs after 40 will make you look unserious,"* or *"You're too old to learn something new,"* or *"What will people think?"* They sound protective, but really they're just repeating old stories you've heard for years.

You don't need to silence them. You don't need to argue with them. You simply need to add another voice to the conversation — one that remembers your strengths, sees your potential, and speaks to you with the same kindness you offer the people you love.

Your supportive voice.

To develop that voice, try this exercise from one of the previous chapters: whenever you're facing a challenge or feeling stuck, imagine someone you care about coming to you with the exact same problem. They ask for your advice. What would you say to them?

Your supportive voice might say things like, *"Just because I can do my old job doesn't mean I should,"* or *"I'm allowed to want a life that feels good,"* or *"I've learned difficult things before; I can learn this too."* It might remind you that you're not on anyone else's timeline, that your experience matters, that changing your mind isn't failure — it's growth. It might gently point out that what other people think is their business, not yours, and that your life is allowed to feel meaningful to you even if it doesn't make sense to anyone else.

Your supportive voice can turn something you once felt ashamed of into a part of your story. One of my favorite examples of this kind of reframing was from Zohran Mamdani, who ran for mayor of New York and won, and said in his victory speech: *"After all, the conventional wisdom will tell you that I'm far from a perfect candidate. I'm young, despite my best effort to grow older. I'm Muslim. I am a democratic socialist. And most damning of all, I refuse to apologize for any of it."*

You might not be a perfect candidate, but you don't need to apologize for who you are. Truly. Women like you with your willingness to grow, to reflect, to try again, make the world softer and wiser. I'm celebrating that in you — and I hope, little by little, you learn to celebrate it in yourself too.

This is what self-compassion looks like in real life. It's a steady, honest conversation with yourself that gives you permission to be who you are.

So many of us have been taught that being hard on ourselves is responsible, that self-acceptance is dangerous, that if you ever say *"I'm okay,"* you'll stop striving, turn into family disappointment, and die unsuccessful — obviously. It's important to acknowledge that inner pressure *did* help you survive certain chapters. But that self-doubt has exhausted more women than it has ever helped. It keeps you in a constant state of tension, as if the only way to grow is to punish yourself into becoming someone new.

You don't have to do that anymore. You don't have to earn your own love and kindness. You deserve to be spoken to with love and respect, even — and especially — by yourself.

Start With What Matters To You

For many people in midlife — balancing work, family, friendships, and responsibilities — life often turns into a set of routines. Nothing is wrong, exactly, but something starts to feel missing. And before you even notice it happening, you find yourself asking: *Why am I unhappy?*

And the only honest place to look for the answer is with what matters to you *now* — not what mattered ten or twenty years ago, not what others expect, not what you once promised yourself you'd become.

Sometimes what matters is obvious. Often, it isn't.

Sometimes it feels like there are too many things pulling at you — too many interests, too many possibilities, too many versions of who you could become. And other times, it feels like everything that once mattered is fading, leaving you unsure of what's left to hold on to.

So the real question becomes:

How do you begin to notice what has meaning for you?

When you ask this question directly, the answer almost never appears. Meaning tends to reveal itself quietly, in the moments we're not trying to notice. So let's approach it from a few other angles.

One way is to notice the people you admire. Think of the friend who stays calm in chaos, the colleague who speaks up even when her voice shakes, the mentor who listens without rushing to fix, the influencer who keeps creating even when no one is watching.

Ask yourself: *What exactly do I admire about them?*

Is it their courage? Their calm? Their creativity? Their humor? Their warmth? Their ability to walk away when something no longer fits?

Your admiration is a compass pointing toward what matters to you. It's rarely random. And here's what will surprise you: once you list the qualities you admire in someone else, you'll notice that these are often the very qualities you're ready to recognize, nurture, or finally allow in yourself.

If it's still hard to accept all your parts, this exercise will show you something surprisingly comforting: the people you admire are often drawn to the same things you are — they just allow those parts to be seen.

Another way to recognize what matters to you is to ask yourself this question: if you could teach your (future) children — or everyone in the world — one thing, what would it be? Kindness? Resilience? Curiosity? Belief that they're allowed to choose their own path?

You can also pay attention to the moments when you feel most alive. Not excited — alive. Maybe also proud. The moments when you lose track of time, when you feel grounded, when something inside you says, "This matters."

Ask yourself:

When was the last time I felt that way?

What was I doing? Who was I with? What part of me was being expressed?

These moments show you where your energy naturally flows.

From Corporate Event Planner to Founder of a Natural Health Center (The United States → The Netherlands)

Sandra once thought she had a clear sense of who she was. She studied accounting, built a solid corporate career in the US, and eventually landed a much sought-after role as a corporate event planner at one of the largest banks, managing million-dollar budgets. Her identity was tied to structure, responsibility, and being good at what she did. And then life shifted—first with motherhood, then with a move to the Middle East with her husband. At 38, she found herself in a quiet apartment in a foreign country, a baby on her hip, totally reliant on her husband—which was very difficult to accept—and with no clear path forward.

And this is how she tells her story.

When my son was born, everything changed. The spreadsheets and corporate events were replaced by feeding times and lullabies. Then my husband's job took us to the Middle East. I was in a foreign country learning to be a mother without my family nearby at the same time yearning for intellectual conversation and a way to earn money as a professional. I kept imagining that once my son was older, I'd go back to the corporate world. But in reality, looking back, I realize I was in a sort of identity crisis for about three years, trying to figure out who I was in this new place.

Everything changed when I got sick in the Middle East. I wasn't feeling well, and doctors mis-prescribed something that made me feel worse. They couldn't figure out what was wrong; it was probably my body trying to tell me something. My mother-in-law, who is a homeopath, suggested a remedy. At first, I was skeptical—after all, I thought homeopathy wasn't "real" medicine. But I felt better after the remedy, and I also saw how fast my son recovered from seasonal illnesses using only homeopathy. That's when curiosity took over.

If you look in a dictionary, health is the state of being free from illness or injury. But in homeopathy, health is defined as the ability to adapt to change and perform without restriction. You can adapt to everything that comes your way as long as you are in good health in both mind and body. Even when terrible things happen, like when a loved one passes away, there is of course grief. Many people stay in this pain for decades, unable to adapt. When we are in good health, our body responds to change in a healthy way. We give ourselves space to grieve, but we still have the strength to do what needs to be done—plan the funeral, communicate with family, and carry on with daily life. Our health offers ways to adapt and let go of the physical symptoms of grief in the body. It's truly about adapting to change.

Studying natural medicine changed more than my health—it changed how I perceived life's challenges. Becoming a therapist taught me to see symptoms, illnesses, and even career blocks not as random events, but as signals waiting to be recognized. They're combinations of factors in your life and environment asking for your attention. When you understand the "why," you can address the root, not just the symptom. That shift in perspective was huge for me.

Around that time, my husband was offered a job in the Netherlands. Another move. Another reset. But this time, I had a direction. I wanted to become a certified homeopath, so I enrolled in a four-year program.

While I was learning, I began a journey of self-exploration, experimenting with various therapies like Reiki and acupuncture. The idea for a center began to form—a place where people could access natural healing in a structured, professional environment that felt safe. This required investment, and while I found many people with the same values, it never felt like the right time or the right fit.

Then, as soon as I graduated, the pandemic started. I realized people needed this more than ever. They were searching for ways to strengthen their health, and I saw how natural medicine truly helped them. It solidified my mission to start a health center dedicated to natural options—an alternative to mainstream medicine, not because mainstream medicine doesn't work, but because it isn't the only option. My husband and I made an important decision: we decided to buy a physical location.

Opening the center wasn't easy. Educating people about how natural medicine works is an uphill battle. Traditional medicine creates very high expectations; people often come to us frustrated, looking for miracles. Sometimes at networking events, people hear what I do and say, "You're a homeopath; we have nothing to talk about," and walk away. They forget how important health is—without it, nothing else matters.

I am positive about traditional medicine; homeopathy can't treat everything. But there's a gap between traditional medicine and what nature offers, and I want people to know there's a natural side they're missing.

Through all of this, curiosity was my compass. I followed small sparks—the things that energized me. I asked myself: *What makes me feel alive? What did I love doing as a child?* Very few people can instantly answer "What makes you happy?" but if you keep exploring the small things that bring you energy, the bigger path reveals itself.

And I didn't do it alone. I learned I'm not superwoman. You need a community that believes in you; their support becomes the safety net that lets you take the leap.

Was I ready for failure? Honestly, I never truly felt it wouldn't work. I have days where I think, "Why am I starting a new career in my 50s?" or "Why am I so passionate about this when people don't recognize how it works?" But I have a core belief that this is my path. It feels like destiny.

Studying homeopathy helped me look for the extraordinary in the simple things. It taught me to look at challenges not as things that happen *to* you, but as signals that life is out of balance. When you understand the "why," you can start to address the root.

It wasn't easy, and it wasn't a predesigned plan. You go through moments of "Who am I? What am I doing?" You figure it out as you go. But now, I feel I'm where I'm supposed to be. If you're passionate and curious, and you're willing to listen and adapt, you can build something truly meaningful.

For Sandra, change arrived uninvited — but it ended up helping her discover the meaning of her next chapter. Sandra's story shows that caring doesn't always show up as inspiration; it shows up as a problem or a frustration. Sometimes it arrives as a spark of "this should be different." The things that irritate you, the problems you can't stop thinking about, the situations you wish someone would finally fix — these, too, reveal what you value.

Ask yourself:

What do I complain about because I secretly care?

What do I wish someone would change?

What breaks my heart a little?

All of these are simply ways of finding the thread that leads you forward. These questions reveal something essential: understanding who you want to be now. When you start with what matters to you, you're not choosing a niche; you're choosing yourself.

Your chosen identity isn't built from titles or achievements. It's built from what you care about — deeply and honestly. And once you know what you care about, everything else becomes easier to figure out.

What You Bring That No One Else Does

At the beginning of this book, we explored the traps that make reinvention feel harder than it needs to be — the invisible rules, the single story, the golden cage, the fog of too many options. None of these patterns say anything about your potential. All they reveal is that you were making big decisions in conditions no one thinks clearly in.

And in the previous chapter, you saw something important: you may already be carrying the skills, instincts, and experiences that your next chapter will rely on. The problem is that the things that come most naturally to you are often the hardest to see. Your strengths feel ordinary from the inside. Your superpowers feel like "nothing special." Your brilliance feels like "just how I am."

That's why this chapter matters. Reinvention doesn't start with the market, or the niche, or the job title. It starts with you, with seeing and recognizing what's already there. With the parts of you that never left — they just got buried under expectations, comparisons, and years of being practical.

When you finally stop and look at what you already have, that's when the real work begins. It's the slower, steadier process of returning to yourself — to the version of you that's been waiting beneath all the noise, quietly holding the diamonds you haven't yet learned to claim.

Let's uncover those diamonds gently and honestly.

Reconnecting With Yourself: Your New Inner Compass

According to the World Economic Forum, roughly two-fifths of the skills you use today will either transform or retire by 2030. Poof. Gone. Like the skill of rewinding a cassette tape with a pencil (if you don't know what that is, don't Google it).

And still, when we look for a new direction, we reduce ourselves to neat CV columns: proficient in Excel, Javascript, C#, data analysis.

It's the same childhood logic: *I'm good at languages, he's good at math.* Familiar. Safe. But incomplete. Those lists show your tools — not the hand that holds them. They don't show how you think, how you solve problems, or how you show up when things get messy.

So I invite you to look at yourself differently — from the inside out, not from the expectations or approval of others. When you notice how much of your identity was shaped by what other people needed from you, this awareness creates space. And in that space, a new question appears:

Who are you when you're no longer performing the version of yourself the world asked you to be?

Think about your own career. There were moments when you stepped into something without fully knowing what you were walking into. You didn't know the jargon, the processes, the unspoken rules. And yet you figured it out. You adapted. You made things work that shouldn't have worked.

That wasn't a single skill. That was *you.*

So what do we call that deeper thing — the thing that stays with you even when your job title changes, even when your industry collapses, even when you're starting from scratch?

It's not *what* you do, it's *how* you do what you do.

It's your superpowers.

I know — the word feels dramatic. You might be thinking, "A superpower? I just organize meetings and send emails." But look closer. What do you quietly fix in those meetings and emails without anyone asking? Why does organizing them energize you instead of draining you? What feels so easy for you — so natural — that you almost overlook it?

There's a consistent pattern in how you approach things, one that becomes unmistakable once you know how to see it. Psychologist Martin Seligman, the father of positive psychology, calls this pattern a *character strength* — the deep, enduring part of your personality that shapes how you move through the world. It's not a skill or a passion, but the invisible architecture of your behavior.

They're why certain tasks feel energizing, while others drain you.

They're why you thrive in some environments and shrink in others.

They're why you can change careers without losing yourself.

From HR to Digital Marketing to Startup Founder (India – Singapore – Netherlands)

Pooja reinvented herself across three countries and multiple industries — fashion, technology, and crypto. For years, she built a sharp, upward-moving career in HR and digital roles at global companies like Google, Tommy Hilfiger, and Calvin Klein, collecting promotions, responsibility, and even a billboard moment in Amsterdam. But after becoming a mother, burning out in a scale-up, and realizing that success on paper didn't match how she felt inside, she stepped off autopilot and rebuilt her life from the ground up. And this is how she tells her story.

I was born in India, in a small town, and moved to a bigger one as I grew up. I was always a good performer, not because anyone pushed me, but because once I tasted what it felt like to be recognized for my effort, I wanted to feel that again.

When I was thirteen, I won a scholarship to study in Singapore. I still remember one of the interview questions — "How will your parents take it if you're not here?" — and my answer, which now feels almost comically bold for a thirteen-year-old: "I can't let their emotions overpower my decisions." That sentence traveled through my family and neighborhood like gossip. Suddenly I was "the bold one," "the independent one," and that reinforcement shaped me more than I realized at the time.

Singapore opened my world. I arrived as the stereotypical Indian scholar expected to excel in sciences, but when I finally had a choice, I picked the arts. Literature, history, philosophy — subjects that allowed interpretation, nuance, and dialogue. Singapore's education system trains you to think on your feet. You walk into an exam hall with your textbook because it won't help you anyway. The question might be something like, "When did the Cold War really start?" and you're expected to write an 800-word essay from your own perspective. That shaped me. It taught me not to take anything at face value, to form my own view, and to articulate it.

After four years, my parents wanted me back in India. I agreed — but only if I got into one specific university. I was waitlisted, devastated, and then suddenly invited to an interview. It lasted three minutes. I walked out confused but hopeful, and I got in. That moment reinforced something I had been building for years: a sense of self-belief that wasn't easily shaken.

I went on to pursue an MBA — reluctantly. I didn't understand why aptitude tests mattered more than conversations, but my mother insisted. My parents, both doctors, wanted security for me. So I did it, got into a top institute, and landed the best placement of my cohort. I was sincere, prepared, hardworking — and it showed. Within eight months of my first job, I moved through three roles because my learning curve was reasonably steep. I found myself sitting in compensation and benefits, helping decide pay and bonus structures for 70,000 employees. And that's when I realized something important: I didn't feel I had earned the right to be in that seat. I didn't understand business deeply enough. I didn't want to pretend I did.

So I quit — without another job lined up.

During my notice period, I received a call from Google telling me I had been rejected for a role I'd applied to months earlier. I asked the recruiter a simple question: "What made me eligible then, and what makes me ineligible now?" She paused, reconsidered, and asked if I was ready to answer some questions. I was. Three rounds later, I had an offer — in digital marketing, not HR. I had no background in it, but I had curiosity, discipline, and a notebook full of handwritten notes.

At Google, my career was anything but linear. I trained new joiners on YouTube, taught analytics, facilitated mental health workshops, volunteered across teams, and eventually moved back into HR — a rare internal shift. I told them I had two superpowers: business acumen and the ability to ask great questions. It worked.

Then I moved to the Netherlands. I could have stayed at Google, but I wanted more impact, more ownership so I started looking for something else. The transition wasn't easy. I faced rejections — 20, 30, 40 of them — because I didn't speak Dutch. I faced cultural blind spots, comments about "why I didn't have an accent despite being from India," assumptions about my background.

And eventually I joined Tommy Hilfiger and Calvin Klein (PVH) as an HR business partner for tech and digital — a world I didn't even know existed within fashion. It became one of the best experiences of my career. I built operating models, set up entities, partnered deeply with stakeholders, and grew quickly.

I learned that rejections hurt most in the beginning, and then they stop hurting. Too often people give up on themselves long before the world gives up on them. And I learned that one good recruiter can change everything.

I think the biggest thing that helped me was one recruiter — Sjoerd. He was the only one who didn't look at my nationality, my accent, or the fact that I didn't speak Dutch. He looked at my thinking. He was the one who reinforced that there's nothing wrong with my profile. And sometimes you just need one person who sees you for your capability, not your passport.

He taught me an important lesson - that you can never be right for a wrong environment. And if you haven't found the right one yet, don't go on a self-auditing spree. Use that effort to find one instead."

I grew at PVH, became a mother, and was promoted during my pregnancy. I returned to work feeling powerful — if I could birth a human, I could do anything. But I also felt something shifting. I wanted a new challenge. I wanted to break another mold. So I joined a fast-growing scale-up in crypto as a director of product and tech HR — a role I landed through LinkedIn, which is almost unheard of at that level. It was chaotic, fast, exhilarating. I built structures from scratch, left my personal imprint on the organization, and became visible as a role model for women in leadership.

In 2024, I had a billboard moment — literally. My face appeared on a major street in Amsterdam as part of a Women's Day campaign declaring me as a 'Role Model for Women in Leadership'. People sent me selfies. My daughter pointed at the poster and said, "That's Mama." For two minutes, I felt proud. And then, almost immediately, I felt something else: Is this it? Is this the peak? Is this the script I chose, or the script I followed because I happened to be good at it?

The titles were growing, the salary was good, the external markers of success were all there — but the internal feeling wasn't. I was postpartum, exhausted, 86 kilos, unable to carry my daughter comfortably, breastfeeding at 1 a.m. while working late into the night.

I asked myself why I was doing all of this, and I didn't have an answer.

So I stepped back. I worked on my body. I worked on my mind. I worked on my sense of agency. And I realized that what I cared about most was women's power — the ability to look in the mirror and feel in control of your life. That's how my venture, Slayrobe, was born.

I didn't abandon HR — I kept my leadership advisory work alive. I didn't abandon business — I used it to build my startup. I didn't abandon my past — I integrated it. I believe pivots aren't mutually exclusive. You can build multiple things, but you must accept that momentum will slow when you're the one driving all of them.

For women, self-belief can waver — with your cycle, with motherhood, with changing countries, with difficult relationships. So many things affect us. But throughout my life, I've had mostly positive reinforcement for my capability. Looking back, my story spans three countries, multiple industries, and several reinventions. I learned that pivots aren't clean. They're messy, iterative, and full of imposter syndrome. But I also learned that every skill I had ever built was transferable. The through-line is clear: I've always chosen growth over comfort, meaning over predictability, and agency over autopilot.

Because I've spent years hiring people in the Netherlands, I know what works for career switchers. Crystallize your narrative. Build a voice in the industry you want to enter. Volunteer. Freelance. Contribute to projects. Own your career breaks instead of apologizing for them. Motherhood and migration aren't gaps — they're lessons. Answer questions directly. Match your communication to the level of the role. Maintain the same positioning regardless of who is in the room — I refer to this as Executive Consistency. Show learning agility — it matters more than skills.

If you work in a company, pay attention to internal opportunities. Internal switches are always a lot easier because you're already visible internally. And the good thing is, if you switch internally, you won't be down-leveled — you'll usually be matched to the level you're already operating at, which makes it much easier to keep your scope and your pay while making the move.

Have you ever felt like something you do is so easy it hardly counts — so obvious that everyone else must do it just as well? Maybe you can calm a room, untangle a messy project, or explain a complex idea in a way that finally lands. You shrug when people thank you for it, because to you it feels like breathing.

Your superpowers are often the things you dismiss as "nothing special." Because they come so naturally to you, you assume they come naturally to everyone. And there's a name for that blind spot: the curse of knowledge. It's a cognitive bias that happens when something becomes so familiar to you that you can't remember what it was like before you knew it. We're trained to think in skills, so we overlook the qualities behind them. These don't show up on a CV. But they shape everything you touch.

Seligman and Christopher Peterson identified 24 character strengths across six domains:

- **Wisdom & Knowledge:** Creativity, Curiosity, Judgment, Love of Learning, Perspective
- **Courage:** Bravery, Perseverance, Honesty, Zest
- **Humanity:** Love, Kindness, Social Intelligence
- **Justice:** Teamwork, Fairness, Leadership
- **Temperance:** Forgiveness, Humility, Prudence, Self-Regulation
- **Transcendence:** Appreciation of Beauty & Excellence, Gratitude, Hope, Humor, Spirituality

When you first look at the list of strengths, it can feel abstract — like someone emptied a box of virtues onto the table. But there's logic underneath. These six families aren't random. They're six different ways humans have learned to move through the world.

- Some of us make sense of life through **understanding** — noticing patterns, asking questions, connecting ideas.
- Some of us move through life with **courage** — showing up even when it's uncomfortable, telling the truth, trying again after failing.
- Some of us are wired for **connection** — sensing what others need, offering warmth, building trust.
- Some of us naturally think in terms of **fairness and groups** —what's balanced, what keeps a team functioning.
- Some of us are anchored in **self-management** — restraint, patience, the ability to pause before reacting.
- And some of us are pulled toward **meaning** — beauty, hope, humor, the things that lift us above the everyday.

Your superpowers don't just describe you. They explain you.

They show you how you tend to meet the world, interact with people, and achieve your goals. They reveal why certain roles felt natural and others felt like wearing someone else's shoes. They explain why you can change jobs, industries, even countries — and still feel like yourself — because the deeper pattern underneath stays the same.

And here's the best part: you already have all these superpowers. The only difference is the order in which they show up for you.

Your Action Plan

Now it's your turn — not to perform, not to impress anyone, but simply to get curious about yourself.

1. Take the VIA Character Strengths Survey.

Go to the VIA Institute on Character website and take the free survey. It's the tool Seligman's team created — the one used in most of the research we've talked about. It takes about 15 minutes, and at the end you'll get a ranked list of all 24 strengths, including your personal "Top 5" or "Top 7." Write them down somewhere you can return to.

2. Reflect — and actually let yourself own them.

Grab a notebook or open a document. For each of your top superpowers, write a few sentences:

- *When was the last time I used this strength?*
  Don't overthink it — it could be at work, at home, or in a tiny moment with a friend.
- *How did using it make me feel?*
  Energized? Calm? Proud?
- *Is this a strength I've always recognized, or is it a surprise?*
  If it's something you didn't expect (like "Appreciation of Beauty" was for me), sit with it. Sometimes the strengths we overlook are the ones we need most.
- *3 ways I can use this superpower more intentionally in the future*

Finding Your Calling

Finding a job that matches your superpowers is good. But finding a calling would've been so much better.

Do you believe there's a calling for everyone — including you?

Some of you might feel certain there is. Others might call it a fantasy, and be a little skeptical. Overall, the idea of a "calling" can sound intimidating — like something that's been determined by some higher power. I want to invite you to approach it differently. Not as a single destiny you must uncover, and not as a perfect path waiting for you to find it, but as an honest conversation with yourself that becomes possible only when you slow down enough to listen.

Earlier in this book, we explored how, in mid-life, the search for a new career often becomes a search for meaning. And sometimes that search deepens even further — into a search for calling.

Calling is a strong word. This is where the first misunderstanding begins. Many people imagine a calling as something you'd enjoy doing 100% of the time. "Find a career you love and you'll never work a day in your life" — it sounds inspiring, but is it realistic?

Let's pause for a moment to consider what a calling actually is. Most of us intuitively know the difference:

A job pays the bills.

A career builds skills and status.

A calling feels meaningful — like it aligns with something inside you.

And I want to be clear here: having work that feels like a calling is not about loving every single task or waking up thrilled every morning. No role is enjoyable 100% of the time — anyone looking for this kind of job will be disappointed, because it doesn't exist.

Every path has friction. Every path has days that feel heavy. A calling isn't about avoiding difficulty. It's about choosing the kind of hard that matters, the kind that leads somewhere true. When your work aligns with who you are — how you think, connect, and make sense of the world — even the hard parts become easier to carry. You feel more at home in yourself. You stop resisting your nature and start drawing strength from it.

After Martin Seligman and his colleagues introduced the framework of character strengths, two researchers — Harzer and Ruch — were trying to answer to the same question:

What makes work feel like a calling?

Their hypothesis was simple: maybe work feels meaningful when you get to use your core strengths — the traits that show up consistently in how you think and act. What they discovered was beyond anything they expected. Across their studies, they found a clear pattern: the more you use your top strengths at work, the more likely you are to experience your work as meaningful — even as a calling. Because the work matches how your mind and personality naturally operate.

They even identified a tipping point: if you use four or more of your top seven strengths in your role, the likelihood of describing your work as a calling rises significantly.

Think about that. It's not about finding the "right" job title. It's not even about doing something specific. It's about finding a role where you can be *yourself.*

Sometimes the problem isn't the job or your skills at all — it's the environment you're doing the work in.

Two people can sit in the same role and live completely different careers. Take project management as an example. Imagine a company where projects move at a steady, predictable pace and people take pride in doing things well rather than rushing through chaos. Teams communicate clearly, deadlines are respected, and thoughtful planning is part of the culture.

Ingrid is naturally organized, calm under pressure, great at breaking chaos into steps, and genuinely enjoys coordinating people. For her, project management feels energizing.

Judgment (seeing all sides clearly)
Prudence (planning and structuring)
Self-regulation (staying steady under pressure)
Teamwork (coordinating people smoothly)
Leadership (guiding a group toward a goal)
Perseverance (following through).

Even when the job is stressful, it feels like the right kind of stress — the kind that makes her feel alive and capable.

Raya, on the other hand, is creative, intuitive, big-picture oriented, and loves generating ideas. Her natural strengths look more like:

Creativity (generating ideas)
Perspective (seeing the big picture)
Curiosity (exploring possibilities)
Love of learning (diving into new concepts)
Social intelligence (reading people and dynamics).

In an environment that is Ingrid's match, Raya can also do traditional project management — she's smart enough — but it drains her. The details feel suffocating. The constant coordination feels heavy. She spends most of her energy trying to be someone she's not.

Same job. Same tasks. Two completely different experiences. For Ingrid, the role might feel like a calling. For Raya, it feels like a mismatch — not because she lacks talent, but because the work doesn't align with how her mind naturally operates.

But this contrast is not a judgment. In the right environment, Raya's strengths can make her an exceptional project manager — sometimes even better than the naturally structured ones. Imagine a creative agency where the PM needs to translate messy ideas into direction, or a startup where the role is less about maintaining order and more about shaping vision. In those settings, big-picture thinking, curiosity, and social intelligence aren't just helpful — they're essential. Meanwhile, Ingrid might thrive in environments that reward precision, predictability, and steady coordination, like engineering, operations, or large corporate programs.

The point is simple: your personality influences how you do the work, not what you are capable of doing. Being in the right environment matters. There are environments where Ingrid is a perfect match. There are environments where Raya is a perfect match. And there are environments where both would struggle. Fit is not about ability — it's about alignment.

When people talk about "career fit," they often focus on skills, titles, or industries. But the deeper truth is that fit comes from the intersection of who you are, how you naturally operate, and the environment you're in. When those pieces line up, the same job can feel energizing instead of draining, meaningful instead of mechanical.

What often happens is that we downplay the superpowers we *do* have and idealize qualities that are completely out of sync with who we are. We chase traits we admire in others while ignoring the ones that come naturally to us. I've seen dozens of women who desperately wanted to be "assertive" in the way they speak. Instead of letting their playful or kind personality shine through, they tried to replace it with something sharper, louder, more forceful — because they felt no one would take them seriously if they showed up as themselves.

Sometimes we confuse the *shape* of a quality with its *foundation*. Assertiveness is a perfect example. You can be deeply assertive and incredibly soft at the same time — if the foundation inside you is solid. That's what people mean when they talk about an iron hand in a velvet glove. The strength is real. The velvet is simply the way it's delivered.

But many of us are afraid to be the velvet glove. We think softness is our flaw that we need to hide. We assume that seriousness must look like sharpness, volume, or force. Yet in life, it's the opposite. The people who shout, demand, and try to make everyone comply are often the ones who feel the least secure inside. Their "iron" is on the outside because there's nothing holding them up on the inside.

Real seriousness — the kind that earns respect — comes from inner clarity. It has nothing to do with outer aggression. When you know who you are and what you stand for, you don't need to raise your voice or perform confidence to defend your truth. You don't need to imitate someone else's shape. Your presence does the work for you.

Mid-life is the moment to become who you already are, embrace it and enjoy it. If you're playful and humorous, let it shine. You can be both playful and serious at the same time — many of the leaders I've worked with were captivating because of that. And if someone looks down on you for it, that has nothing to do with you. It's a signal about whether you're in the right environment, not a sign that you should change who you are.

Sometimes it's not a full career change you're craving. It's more autonomy. More space to use your strengths. More room to work in a way that feels like you, instead of squeezing yourself into someone else's system. Even the "right" job will feel wrong if every step is controlled and you don't have room to breathe.

And let's make something clear: I'm not saying you can't develop qualities that don't come naturally. If assertiveness isn't something that comes naturally, and you want to become more assertive, you can absolutely build that skill over time.

The real question is what kind of assertive you are. Assertiveness doesn't always have to look like raising your voice or becoming someone you're not. Built on top of your natural strengths, it looks different for everyone. For some people, it's direct and warm at the same time — an iron hand in a velvet glove. For others, it's calm, steady, and quietly firm.

You can certainly develop any skill. But the most powerful version of assertiveness — or confidence, or leadership — is the one that grows *from* who you already are. Any quality will be most sustainable when it's built on top of your strengths, not in opposition to them.

That's the difference between expanding your abilities and abandoning your core. Climbing your mountain is a lot easier when you're not carrying the weight of pretending to be someone else.

This doesn't mean every moment of your new career will be joyful. No job is free of friction. But if most of your work lets you use the parts of you that come naturally, you're already much closer to fulfillment than you might realize.

A calling isn't about finding the perfect career or role. It's about having the freedom to be yourself in the work you do — whether that's inside a company or in your own business.

And this is where the next part of the journey begins. Because autonomy doesn't appear out of nowhere. It grows from how you show up in the world — the signals you send, the way you communicate your strengths, the clarity you bring to your story — and most importantly, how you show up in relationships with other people.

Your Action Plan

These exercises help you move from imagination to intention — from the dream to the draft.

Step 1: Block 2–3 hours for yourself

Put it in your calendar. Treat it like a meeting with your future self. Open the result of your test.

Step 2: Connect Your Strengths to Your Core Values

Your superpowers are the *how*. Your values are the *why*. Together, they form the backbone of your internal compass.

1. **What values do your superpowers point to?**

    - If your top strength is Fairness, you likely value justice.
    - If your top strengths are Love and Kindness, you likely value compassion and connection.
    - If Creativity and Curiosity lead your list, you might value growth, innovation, or exploration.

2. **Reflect on your top four personal values.**
    How do the top 4 superpowers show up in your life? Which of them have you used this week?

Step 3: Bridge to Your Future

Reinvention is not only about realization. It's about taking action. So let's make this real — without pressure.

1.   **Find a job description you're curious about.**

Even if you don't feel "qualified." Read it not for the required skills, but for the *strength clues*, and match those clues to your own:

- "Build collaborative teams" → Teamwork, Social Intelligence
- "Navigate ambiguity" → Judgment, Bravery
- "Drive innovative solutions" → Creativity, Zest

Highlight roles where you see opportunities to use at least three of your signature strengths. So when a recruiter asks, "Why are you the best fit for this role?" you suddenly have an answer that goes deeper than diplomas or job titles: "I deeply value [your value], and my strength in [your strength] allows me to bring that to life in this role with honesty and energy."

2.   **Connect your past career to your future career using your superpowers.**

If you're drawn to a certain profession, it's not random. There is always a thread — a strength, a value, a way of thinking — that connects where you've been to where you want to go. Even if you're switching from law to data science, or hospitality to UX design, something in your past aligns with the new direction.

Your job is to make that thread visible — to yourself first, and then to others. And please don't leave this part in your head. Put it somewhere outside of you — on paper, on a board, in a file, whatever feels natural.

3.   **Return to the role that sparked your excitement.**

Look again at the qualities they're seeking. Now write a cover letter explaining why you're the best candidate — not because of your past job titles, but because of your strengths, your values, and the way you naturally operate.

Step 4. Create your new story

Answer these prompts in detail:

- What kind of person do I want to grow into?
- What is my mission?
- Who do I care for?
- What does my work give to others?
- What does it give to me?
- What is important to me at this stage of my life?
- What do I want more of?
- What do I want less of?
- What am I no longer willing to tolerate?

This becomes the foundation of your chosen identity.

It's only natural if you can't answer all these questions in a single day. Let them sit with you. Return to them. And most importantly, write down whatever surfaces — even the small, uncertain pieces.

In the next chapter, you'll learn how to take this chosen identity — the one you've been quietly uncovering — and translate it into a clear, confident presence in the world, so others can finally recognize the person you're becoming.

The Conversation With Your People

The conversation about finding your new career — especially after moving countries — is really a conversation about building a new life and choosing who you're becoming next. And as we keep exploring the question of identity, one thing becomes clear: it begins in the body.

Yet very often, when we move and start over, the body slips into survival mode — stress, exhaustion, tension, loneliness. In that state, it's not interested in reinvention; it's simply trying to get you through the day. So the real question becomes: how do we support the body enough for identity to have space to grow.

And this is where the story widens. Because the moment you start caring for the body, you're no longer just talking about identity — you're talking about health, longevity, and what helps a human being stay grounded through change. People have spent centuries trying to understand how we live longer and live well. We've searched for miracle foods, fountains of youth, and all sorts of "secrets" that promise to add years to our lives. And whenever we found an outlier — a place, a community, a habit — we tried to learn from it.

In the previous chapters, you've already met a few of these familiar ideas — sleep, walking, food. You've heard them many times. Now it's time for the less obvious one — something that truly keeps your body – and identity anchored.

In the 1950s,heart attacks were the leading cause of death for men over 65 in the United States. In *Outliers*, Malcolm Gladwell follows a physician who noticed something groundbreaking: a town where heart attacks simply... didn't happen.

How could it be that in Roseto, Pennsylvania there were no deaths from heart attacks at all? No one under 55 had ever had one. The overall death rate was 30–35% lower than expected.

The first hypothesis was food. It wasn't true — there was nothing special about their food. The second was genetics — also not true, because relatives of Rosetans living elsewhere in the U.S. didn't share the same health outcomes.

So the researchers did the simplest thing: they talked to people. Conversation after conversation, they realized the real reason.

And then, thousands of miles away, and decades later, another outlier appeared. Okinawa, Japan is one of the world's famous "Blue Zones," known for its unusually high number of people living past 100. According to the United Nations and World Population Review, Japan's centenarian rate is 80.6 per 100,000 people. The U.S. average is 28.8. The global average is 11.6.

Clearly, something interesting is happening there.

So Héctor García and Francesc Miralles, authors of *Ikigai*, set out to investigate it. At the time, Okinawa had 24.55 people over 100 for every 100,000 inhabitants. In their book *Ikigai*, they describe their journey to Ogimi, a small town of 3,000 people with one of the highest life expectancies in the world. In Ogimi, the number of people living past 100 wasn't just high — it was astonishing. Naturally, they got curious. And what they discovered surprised them.

Because what they found in Ogimi was remarkably similar to what the physician had discovered in Roseto. In both places, the first thing researchers noticed was the friendliness — a kind of everyday warmth.

In Roseto, many families lived with three generations under one roof. People visited each other constantly. They shared meals, stories, and burdens. It was the kind of community where someone always sits beside you, day after day, making sure you never have to carry your life alone.

In Ogimi, the pattern was the same. The people were deeply connected to one another. Okinawans live by the principle: "Treat everyone like a brother, even if you've never met them before." They belonged to *moai* — small circles of friends who stayed together for life. They checked in on each other. They shared meals. They gardened side by side. They talked every day.

In both communities, people found connection and belonging. And loneliness — the invisible stress that wears so many of us down — barely existed.

It turns out the real secret to a long, meaningful life isn't hidden in a supplement or a routine. It's in the relationships that you have with the people who walk beside you.

It's human connection. Belonging.

Feeling loved.

From Non-Profit to Her Own Consulting Business (The United States → Netherlands)

"The whole act of being seen—of being a messy human—is terrifying. But it allows people to move quicker to support you."

Zanni has gone through more reinventions than she ever expected — from forensic anthropology to nonprofits, from logistics to operations, from the US to the Netherlands, and finally into running her own consulting business. Each shift came from a moment of pressure, burnout, or life upheaval, and each time she rebuilt her path from scratch. What stands out most when she speaks is her honesty: she doesn't pretend transitions are clean or linear. She talks openly about burnout, uncertainty, and the fear of being seen — and how vulnerability, strangely enough, became the thing that helped her move forward.
And this is how she tells her story.

I went to college to do forensic anthropology. I loved my internship at the morgue but got really burned out when I continued my education in a Masters program immediately after my 4 year university degree. This program was more theory work and I had wanted to continue more practical education, like my internship at the morgue in Arizona. I got really burnt out. So I took a job at a non-profit. That was my first switch. My brain really enjoys helping people and feeling useful and I didn't have any corporate sort of bone in my body, really.

After that, there were a couple of switches too.

In 2008, the financial crisis hit. Both me and my husband have really been feeling stuck in our jobs because we've been there for a few years. At that point, my husband worked in tech in product management and the only place hiring people at that point was San Francisco. So we moved from San Diego to San Francisco. I switched again, going into logistics with a big furniture company.

When we moved from San Francisco back down to San Diego for family reasons—we had just had a baby—I had to put my career on hold for nearly 4 years. Then I went back to nonprofits. I moved into the operations side, which felt familiar yet new. I'd done events before, and now I was handling events and operations together.

We had two little kids then. Life was... a lot.

2020 hit, I started a master's degree in nonprofit management, and also began remodeling our house. Then my husband lost his job in a restructure.

Everything just stopped. We looked at each other, and it was like, okay. If everything changes, maybe it's time for us to change too. We needed to reset. Our minds, our bodies, everything. The kids were so small. And we were just... fried. The pandemic had left us burnt out, turned inward, taking on more and more until we couldn't anymore.

So we decided.

Okay.

Let's move.

That's how we moved to the Netherlands. My job changed. I'm still doing nonprofit operations work, but now I'm a consultant instead of being in-house.

Luckily, there was a visa program for Americans in the Netherlands. I have to continue my work as a self-employed person. I still work mostly with US clients, but I recently got my first Dutch client, a small business needing growth support.

I've gone through several career transitions, but the transition from being a practitioner to being a business owner is so different. Running a solo business as a self-employed person is nothing like being an individual contributor at an organization. That transition alone is a massive shift.

I was very lucky to have a lot of referrals from my last position as an in-house director of operations. They're from an organization in California that already works with nonprofits.

I've been getting roles from them and have been lucky to have a few clients come from those referrals. But they're all on California time, so I need to expand my network—maybe to the East Coast or find clients here. I've invested heavily in networking over the last year.

I can't help but see that being a business owner requires at least 50% of your time being out there. Somehow online, offline, promoting yourself, promoting your services. If you're a solo operation with no employees, you have no help. So that leaves you with 50% of your time, and you can only take on about 50% of your capacity.

I also joined Female Ventures, a non-profit supporting fempreneurs, as a volunteer. I joined many, many online networking groups for other nonprofit consultants to meet people, hopefully find my tribe, and expand my network that way. I also joined The Humanity Hub; it's a great space to meet non-profits and NGOs.

Sometimes you feel like you're doing lots of actions, but you're not sure what's bringing results. Distilling one from another takes time and a lot of effort.

And my husband had his own career transition.

He was in tech when we moved, used to do product management and manage teams. He was trying to find a job after burning out, but it was a tough market, and he also didn't want things to be the way they were before. He ended up declining some offers because he knew they weren't a good cultural fit.

> At this stage of life, we felt the need to really invest in our local community, to figure out how to be good citizens and invest in the place we were living. We had felt a little disconnected from that in the US.
>
> So he did things he'd never done before. He became a musician, a singer, and a poet, diving into his creative past. And he first got a job at Post NL here in the Netherlands, as a delivery guy. He really wanted to be in the community, and it was an exciting opportunity to learn the language. Now, he works in tech again and has better balance and boundaries after recovering from burnout.
>
> When you move, you're blowing up every single thing in your life. You try to have the perfect plan all laid out, and it will never go exactly that way. It's okay to not have everything figured out, accept the changes, and learn the lessons.
>
> One thing that turned out to be pretty important for me is figuring out my boundaries in the process. You're going to put yourself out in the community, but if you don't know your own limits, there will be opportunities where you take on things that are mismatched to what you desire to do. You have to really put the guardrails in place. So when you're figuring out the things you find most important, you can't waiver.
>
> I've found that tapping in and being really honest and vulnerable about where you are invites people in. In a world of inauthenticity on social media, where we only see snippets, the more you can open up, the more genuine the response you're going to get. It's very scary. I still feel very scared to do it. The whole act of being seen—of being a messy human — is terrifying. But it allows people to move quicker to support you.

The longest-running study on human happiness, the Harvard Study of Adult Development, found that the strongest predictor of well-being and long-term health wasn't wealth, career success, or even genetics. It was the quality of your relationships. Again and again, the data points to the same truth: we are built to belong.

And yet this desire to belong often collides with the fear of being seen. Many of us struggle with visibility — especially in the vulnerable beginning of a new career. *What if someone sees the real me?* But presenting a polished, edited version of yourself only pushes you further away from the connection you're craving. A perfect plan is a trap. Perfection leaves no room for growth. Holding yourself to that impossible standard only makes you feel stuck.

Real progress is messy.

It happens when you allow others to see you before you're ready.

The stories in this book — including Zanni's — show that real change begins when you choose connection and belonging over being "ready" or "perfect." When you start over in a circle that feels safe, you build the confidence to move forward and pursue something bigger.

But if being yourself still doesn't feel safe, you don't have to show up to the whole world yet. You start by showing up to the people you trust. Let yourself connect with the people around you as a person in motion — someone exploring, learning, adjusting as she goes. You don't need to present yourself as a finished product. You don't need every detail figured out. What you need is the willingness to take one small step outward, to let yourself be seen just enough, and to remember that the next chapter of your life will be shaped through connection.

This chapter is about stepping out to your people before you feel complete — moving with the version of you that exists today: curious, imperfect, becoming. It's about finding belonging and the feeling of being loved, because no one writes their next chapter in isolation. It's written through choices, relationships, and the small, brave moments when you let yourself be seen.

In the pages ahead, we'll explore how to make this early testing gentle and grounded, so you can move toward your desired career with clarity and confidence:

- testing your ideas in small, safe conversations;
- gathering feedback that helps you refine your direction;
- approaching the right opportunities through people who already believe in you;
- learning to move through the world without letting the fear of rejection shrink your life.

And finally, putting together a simple plan for building real human connections — the kind that feels natural to you and aligned with your values.

You don't have to "fake it until you make it."

Nor do you have to create a persona or build a personal brand.

You just have to open your heart.

Testing Your Idea

When you imagine starting something new in a new place — a career shift, a project, a business — the mind often jumps straight to the biggest, loudest step: telling the whole world. Posting on LinkedIn. Updating your headline. Creating a website. Announcing your new venture with confidence and a perfect photo.

It makes sense. First, the need for recognition is one of our deepest human needs. Every person wants to feel seen and appreciated. And in the modern world, we're surrounded by exposure. Everyone seems to be building a brand, collecting likes, sharing updates, and staying visible. It creates the illusion that visibility must come first.

But I want to invite you into a different approach. Instead of focusing on exposure, as we've discussed earlier in the book, I invite you to turn your attention inward — to test your idea and get your own inner confirmation first.

Testing your idea gives you three powerful advantages:

- **You discover whether the path truly fits you.** Dreams are hypotheses. You can't know if something is right for you until you try it in real life, even in the smallest way.
- **You build confidence through experience, not imagination.** The first tiny results — a good conversation, a small win, a moment of flow — dissolve doubt far more effectively than any amount of thinking.
- **You avoid overwhelming yourself.** You don't have to fight fear or "fake it until you make it." You can move gently, with baby steps, giving yourself space and time to grow into this new direction.

The moment you shift from "I must announce this to everyone" to "Let me quietly see what this feels like," everything softens. And that softness does something important: it turns your gaze inward again. Instead of performing for an imagined audience, you begin listening to yourself — to what feels right, what feels alive, what feels like *you*.

The natural question becomes: *Alright, but with my gaze turned inward, what would be the first step to test that new career?*

This is where modern life misleads us. It whispers that the first step must be public — send a CV, build a website, create a brand, post online. These steps look productive, but they're often the worst place to begin, because they skip the part that actually grounds you in your new field: building connections and trust.

Two Approaches to Reinventing Your Career

When you're ready to start a new career, it can feel like the number of possible next steps is endless — and somehow still not enough. There's no single "right" way to begin, but to make things simpler, let's look at two broad paths you've already seen in the stories throughout this book.

The first is the *classic path*. This is the route most of us were raised to believe is the "right" way: choose a profession, get the degree, follow the steps, earn the credentials, and move forward in a straight line. And for some careers, this path is non-negotiable. If you want to become a university professor, a medical doctor, a licensed therapist, an architect, a lawyer, or any profession that requires formal certification, education isn't optional — it's the gateway.

Because this path is so familiar and it provides reliability, it might seem like it's the only legitimate way to start over. And that assumption can feel suffocating. A new degree is expensive. It takes years. It may not fit your life right now. You might not even know yet whether the field is right for you. And if your dream career is emerging, unconventional, or entrepreneurial, there may not even be a degree for it.

That's where the second path comes in — *the entrepreneurial path*. It's very different because in entrepreneurship, no one can give you permission to become an entrepreneur. There's no diploma, no official stamp that says you're ready. You start because you decide to start, and then figure everything out as you go — trying, failing, learning, and adjusting.

You've seen this path in many of the stories in this book: women who didn't have a blueprint, but built something meaningful by following their curiosity, testing ideas, and learning in real time.

As Renée — one of the brilliant women I spoke with — pointed out: *"The entrepreneurial mindset really helps when you're trying to settle somewhere. Whether that means running your own business or channeling your frustration into finding a role that truly fits you, it makes you less reliant on someone else paying your way. Sometimes I feel a bit hypocritical, because my own business is by no means wildly successful—but I've kept it going, and it has supported me and my children in several ways."*

Just like switching careers, there is no single "right" way to become an entrepreneur. Every story is different. Some begin with a tiny project. Some start with a single conversation. Some grow slowly, some skyrocket. But beneath all these variations, there is one element that appears again and again — an element so obvious we often overlook it.

Human connection.

In a world full of technology, likes, and AI, it's easy to believe you need to be "out there" immediately — visible, polished, and present on every channel. But you don't. Visibility is not the same as opportunity.

Imagine you're offering your first service — coaching, consulting, photography, design, tutoring, anything you're exploring. Which step is more likely to bring the first customer?

- listing yourself on a platform;
- creating a beautiful Instagram profile;
- reaching out to people you know and offering your help.

In entrepreneurship, we often talk about "low-hanging fruit" — the actions that require the least effort but create the biggest impact. The third option is almost always the low-hanging fruit. Not because it's easier, but because it's warmer. Your friends, former colleagues, and acquaintances already trust you. You don't need to prove yourself. You don't need a brand. You don't need a perfect pitch.

Sometimes simply connecting with the people who are already there can speed up your transition more than anything else.

Not websites.

Not business plans.

Not perfect branding.

People.

From Acrobat to Director of a Multidisciplinary Theater (Belarus → Uruguay)

Masha's life has never moved in straight lines. She grew up in the discipline of acrobatics, rose through the circus, built a career in directing and show production, raised two children between rehearsals and client meetings, filmed protest videos that shook Belarus, faced the KGB in her own living room, and fled across the world with her mother Tatiana — who you met earlier — before the walls closed in. In Uruguay, she rebuilt everything from scratch — community, work, identity — starting over once more.

And this is how she tells her story.

I'm Masha, and I'm from Minsk, Belarus. My story starts in sports — from the age of five I was an acrobat. No weekends, no summers, just training camps and competitions. I became a Master of Sport, but my discipline wasn't Olympic, so the highest dream was the World Championship. I broke my arm, had setbacks, but still finished my sports career with the title.

I worked in a trio — two girls at the bottom, I was the top. By fifteen my body had grown, and the only way to stay on the team was to move "down," which I didn't want. So I left sports and continued in the Belarusian State Circus. I changed partners — now they were men — and continued performing. I was the youngest performer there.

After some time, I got contracts abroad: Taiwan, Korea, Italy. I traveled a lot. Parallel to that, I worked on film projects, in theatre, did choreography, staging — different creative things. Eventually I understood what I really wanted: to study directing and producing. The options in Minsk were limited, so I enrolled in the Institute of Culture in St. Petersburg. I studied part-time, and worked on short-term contracts to be able to pay for my studies.

My daughter was born in my final year of university, so I had to complete my entire diploma project while caring for a newborn.

That diploma project was huge: the 60th anniversary of the UN. A branded train traveled through all major cities of Belarus. We flew ahead of the train every day, built the stage, welcomed the delegations, then dismantled, flew to the next city, and repeated. A full week without sleep or food. After that, nothing scared me anymore.

I graduated as a director and producer of show programs — and I actually worked in my profession, which is rare. I was hired immediately and quickly became a creative director. After that, I worked in the event industry for six years, creating shows for the stage — concepts, scripts, visuals, contractors, budgets, everything from A to Z. I filmed videos, designed visuals, and oversaw installations. It was nonstop.

By then I had two children. I never had maternity leave. My kids grew up in offices, in cars, backstage. Clients held my babies while I delivered presentations. So at some point it was only logical that I burned out badly. I felt I had hit a ceiling in Belarus — I had done big projects, and there wasn't much room to grow.

At some point, when the pandemic hit, I realized: that was it. I wrote an email to my company: "Thank you for everything, but I'm done." For the first time in my life, I didn't know what to do next.

The same year Belarus had presidential elections. For the first time, we had candidates who we genuinely believed could change something. But every opposition candidate was detained beforehand and not allowed to run.

One night, I had a dream, and in it was a video idea that made sense of everything unfolding around me. I woke up with the idea still burning in my mind, and I knew I had to film it. I gathered a team of top professionals — even reached out to a girl who had always been my competitor. She was the first person I called. We became close friends after that.

We made a short video called *Freedom Belarus* — stylish, modern, showing that Belarus is not just "a woman in a wreath and a tractor." It went viral instantly.

After the results of the elections were announced, the country erupted in mass protests. We filmed another video — a video about the women's protest movement. In the video, women in white — the leading force behind the peaceful protests — bury weapons, a symbol of evil, in a symbolic grave. The video went viral again. In a few years, we were invited to present it at the Berlin Film Festival.

We filmed until it became dangerous.

One day the KGB came to my home. They questioned me for two and a half hours — asking where the weapons from the video were. Everything was of course props, but they still kept searching for "the real weapons." They also searched the homes of my actors and cinematographers.

I didn't get arrested then. But soon letters started arriving at my children's kindergarten saying we were an "unsafe, troubled family." We knew what was next — a random excuse for 15 days in jail, then 30, then something harsher.

By that time, we already had our Uruguayan passports. So we left.

My husband works in IT. His remote job allowed us to have some stability. After that, his employer decided to open an office in Uruguay, and to do that they needed a Uruguayan director. As I had a Uruguayan passport through my grandfather, we agreed that I'll take the role of the director.

I got swallowed by the research: opening a company, taxes, hiring, contracts, offices, accountants — all of it. I opened the office, hired staff, helped with everything — even things that weren't my job. Parallel to that, I helped local businesses with growing their Instagram accounts, content, and promotion. I also created a chat for the Russian-speaking diaspora — it grew from four people to around 750 in three years. I organized events, meetups, barbecues, quizzes, 90s discos — anything to help people connect.

But eventually I burned out again.

I was doing everything except what I wanted. I told my husband I couldn't continue. He supported me, and I dropped all my side projects.

And then I asked myself:

Who am I now?

What do I do at 37?

What do I want?

I looked for answers and went to therapy for the first time in my life. I had always disliked psychologists because of bad experiences, but this time I found two great women who worked together. I told them: "I feel like I'm falling into depression. Or a midlife crisis. Or immigration shock." They said one doesn't exclude the other.

I felt like everything I had built in my life was useless here, in a new country, in a new language, in a new culture. Like all my skills didn't matter. And the hardest thing was finding what exactly I wanted to do.

My husband was also struggling. In normal life, our crises would have happened at different times. But here — immigration, midlife, depression — everything hit both of us at once. We were both overwhelmed, both scared, both unable to help each other.

And then I accidentally saw a video of Slava Polunin — a world-renowned, highly decorated clown from St. Petersburg — saying that to be happy you need three things:

Work where you feel joy.

With people you want to hug.

Doing what makes your heart sing.

I loved those three points. My mind went straight back to my student years and what I dreamed of creating back then: a wordless theatre performance. Physical theatre that blends multiple genres — circus arts, puppetry, mask work, multimedia projections, and movement-based storytelling. As a creative person, I've always needed to express whatever feels most alive in me at the moment — and at that time, it was the experience of migration.

Suddenly, everything connected.

Inspired by Polunin, I told my therapist: "I want to stage a show about the five stages of migration — from euphoria to depression — and how to find your way through. And I want to go to Polunin's Yellow Mill in France for my 38th birthday." I had no idea how to get there though.

Now that I had an idea of the show, I started asking around. Someone introduced me to a guy in Montevideo who "did something in theatre." I met him — he turned out to be from St. Petersburg, trained in the same theatrical tradition. We matched immediately. I showed him my presentation, my ideas, and the structure of the show. He said: "I'm in. When do we start?"

So we started building everything: sewing, gluing, constructing, rehearsing.

Meanwhile, my friend — the same former competitor — bought all ten tickets required for a tour of the Yellow Mill. That was her birthday gift to me. We went together. I met Polunin, cried from emotion, felt inspired again.

Our show is now live. The first big run-through happened recently. We performed in Maldonado — almost a full house. The theatre was old and cold, technically challenging, but we did it.

We also got coverage in *El País* — the biggest media outlet in Uruguay — a full page with photos. My story, including the detail that my ancestors came to Uruguay 100 years ago and now I have returned, caught their attention.

There was a moment when I genuinely thought I had to start over, that nothing I'd done before held value here. But slowly, I learned that wasn't true at all. Everything is possible — you just need to find where, with whom, and what. That's the formula.

From Being a Stranger to Being a Friend

In the early 1960s, a young psychologist named Robert Zajonc became fascinated with a question most people never think to ask: *Why do we like the things we like?* Not the big things — not art or music or people we admire — but the tiny, almost invisible preferences that shape our everyday choices.

So he designed an experiment that looked, at first glance, almost pointless. He showed people nonsense. Literally. Strings of letters that meant nothing. Symbols no one recognized. Faces of strangers they would never meet. Some of these images appeared for so little time that the participants couldn't consciously register them at all. A flash, a flicker, gone.

And then something strange happened.

When Zajonc later asked which images people preferred, they consistently chose the ones they had seen before — even if they had no memory of ever seeing them. That led him to conclude that they weren't choosing meaning or beauty. They were choosing familiarity. Their brains had recognized a pattern. And familiarity, it turned out, felt safe.

Zajonc called this the *mere-exposure effect*, and it became one of the most replicated findings in psychology. We like things more simply because we've seen them before. A melody on the radio. A logo on a billboard. The face of a celebrity. The more familiar something feels, the less risky it seems. And the less risky it seems, the more we trust it.

Which brings us to a quiet truth about reinvention — one that most people overlook. When you're changing careers, starting a project, or stepping into a new identity, you are — in the eyes of others — a stranger. Not because you lack talent or potential, but because people don't yet have a pattern to recognize. They don't know what you care about, what you're learning, or where you're heading.

Reinvention becomes harder not because you're unqualified, but because you're unfamiliar. And unfamiliarity, as Zajonc showed, is something our brains instinctively resist.

That's why when you're looking for that first opportunity, it makes a lot of sense to turn to people who already know how good you are.

You begin with people who already trust you.

People who open doors.

People who say, "I know someone you should talk to."

This is the foundation of the entrepreneurial path — and, in truth, it's also the foundation of most career transitions. The first opportunities rarely come from strangers. They come from the people who already see your strengths, even before you fully see them yourself.

**From Financial Auditor to Financial Well-Being Coach & Mentor (Romania →
Netherlands)**

*Andreea spent sixteen years building a solid career in finance — auditing, controlling, management —
when she suddenly found herself questioning whether this was really the life she wanted. Her reinvention
began not with a plan, but with exhaustion, dizziness on a Bucharest street, and a question that changed
everything: "If I were to die tomorrow, would I be fulfilled with what I've done?"*
This is how she tells her story.

I've always been a good student. As a teenager in Romania, I wanted to attend a high
school focused on foreign languages — I loved the idea of speaking many languages and
traveling the world. But the school didn't have a great reputation, and both my teachers and
my parents pushed me toward the best high school in the city instead. It was focused on
mathematics and physics. I accepted the challenge. The trade-off was that it offered
intensive English — six or seven classes a week — and that made the choice easier.

When high school ended, I was drawn to psychology or journalism. I loved understanding
people, how they think and react. But everyone around me insisted that economics would
offer more stability and more options. So I chose international transactions — a mix of
economics, diplomacy, and foreign languages — and later completed a master's in financial
auditing.

That's how I entered the world of finance. I started with an internship at an audit
company, they liked my work, and I stayed. That became my first career — and eventually
my identity.

There were parts of the job I enjoyed. I had great mentors, supportive managers, satisfied
clients, and successful projects. I became good at what I was doing, and that made the work
feel meaningful.

But there were also moments — many of them — when I wondered: "Is this really what
I'm supposed to do? Isn't there something closer to who I am?"

I was always searching for my mission, my natural gifts, the thing that wouldn't feel like a
struggle. And I noticed something important: the colleagues who excelled weren't
necessarily more talented — they simply enjoyed the work more. That realization made me
feel less guilty for not wanting to go deeper into something that didn't feel like mine.

After three years in auditing, I even tried to switch to HR. I was drawn to talent
development, motivation, and creating a healthy work environment. I almost got the job —
but it was entry-level, paid far less, and I had rent to pay in Bucharest. So I stayed in finance.
Yet the idea of switching never left me.

By 2017, I had climbed the ladder. I was a partner in my department — the highest level I
could reach without switching companies. Meanwhile, my husband got a job in the

Netherlands and moved there alone. I stayed behind with a full-time job, constant travel, and two small children.

I was exhausted. One day, walking on the street, I felt dizzy — really dizzy — and two questions hit me:

"If something happens to me right now, who will take care of my kids?"

"If I die tomorrow, is this the professional life I want to leave behind?"

The answer to the second question was a clear no.

I reduced my job to part-time, but in reality it was still six or seven hours a day. I loved my colleagues and my team, but I was drained. In 2020, during the pandemic, my husband received a permanent contract in the Netherlands. He asked: *"Are you coming with me?"*

I knew that if I didn't take the chance then, I never would. So I moved to The Hague. I worked remotely for six months to ensure a smooth transition — and then I quit. I told myself: *"I want to do something completely different."*

The first months were peaceful. I needed rest. But then the pressure came:

"I'm almost 40. I can't afford to play games. Whatever I do next must work."

I didn't allow myself to experiment. I didn't allow myself to fail. Everything had to be purposeful, goal-oriented, result-oriented. It was suffocating.

But then I met people online — it was still the pandemic — and joined a course about exploring passions. It helped me reconnect with what I naturally loved: listening to people, understanding them, communicating, organizing, writing.

Two paths emerged: writing and coaching/counseling. Writing was cheaper and easier to start, so I tried it first. It was nice, but not enough. I needed something deeper. So I enrolled in a counseling program — an introduction to a coaching school — and I loved it. It felt meaningful. It felt like me.

That's how I decided to pursue coaching seriously. I wanted proper training, ethics, structure — so I chose an ICF-accredited school. I didn't want to be "just another coach." I wanted to be trustworthy, professional, and responsible.

After finishing the program, I faced the hardest part: finding clients.

Selling terrified me. Even in my audit career, networking was the part I hated most. But now there was no one else to do it for me. I had to step out and say: *"This is me. This is what I do now."*

I was scared of what people would think. Sixteen years in auditing — and now coaching? Would they think I'd lost my mind?

But the opposite happened. People congratulated me. They admired the courage. And then something unexpected happened: people started reaching out.

Not for general coaching. For financial coaching.

I hadn't mentioned finances at all. But they saw my background and assumed I could help. My mentor told me: *"If people come to you for something, embrace it. See where it leads."*

So I did. And it worked. My first clients came organically — from my old network, from peers in coaching school, from people who trusted me. I created workshops and newsletters on financial well-being. I worked with couples, professionals, companies, business owners.

One couple even said, "We're terrible with money. Can you help us?" That's how my new career began.

The biggest challenge wasn't the market.

It wasn't clients.

It wasn't money.

It was me.

My limiting beliefs, impostor syndrome, perfectionism, fear of failure. My guilt about not contributing financially while my husband supported us.

I was my own biggest barrier.

Moving to the Netherlands changed me. In Romania, perfectionism is a cultural norm. You don't try unless you know you'll succeed. If you can't do it perfectly, step aside.

Here, people try. They fail. They learn. And it's okay.

That mindset helped me breathe.

Trust Is Your Starting Point...

Before you go out into the wider world, you can start by having a simple, honest conversation with the people closest to you. Keep in mind that you're not asking for permission to proceed with your path — you're looking for kindness, connection, perspective — the kind of support that comes from people who already know and trust you.

Starting with real-life conversations gives you something else that matters just as much: it grounds your fears. The mind is a prediction machine, but it's notoriously bad at drawing an accurate picture of the future. When you're worried about how others might react — and we all are — actually talking to people and getting real feedback shows you that the world is far safer than your imagination suggests. A little encouragement from real humans shifts everything. It makes the world feel more welcoming, and it strengthens your confidence to take the next step.

That's especially true with your closest circle. With the people you trust, you can:

- Ask for opportunities.
- Offer your help to build a portfolio.

- Search for people in the industry you'd like to enter.

...Yet There's More

Earlier in the book, we looked at how using your top four superpowers can make your work feel less like a job and more like a calling. Take a moment to review them again:

- **Wisdom & Knowledge:** Creativity, Curiosity, Judgment, Love of Learning, Perspective
- **Courage:** Bravery, Perseverance, Honesty, Zest
- **Humanity:** Love, Kindness, Social Intelligence
- **Justice:** Teamwork, Fairness, Leadership
- **Temperance:** Forgiveness, Humility, Prudence, Self-Regulation
- **Transcendence:** Appreciation of Beauty & Excellence, Gratitude, Hope, Humor, Spirituality

Whatever steps you're taking next, remember this: when you actively use your top four superpowers, everything you do starts to feel aligned — like something you were meant to do. And you don't have to wait for a job title or a promotion to begin.

Your superpowers are the bridge between who you are on the inside and how you show up in the world. Once you start using them intentionally, the world starts meeting you differently. So try connecting with people in ways that feel aligned with your superpowers.

If creativity is one of your superpowers, think of a creative way to comment on someone's achievement.

If your strength is love of learning, ask your friend about their expertise and genuinely enjoy learning from them.

If it's kindness, connect someone with a person who could help them, expecting nothing in return.

If it's fairness, treat everyone with the same respect, not just the people who seem "important."

You get the idea. When you lead with your superpowers, you stop trying to impress people and start trying to connect with them in a way that feels true to you. And whether you notice it or not, you're already using these strengths every day. Now

I'm inviting you to explore new ways to bring them forward — to put your superpowers into action with intention.

We're so used to walking into conversations trying to prove something — talking business, listing achievements, trying to get attention. But when you start to use your strengths, you're not performing anymore. You're simply showing up as the most natural version of yourself. And people feel that. They respond to it. They trust it.

When you use your strengths:

- conversations feel lighter;
- connections feel real;
- you stop worrying about saying the "right" thing;;
- you start attracting the people who actually get you
- you feel like you belong in the rooms you walk into.

And that's the real point.

Using your superpowers is about being true. *Authentic.* It's about letting the parts of you that are already strong do the heavy lifting, instead of forcing yourself into a version of you that feels stiff or unnatural.

Reinvention, turns out, isn't about becoming someone new. It's about finally giving yourself permission to be who you've always been — out loud, in front of others, without shrinking or apologizing — and letting the people around you support and love you along the way.

Let's see how you can start.

Your Partner

Not everyone has a partner — and you absolutely don't need one to reinvent your career. But if you do have someone close to you, and your relationship feels safe and intimate, it's worth pausing here for a moment.

When you're switching careers, the support of the person closest to you matters more than most people admit. Your partner doesn't need to take action, solve anything, or become your career coach — but they do need to be on board. Their emotional support creates stability while everything else is shifting.

Now sometimes you might feel hesitation from them. It's human. Change is stressful, even when it's positive. They may worry about how your new direction will affect your relationship, your time together, or the version of you they've grown used to.

I once had a moment like this myself. When I joined an entrepreneurial program that required evenings and weekends away from home, I was thrilled. My partner… not so much. Years later he told me, half-joking, "How could I be excited? You were suddenly spending all your time away, surrounded by other men." It was a joke — but also a reminder that we assign different meanings to the same event. Where I saw opportunity, he saw threat.

This is meant to show something simple but important: two people can look at the exact same moment and see two completely different realities — not because one of them is right and the other is wrong, but because each person brings their own fears, hopes, and assumptions into the room.

That's why bringing your partner along emotionally matters.

Not to persuade them or to win an argument.

But to let them *see* you.

To let them understand what this transition feels like from the inside.

Maybe that looks like sitting across from them at dinner and finally saying the thing you've been carrying in your chest for months.

Maybe it's taking a walk together and admitting, "I'm scared, but I'm also excited, and I don't want to do this part alone."

Maybe it's letting them hold your hand while you say out loud the dream you've been whispering only to yourself.

It's these small, human moments that shift the ground between you.

A few principles help:

- Reassure them that your love and commitment remain steady.
- Let them voice their fears without absorbing them as your own.
- Clarify that any temporary disruptions — evening classes, extra workload — are just that: temporary.
- Show them how your growth will benefit both of you.

In practice, it might sound like:

"I can see this change feels unsettling. I get it — it affects both of us. But I've thought this through, and I truly believe this is the right way for me. It will require some work, but when this phase is over, we'll have more energy and more freedom together."

Your partner's support is not mandatory — but if you can have it, it becomes a powerful foundation.

By now you've probably noticed that many stories in this book go even further: they show how a partner can play a key role in a career switch. Sometimes a partner becomes a guide into a new field — especially in areas like IT or entrepreneurship. In some cultures, this kind of partnership within a marriage feels natural; in others, work lives stay more separate. But one thing is universal: if you already have someone who knows you deeply and trusts you, cherish that.

Your Family

Reinvention is messy. It's raw. And in the early stages, your dream is fragile — like something still forming, not ready for bright lights or loud opinions. You don't show it to everyone. In fact, you *shouldn't*.

Family is often the first place we turn. In some households, everyone feels entitled to offer guidance; in others, stability is deeply valued; in others still, a career decision is seen as something that reflects on the whole family. But even in the closest families, the boundary between emotional support and career advice might not exist.

If you're lucky enough to have people who truly understand and support you, they can become the first safe audience to hear about your plan. Still, there are a few things worth keeping in mind so these early conversations feel supportive rather than overwhelming.

1. Be mindful of who you turn to for advice

Our instinct is to go to the people we love most — parents, siblings, best friends. But love doesn't automatically translate into relevant guidance. My mother worked in the same university for 30 years. I adore her. But she's not the person to advise me on entrepreneurship or career reinvention. Her world is different. Her fears are different. Her definition of "safe" is different.

2. Remember that your choices are yours

When we feel lost, it's tempting to hand over responsibility to someone you trust: *"Just tell me what to do."* But your path is your own. Advice can inform you, but it shouldn't direct you. No one else carries the consequences of your choices — only you do. So keep the ownership where it belongs.

If you treat their input like your inner voices — "I'll listen to you, but I won't obey you" — their words become perspective, not permission.

3. Be clear about what you're asking for

Before you talk to someone, pause and ask yourself: *What do I actually need from this conversation? Is it emotional support, contact, or feedback?*

Speaking about your needs directly — first with yourself, then with others — is one of the most powerful things you master. Otherwise, you might share your dream hoping for encouragement — and instead receive their fears, their insecurities, or their horror stories about someone who failed. Not because they want to discourage you, but because they're projecting their own anxieties.

Clarity about your needs protects your dream.

When these three things are in place, your close circle becomes a powerful resource. They can help you:

- find people who already do what you want to do;
- get introductions into the field you're exploring;
- learn about opportunities that aren't visible from the outside.

But remember: **their stories are not your story. Their fears are not your fears.** Your path will be different — and that's exactly the point.

Your Friends

Friends are the natural next circle after your partner and your closest family — the bridge between your private world and the wider one you're trying to enter. They sit in that easy middle space: close enough to know who you are, but far enough to see possibilities you might miss. And because they live in different workplaces, different social circles, different corners of life, they often hold the very connections you don't yet have.

What makes friends so helpful at this stage is that the stakes are lower. You don't have to impress them or present a polished version of your new direction. You can simply talk — loosely, honestly, without the pressure of having everything figured out. A coffee chat, a walk, a message that starts with "I've been thinking about something…" can open more doors than a perfectly crafted LinkedIn post ever will.

Reflected identity with strangers is often labels and generalizations. Reflected identity with friends is something entirely different: it's a reminder of who you are. They reflect back the parts of you that are easy to overlook when you're deep in uncertainty. And sometimes, without even trying, they say the one sentence that changes everything: *"You know, I think I know someone you should talk to."*

From Sales to Contemporary Art (Russia → The United Kingdom)

Sveta never expected to find herself in the world of contemporary art. For nearly twenty years, she built a career in corporate sales. She lived inside the rhythm of a large international company, juggling time zones, complex projects, and a team that grew under her leadership.

But after a move to the UK, two small children, a lockdown that broke her open, and a long, painful recovery, she found herself pulled into a completely different universe — one she had loved since she was a teenager but never imagined entering professionally.

And this is how she tells her story.

I spent ten years in a technology company in the pricing department. This is the department responsible for pricing, licensing, upgrades, downgrades, early renewals, late renewals — all the internal movements inside the product line. We did quarterly assessments, competitive research, and constant feedback loops with local offices. Someone would release something, someone would drop prices, and we had to react.

My team eventually grew to seven people. I led the pricing function. Then I got married and moved to the UK. Because of that, I stepped down from my managerial role — at the time, they didn't think I could handle remote work and endless business trips. I created a new position for myself inside the same department, and two years later they offered me my old role back. Everything seemed fine.

Until COVID.

At that moment, I had two small children — two and a half and almost four. We moved into a new house a week before lockdown. And suddenly I was trapped at home with two kids and a full-time job in an international company where everything runs 24/7, where projects last for years, where you need deep focus and long stretches of uninterrupted time.

A year of trying to combine work and childcare — and I burned out completely. I was diagnosed with depression and an anxiety disorder. I didn't recognize myself then. It was frightening to look at who I had turned into. Something in my system had malfunctioned.

I kept working through all of this. My manager at the time treated me with incredible humanity. We had one conversation. I shared what was happening with me. He said:

"Delegate everything you can. If you can't keep up or need help, let me know." So in 2021, I finally learned how to delegate.

I worked with the tiniest amount of energy — just enough to function. But slowly, over the course of a year, life started returning in small colored pixels.

Then we had another reorg. My new manager was fine, but he had different expectations: 24/7 availability, business trips to Moscow twice a month. I tried. I really did. I loved the work, the function, the company. I lasted a couple of months — and then took my first sick leave ever.

After the Christmas break, I realized I still wasn't ready to come back. I took another four weeks off.

Then the war started. And it crushed me.

Everything collided at once: my mental state, the external world, the company's security situation in Russia. When I finally returned, my manager and I agreed — calmly, respectfully — that I would leave. Honestly, it wasn't the corporate world that broke me. It was the combination of a 24/7 job and 24/7 childcare. No one can survive that.

And that's how I ended up not working for two and a half years.

The first year after leaving — I barely remember it. I volunteered, helped Ukrainian families — half my family is in Ukraine, and some came to stay with us. I was emotionally all over the place.

And then, slowly, my story with contemporary art began.

It actually started long ago. In tenth grade, our school took us from Kaluga to the Tretyakov Gallery. I saw Kandinsky's paintings — and time stopped. They had to pull me away from the painting.

Since then, I have looked at contemporary art whenever I could. I never went to art school, never studied it formally. But abstract, modern art did something to me that nothing else did.

When I started traveling for work, I combined business trips with exhibitions. Everyone else went drinking; I went to Frieze. I made a few acquaintances in the art world — just a handful.

One of them was a Russian artist studying in France. I admired her work. She asked me to help with her promotion. We worked together for about six months, made a roadmap — and then COVID hit. Everything stopped.

We stayed in touch though. And after I left my job, and she finished her studies, she messaged me: "I'm having my first solo exhibition in France."

I was happy for her and ready to fly over. The day before my flight she texted: "Oh, by the way —I already told everyone that my agent is coming — that's you."

I was baffled. I had no education, no market knowledge, no network, no experience. But I couldn't let her down so I took a chance.

We didn't sell anything that day. I stood there in a dress and heels, everyone speaking French, me understanding nothing. But I thought: at least one person already knows the new me and still wants to work with me.

That was the moment everything shifted. I realized that I can become part of this world. I started traveling to fairs and exhibitions: Art Basel, Frieze, the Venice Biennale. Every two months — somewhere. My husband still works full-time, the kids still exist, so everything had to be coordinated.

I embraced my strength — networking. I love people, I love talking, people gravitate toward me. So I reached out to everyone I knew who had even a distant connection to the art world, joining a couple of art-related clubs.

And then I realized that I enjoyed art dealing. Through one of the clubs, a woman with a collector base reached out. A collector came to London and wanted to buy something. I made a selection — nine works in three price ranges. Most of the time went into finding the actual prices. And I've made two sales.

In the process, I also met so many people — gallery owners, managers, artists. I even bought a piece myself — I wanted to experience the full customer journey: compliance, logistics, insurance.

Now I'm working on a sculpture project in Scotland. The owner of a private airfield wanted to create a sculpture trail at their premises. My husband said: "My wife works in art." I thought: "I know nothing about sculpture." But I took it on.

I searched for sculptors, went to degree shows, held interviews. Three sculptors basically told me: "For that money, don't even approach us." I almost gave up — until I found a young woman who had just graduated from Glasgow School of Art. Her sketch was perfect. Now we're applying for funding.

This whole thing — it was unexpected. I don't control it. But I enjoy it.

Financially, it's not sustainable yet. And I know I'm not willing to be a starving artist or a starving art agent. But I'll keep doing art projects. Maybe by the time I retire, I'll be able to switch fully — drink champagne with collectors at auctions.

I don't know where this path leads.

But I know that I belong here and I'm happy.

This is how reinvention often begins — not with a grand plan, but with a small, human conversation.

A colleague who listens.

A friend who sees in you the skill you barely notice in yourself.

A manager who supports you in the moment you need.

It's softer than strategy, but often far more effective.

And because you're not asking them to solve your career, just to witness your direction, the whole thing feels lighter. More natural. More like the beginning of something real.

As you think about your next step, is there a friend who feels like an easy, low-pressure place to start the conversation?

Your Mentor (Coach)

If you've never had a mentor, the idea can feel strange or overly dramatic. There's that inner voice insisting, *"Come on, I'm a grown-up. I can handle this on my own."* But when you're changing your life, having someone walk beside you can shift the entire experience. A mentor gives you something rare: a person who supports your desires without dismissing them, who listens without projecting their own fears, and who can see possibilities you can't yet see. And if they've been where you are, they can guide you through the fog — by helping you trust your own steps.

Naturally, mentoring brings up a lot of questions — how do I find the right mentor, how do I know they can truly help, and how do I make this person want to work with me.

There are people who do mentoring professionally, and you can explore that path — most offer an introductory conversation where you can get a sense of their approach. But meaningful guidance doesn't have to come from a single "official" mentor. You can find it in places where people naturally share what they know:

- **Non-profits** that run career or transition programs.
- **Coaching communities** or peer-mentoring circles.
- **LinkedIn**, where many professionals are ready to generously share insights when someone reaches out with intention.

Your natural inclination might be to look for that one perfect role model — someone who has the life you want and can guide you through every step. But that person is rare, and if you find them, you're lucky. More often, the support you need comes from a few different people who each offer a piece of the puzzle: someone who inspires you, someone who listens, someone who challenges you, someone who opens a door.

So if you don't see a perfect guide around you, don't give up. What matters most is gathering a small constellation of people who help you stay connected to your direction when doubt pulls you away from it — especially during the moments when support from your closest people isn't enough.

And the first step to finding any of them is simply being open about the fact that you're looking. You don't have to announce that you're searching for a mentor. You can share something much simpler: *"I'd love to connect with someone who has experience in X or Y."* Don't overthink it. Trust your circle.

Your Safe Space

Your family and friends are supposed to be the safe space. Unfortunately, in reality, that's not always how it works. Some of them might not be fully on board with your new path. Or they may love you deeply, yet still mirror an older version of you — the identity you've already outgrown. And when you're trying to change your life, that lack of support can feel suffocating.

This is why so many people feel more alive, more honest, and more themselves with strangers than with the people who know them best. Strangers don't carry your history. They don't have expectations for who you should be, and they haven't seen you becoming. They meet you in the present moment — the version of you that's emerging, not the one you're trying to shed.

That's the power of finding a safe space: a place where you can show up without performing, without defending your choices, without being pulled back into an identity that no longer fits. A place where you can say "I'm lost," "I'm trying," or "I'm changing," and instead of fear or confusion, you're met with recognition.

And the easiest way to find that kind of safety is to find your people — the ones who are going through the same challenges. People who are also questioning, rebuilding, experimenting. Their presence validates your experience. Their fears sound like your fears. Their hopes mirror your own. Suddenly, you're not the odd one out. You're part of a shared journey.

That's exactly what you can find in Reinvento Club. A community of people who are in the same transition, asking the same questions, navigating the same uncertainty. A place where you don't have to explain yourself or justify your desires. You're understood simply because everyone there is walking a similar path.

A safe space doesn't magically solve your problems. But it changes the emotional climate you're operating in. It gives you room to breathe, to experiment, to be curious without being judged. And when you feel safe, you take bolder steps — not because the path is easier, but because you finally have the space to walk it as the person you're becoming.

The Golden Rule of Connection

By now, you've probably had that feeling more than once.

"Even my closest circle — they're living their own lives with their own problems. Why should they help me? How do I even ask?"

Strong women often struggle with asking for help. Somewhere along the way we learned that strength meant self-reliance. We learned that being the one who holds everything together keeps the peace. We learned that needing less makes us easier to love. We learned that asking for anything — time, attention, support — might create tension, disappointment, or conflict. And once those lessons settle into your nervous system, asking for help doesn't feel like a simple request. It feels like a risk.

So if you find yourself hesitating to ask for help, I invite you to see that hesitation not as a flaw, but as a story that once protected you, a story that makes perfect sense.

The first step isn't to force yourself to ask for help. It's to understand why it feels so hard. Notice the thoughts that come up when you imagine reaching out:

I don't want to bother them.

I should handle this myself.

They'll think I'm weak.

They have their own problems.

For many of us, the instinct is to tuck our problems away. You don't want to become the person who's always overwhelmed, always asking, always needing.

But I invite you to gently notice what this habit creates. When you hide what's heavy for you, even from someone you love, the relationship starts to feel slightly out of sync. People around you can't support what they don't know. Most people genuinely want to help, to show up, to be there — and without meaning to, you take that chance away from them.

From Business Development to Burnout Coach (Russia → Netherlands)

Nadia's career change didn't begin with a plan. It began in 2023, when her relationship ended, her job disappeared, and her tumor returned — all within weeks. She says that's when her entire identity collapsed, and when her focus shifted inwards.

And this is how she tells her story.

I had graduated with a bachelor's in general management and a master's in international business in Russia and four years later moved to the Netherlands. That was twenty years ago. I worked exactly according to what I studied — business development, partnership management, stakeholder management. Corporate jobs, international teams, travel to London every other month. It was convenient, well-paid, remote, undemanding.

If you look at my life chronologically, the first big career shift came in 2013. Next to my 40-hour job, I founded a side project around my passion: a Russian chamber music festival in Amsterdam. I always had a passion for classical music. Little by little, I realized cultural management excited me more than technology.

But the real story — the one that changed everything — begins earlier.

In 2012, I got divorced. I was raising my son alone and had enough things on my plate. Around 2013–2014, my hormonal system was going in all directions, and I didn't know what was happening to me.

It wasn't until 2019, they finally discovered the tumor in my head. In 2020, I had my first neurosurgery. It took me a year to get my body to a fully operational mode again, but I was happy — I finally got my health back. Only after that I finally got my health back. I became a normal, healthy person again.

And then I got into a relationship. After ten years living by myself, fighting a difficult disease, I put all my identity into that relationship. I felt like I was finally a woman again — healthy, loved, in a partnership.

So when the relationship fell apart in 2023, I felt like everything collapsed. Even though I had a career, my whole identity was standing on a pillar of being his girlfriend. I didn't know who I was anymore if I wasn't his girlfriend.

It is probably our background. It's how we were raised — that as a woman, you can do anything like career or creativity, but your main goal is to have a family and a child. That's why you're born a woman. That was so deeply embedded in my subconscious and in my genetic code.

And then my work contract, which was temporary, wasn't prolonged. I felt so ashamed I didn't tell anyone. I felt like it was my fault. I knew it was nonsense, but feelings don't follow logic. I kept it a secret like there was no tomorrow.

And then, within two months, I heard that my tumor came back.

Relationship gone.

Job gone.

Health shaken again.

That's when everything changed.

I went to therapy. At first, it was just to clarify my internal positioning — my identity. She suggested a course. I took it. From that course, another course emerged. Before I noticed it, I graduated as a psychologist myself.

During that time, I was exhausted. There were days I couldn't get out of bed. Days when I didn't see the reason why.

In 2024, I had my second operation. They told me it was not successful and they could not remove the tumor fully.

Almost nobody knew. I wasn't open about my situation. I didn't ask for help. If asked now what I'd do differently, my answer would be simple: I'd ask for help — emotional, physical, operational, logistical, psychological.

But studying psychology became my lifeline. I understood patterns — why the relationship fell apart, why I felt the way I felt. I stopped blaming myself. I stopped blaming him. I just understood it.

And I realized something else: I wasn't doing professionally what excited me anymore. Helping people — that became my biggest motivation. Business development is still nice. I still exercise. But business development is a job. Helping people is a life purpose.

So I started working with people approaching burnout, in burnout, or losing their sense of purpose — people who feel disconnected from themselves. I know that place. I've been there. Together with a group of enthusiasts, we founded a startup about burnout prevention, where I'm the Chief Commercial Officer. I look after sales and business development. So now I'm developing two businesses: myself as a coach, and our startup, which combines the best of my 2 worlds: the passion for helping people and the creativity of business development.

Today, things are different.

Professionally, I'm happy. I have a very nice relationship. I'm still working on my health — I'm going to soon have another operation, and hopefully it will be the last one.

But the important thing is, I got myself back. And I'm proud of that. It fills me with confidence, self-love, self-trust. When you're happy with what you have, you feel different from the inside out.

The moment you start leaning on external validation — support, opinions, evaluation — that's when you lose yourself. That's when you become shaky. That's why turning my attention inward — into my emotions, my beliefs, my values — made the difference.

And one more thing:

You are the center of your life.

You are the most important person in your life.

And you are the only person who will always love you.

So make sure you do.

Nothing is more distancing than someone who never cracks, never doubts, never shows the slightest fracture — and yet that's exactly how many of us appear when we're holding the weight of the world on our shoulders. Vulnerability is what makes us human, and it's the only thing that creates real connection. Showing your uncertainty to the world might feel unsafe, but it's what allows others to recognize themselves in you — and step closer instead of pulling away.

From that place, asking for help becomes less about the request itself and more about allowing connection. You can start small — not with the biggest task or a disguised therapy session, but with something manageable. Share a worry with a friend. Ask your partner for a bit of support. Let someone know you're overwhelmed instead of pretending you're fine. Each time you do, you teach your nervous system that the world doesn't collapse when you lean on someone. In fact, most people feel honored to be trusted.

If asking for help is difficult for you, there is a hack that can make it easier.

Start by helping others.

Be the change you want to see.

But first, let's redefine what "help" actually means.

As we've seen in the earlier chapter, many of us were raised to care for others first. So "helping" often gets confused with over-giving — showing up when you have no energy, saying yes because you feel guilty, or supporting for free simply because someone asked.

In my conversations, women often told me they feel they must "give their all" every time just to earn the right to receive anything back. One business owner told me she kept making her workshops — her only income in a new country — almost unprofitable because she felt she had to offer the best room, the best snacks, the best equipment every single time. She was barely getting by, always stressed out, and no one knew.

Do parts of this feel familiar to you?

Caring for others is wonderful. And there's nothing wrong with improving the experience for your customers. But if you notice yourself giving away food when you're dying from hunger, it's time to listen to what's driving this desire.

If there's the pain of having no choice, of emptying yourself; if you believe you must shrink so others can shine; if you feel you must give everything just to receive a little — the world cannot meet you at that level of sacrifice. It simply doesn't know how.

So you end up flattering your ego — "I'm providing the best customer experience" — while quietly resenting the world because "they don't understand."

But is this really the person you want to be?

Real helping feels different — on the inside.

I invite you to see help as something that comes naturally to you — something you offer to others *and* to yourself, something that fills you rather than drains you. Because filling yourself has nothing to do with taking away from others. And helping others isn't measured by how much effort you put in. You never know when a single word or a simple connection might shift someone's life.

Most importantly — when you offer your time, your knowledge, your presence, something inside you heals. You feel useful. You feel connected. You feel like you matter — and that feeling makes it easier to believe that you, too, are allowed to receive support. Helping others doesn't just make a difference in their lives; it restores your sense of belonging in the world. And belonging makes asking feel less like a burden and more like a natural part of being human.

Here a few ways to begin helping people around you:

- Introduce two people who could help each other.
- Share a resource with a colleague who might benefit from it.
- Find an organization where you can volunteer your skills.
- Support a friend with something that comes easily to you.

Each act of giving builds the muscle that lets you welcome support in return. It deepens relationships.

Yet once you open yourself to support — whether by asking for help or offering it — another fear rises: the fear of being turned away. The fear that someone might say no, misunderstand you, or not show up as you hoped. And we need to talk about that, because every meaningful change requires you to reach out, try, ask, apply, step forward. And with that comes the possibility of hearing "no." So before we go on, we need to explore one more thing: how to meet rejection without letting it define you.

Preparing To Meet The World

After reconnecting with the people who feel safest to you, the next step is gently re-engaging with the wider world. For many of us — especially those who lean toward introversion — this can feel a bit overwhelming. And that's completely understandable.

But I'm inviting you to consider a different perspective. At one of the personal and professional development events on human connection that I attended, the host asked a simple question:

"Raise your hand if you would like to have one more friend in your life."

How many hands do you think went up?

Every single one.

That moment stayed with me. It reminded me that most of us — no matter our age, culture, or personality —long for more connection. Not necessarily another best friend, but at least one more person we feel good around. Someone who values us, supports us, and makes life a little lighter.

Connection is in our nature. We're wired for it.

And yet, when it comes to building these new connections, many of us freeze. Networking, the word itself, often feels cold and transactional. Especially in a new country, it often turns into a script:

"What's your name?"

"Where are you from?"

"What do you do?"

People walk away thinking they've made a connection, when in reality, they've only exchanged some basic information. We forget what real connection feels like — the warmth, the curiosity, the sense of being seen.

The next chapter is about rebuilding that sense of connection. It's about making networking less stressful, even if you're an introvert. It's about learning how to talk to people without feeling awkward or "too much." And it's about understanding that switching jobs is rarely a straight line of education → credentials → job offer.

If you've read the stories earlier in this book, you've probably noticed a pattern. Education plays a role, yes — but it's never the whole story. Every single person I spoke with mentioned, directly or indirectly, the same essential ingredient:

Switching careers requires someone to believe in you — and someone else to give you a chance.

A future manager who sees your potential.

A future customer who trusts you enough to try your service.

A person who opens a door you didn't know existed.

And that always begins with connection.

From Tax Lawyer to a Quality Assurance Engineer (Kyrgyzstan → Russia → Singapore)

"When you're a non-standard candidate, you need non-standard solutions."

In Russia, Veronika was a respected lawyer with her own consulting practice. After her husband's job took her to Singapore, she found herself starting from zero — no work visa, no clear path, and a global shift that made her entire field feel unstable. What began as fear turned into curiosity, and curiosity led her somewhere she never expected: into the world of technology.

Veronika graduated with honors as a lawyer, specializing in building corporate structures for international businesses. For eight years, she worked her way up diligently in legal firms.

After switching companies a few times, Veronika noticed that her firm was taking on unethical projects. It was not something she could accept. She drew clear boundaries, rejecting assignments that violated her standards. Nine months later, unwilling to compromise her values, she left and started her own consulting business—with her husband's support.

Veronika was good at what she did—optimizing taxes for international companies. As soon as her clients learned she was starting her own firm, many followed her.

"Within six months, I reached the same level of compensation. That same year, we decided to move to Singapore after my partner landed a great job there. I didn't have a work visa but I could still stay as an entrepreneur providing consulting services remotely.

Then, international regulations changed, making it cumbersome for clients to maintain their existing company structures. They began asking me to manage private assets—boats, villas—which wasn't what I wanted to do.

I felt stuck, unsure of my next move, and eventually hit a burnout.

Around the same time, news broke that AI might replace lawyers. As an anxious person, I panicked at first. The only way I could ease my fear was to learn everything about AI and its capabilities. I took several AI courses and realized it wasn't going to replace me—not yet, at least.

Beyond bringing peace of mind, those courses sparked a genuine interest in IT. I'd always wanted globally valuable skills with the flexibility to pivot when needed. The tech industry seemed perfect—constantly evolving, with endless new things to learn.

So, the question was: what is the profession I will be pursuing?

Jurisprudence is very structured. If you want to become a lawyer, the path is clear and linear. Go to law school, practice and you'll have a job. Technology and IT were anything but linear—there was no obvious way to break into the field from scratch.

Luckily, I knew someone who could help make this decision. My husband, a software engineer with 20 years of experience. I shared my idea with him, and like any seasoned professional, he had a lot of advice—some fascinating, some overwhelming. Together we identified an entry-level role I could pursue: quality assurance engineer. This is someone who helps software companies test their products and catch errors before release.

Ok, so I needed to somehow become a QA engineer. How do I make the switch?

To me, the logical first step was education. Learning is one of my most favorite things in life, after all. After researching Coursera, I found the University of Pennsylvania's Master's program for career switchers, covering programming fundamentals, software architecture, and networking.

The program was a perfect fit. But a Master's takes years, and I had no tech background whatsoever. That's when it hit me: When you're a non-standard candidate, you need non-standard solutions.

I started with earning a basic quality assurance certification. But employers always want experience, right? I joined uTest, a global crowdsourcing platform for testing. This meant working with software startups that needed help catching errors in their apps but lacked resources to hire full-time QA staff. The path was similar to any freelance platform: complete projects, boost your rating, and get more work. I spent over a year there and added it to my CV. Some people dismiss this opportunity as "not real experience," but I disagreed—you're solving real business challenges for real pay.

I also needed connections. In Singapore, expat networking is huge. I attended all women-in-tech events I could find, met career switchers who inspired me, and even landed interviews through their referrals. Yet every networking event was a challenge. As I'm a very introverted person, sometimes I'd force myself to go because I was afraid I'll unlearn how to talk to people. Seriously! In the end, I can't emphasize enough how crucial it is to have role models—to meet real people who've made the transition you're attempting.

At the same time, I spent a lot of time on LinkedIn looking at profiles in my target field, asking: What are my unique strengths? My bilingual skills (Russian and English), for one. After that, I researched companies in Singapore that would be a great fit for me.

One specific company stood out to me. I really wanted to work for them. So I made a few very intentional moves to make this reality. For example, I added several QA engineers from that company to my network on LinkedIn. After connecting with a few employees, I modeled my uTest experience after one woman's profile—focusing on metrics: use cases handled, projects completed, UI research conducted. Of course, I never seriously assumed they would hire me.

After I edited my LinkedIn profile, it was time to apply for several roles. When I started applying for jobs and getting interviews, psychologically it was a nightmare. Because you'll get rejected.

Another challenge during interviews were the tough questions any career switcher will probably face. During interviews recruiters would ask: 'Are you sure you're committed to switching careers? What if it doesn't work out—will you go back?'

And I thought: "There's no going back. I'm only moving forward."

But how do you convince strangers who are meeting you for the first time?

Yet luck finally found me. Right after finishing my first semester, I opened LinkedIn to a message from a QA manager at that very company I pursued—the very woman whose profile had helped me reframe my experience.

I couldn't believe my eyes, but her core message was clear:

"Are you interested in joining our team as a senior QA engineer?"

I was honest. "I'm not ready for a senior role yet," I told her. She invited me for an interview, and a few weeks later, I joined as a QA engineer. The entire transition took about a year.

At first, the job was overwhelming. I'd never worked for such a large company. But after releasing one of my first projects, I noticed that compared to the engineers around me, I brought a different kind of maturity and communication skills. I wasn't afraid to ask for help, "Can you show me how this works?" My teammates reported that it was easy to work with me because I researched things deeply before seeking help and was able to ask the right questions.

For a career switcher, it's crucial to recognize your value beyond hard skills. You may not see it this way, but every experience you've accumulated so far is valuable. Understanding processes, navigating communication, managing hierarchy, and solving problems—this is professional maturity. I've developed it, and you likely have it, too.

These abilities—like collaborating effectively and seeking help when needed—form the foundation of any successful career. No matter what path you're pursuing, you bring this entire wealth of experience with you.

Surprisingly, QA and jurisprudence have a lot in common. Both require analyzing documents, spotting inconsistencies, and clarifying ambiguities. And in both fields communication is key. You need to truly understand what the client (or stakeholder) needs. So I wasn't really starting from scratch—I brought years of developing the same core skills.

I owe so much of this to my husband. While I was deep in learning, he took over cooking and chores. That support was the reason I was able to make this leap. He's literally a saint (but don't you dare tell him).

In terms of careers, women often achieve less than men. Not because they are less capable, but because their time is dedicated to the unpaid, and often unacknowledged, full-time job of running a household and raising a family. Household labor is real labor, and it drains time and energy. I was truly blessed—I could afford my education and had a partner who supported me through the career switch. Not everyone gets that. Yet I firmly believe there's a chance for anyone to start a new career."

You can't meet the world with confidence until you meet yourself with honesty — and that begins with accepting the real version of you, not the polished or performative one you think you're supposed to present.

And the real version of you includes your superpowers.

If you're quiet, remember that quiet people listen deeply, notice what others miss, and create safety in rooms where everyone else is performing.

If you're intense, remember that intensity is passion and depth — the refusal to skim the surface of life. It isn't "too much"; it's the energy that brings meaning to everything you touch.

And if your path has been unconventional, remember that unconventional people see possibilities others overlook. They imagine, innovate, create — and they're the ones who bring vision into the room.

Every quality is precious in the right setting. There's no perfect — only the mix of traits that make you *you*. Some you've hidden, some you're reclaiming, some shine differently depending on who's looking. You don't control their gaze. You control your light.

Value, turns out, isn't a fixed trait. It's not something you either have or don't have. It's born out of a need someone else has. And even when you're still growing, still learning, still figuring things out, you have value simply because you carry a unique mix of experiences, perspectives, and strengths that no one else does. You don't need to be perfect to be valuable. You don't need to be fully formed to be worthy of being seen.

What you might need is just some luck.

As Veronika put it: *"You'll need some luck, but luck isn't passive — we create it through action. Put yourself in the right rooms. Be in the right place at the right time. Introduce yourself: 'I'm an [X] professional exploring [Y] opportunities.' I know it's uncomfortable (I'm an introvert too!), but without this, I'd never be where I am today. Opportunity always meets those who show up."*

Yet the moment we put ourselves in those rooms, we inevitably meet rejection. And this is where something essential comes to light. Accepting yourself is only half of the equation. The other half is accepting rejection.

This might sound too good to be true, but... Imagine that you're not afraid of rejection anymore. How would that feel?

You walk into a room and your mind stays quiet instead of scanning for danger, because you're no longer bracing for the possibility of being dismissed. You speak without shrinking your voice, because you're not trying to pre-edit yourself into something safer or smaller to avoid being judged. You reach out to people because you're curious, not because you're calculating the odds of being ignored. You try things simply because they matter to you, not because you're guaranteed applause. And when someone doesn't respond the way you hoped, it stings for a moment and then passes — it doesn't spiral into a story about your worth.

Rejection becomes a moment, not a threat.

Of course, this is much easier in theory than in practice. When rejections pile up, even the strongest mind can wobble. You can remind yourself that rejection doesn't define your value, but your nervous system often tells a different story. That's why your strength circle matters so much — the people who remind you who you are when fear tries to convince you otherwise. At first, this might be someone close to you, but over time you'll notice others joining that circle too.

Switching careers always requires two things: having people who believe in you, and someone who is willing to give you a chance to prove yourself. And truth is, both of those require you to face the possibility of rejection. That "someone" — a future manager, a future customer, a future collaborator — can only find you if you're willing to be seen, even when being seen feels risky.

For many of us, new connections feel stressful because the fear of rejection lingers in the background. You worry if you're clear enough, because you're not speaking your first language. You might prefer quiet time with your family and find socializing draining. You might be navigating mid-life responsibilities — moving countries, arranging schools, dealing with paperwork, working full time — and the idea of "networking" feels like one more exhausting task on an already full plate. In all of these situations, the fear of rejection doesn't just exist — it multiplies.

Your personality can add its own flavor too. A brain wired with ADHD brings creativity and intensity, but it can also make social interactions feel unpredictable or overwhelming, which makes the fear of rejection louder.

Yet reinvention is relationship-building. It's learning new ways of interacting with the people around you. And relationships are a verb — they need consistency, attention, and a bit of courage, especially the courage to risk rejection. There are no shortcuts, but there *are* ways to make the process lighter, more human, and far less stressful.

When you're in a new environment, building new connections is a part of creating a new life. But it doesn't have to feel like a performance or a burden. When you understand rejection differently, it stops being a verdict and becomes another step to becoming more you.

And that's where we're headed next — because before you can build meaningful relationships, you need one foundational skill: the ability to accept rejection without losing yourself.

The Secret of Embracing Rejection

When it comes to building new connections in a new place, most of us aren't held back by lack of talent or lack of opportunity. We're held back by something much less visible and much more powerful:

The fear of rejection.

Showing up in a world that speaks a different language and follows different cultural norms can feel incredibly raw — even dangerous. Your system goes on high alert. Every next step feels like a decision with consequences. And when you're considering a pivot, the sheer number of possible directions can feel overwhelming. You sense the pressure to act, yet choosing the "right" action becomes its own source of stress. Do you take another course? Rewrite your CV? Build a personal brand? Or simply tell people, honestly, what you've been exploring?

This lack of clarity creates pressure before you've even begun. And then, the moment other people enter the picture, everything becomes even more overwhelming. As soon as you imagine announcing your pivot to the world — especially on LinkedIn — the old fears rush in:

- How that former colleague will roll their eyes this time.
- How that company will gossip using every version of "did she go nuts."
- How that one acquaintance will dramatically whisper, "She's really doing that now?"

Sometimes you even know exactly what they would say — and those imagined voices settle in your mind, freezing you in place. Because you care. We all do. Belonging is one of the oldest instincts we carry, and the thought of stepping outside the version of you people are used to can feel like risking that belonging.

And underneath all of that sits another, quieter pressure: financial reality. Few of us can afford to sit at home endlessly debating which path to take. You need your journey to be financially sustainable. So suddenly it feels as if you must sell a perfect version of yourself before you've even had the chance to build the skills, as if you're expected to be convincing before you're allowed to be curious.

This creates an impossible standard: you're supposed to present a polished version of something you're only just beginning to explore — and to do it in a world that doesn't always feel safe. Not safe because every step seems to invite someone's opinion, someone's judgment, someone's quiet (or not so quiet) evaluation of whether you're good enough.

When you're vulnerable, rejection feels like it's everywhere: in a friend's offhand comment, in job applications, and in tiny moments that suddenly feel much bigger than they are.

Here's why rejection is so powerful. As we've seen in the earlier chapters, for each of us three basic needs must be met:

- "I'm enough."
- "I'm loved."
- "I'm appreciated"

When any of these needs is threatened, your sense of agency collapses. And rejection — even small, everyday rejection — hits *all three* at once.

First, rejection takes away your sense of control because it makes you feel like someone else is deciding the direction of your life, and your choices no longer matter.

Then rejection takes away your sense of capability because when someone doesn't hire you, it can feel as if they've just made a decision about who we are and what we're allowed to become.

Finally, rejection takes away your sense of belonging because it whispers that you're on the outside, that you don't fit, and that others have a place you're not invited into.

But what if you learned to work with rejection and it didn't have the power to stop you anymore?

In this chapter, we'll explore five psychological shifts that help you move from fearing rejection to feeling free from it. They're grounded in motivation theory, emotional intelligence, and the lived experiences of people who have rebuilt their careers, their identities, and their confidence from scratch.

Each shift is a way of reclaiming your agency — especially when you're switching careers, networking, or stepping into a new professional identity.

And reclaiming agency always begins with reclaiming control.

1. Reclaim Control

There's a well-known list in psychology called The Holmes–Rahe Stress Inventory. You've seen it before. It ranks the most stressful life events a person can experience. Here are some of the top ones:

- death of a spouse;
- divorce;
- separation;
- imprisonment;
- personal injury or illness;
- marriage (yes, even positive change is stressful);
- job loss;
- retirement;
- major financial changes;
- moving to a new country;
- pregnancy;
- major change in responsibilities at work.

When you look at this list, it seems random at first — a mix of tragedies, transitions, and milestones. We look at these events and think, *"Of course they're stressful — they're painful, they're complicated, they're life-changing."*

But there's one thread running through all of them:

Every single one involves losing control.

Our brain is wired for predictability. It needs to feel like you have some kind of steering wheel, even a tiny one. When that disappears, even for a moment, your nervous system reacts the same way it would if you were standing on a cliff edge with no railing.

It doesn't matter if the event is tragic, joyful, or somewhere in between — your system doesn't distinguish. A wedding, a move, a job loss, a breakup… they all shake the ground under your feet. They all force you to rebuild routines, identities, expectations, and roles.

Your body reads loss of control as danger. Until you claim it back, it will keep bracing for impact — even when nothing is coming. Being grounded in the fact that you *do* have control over your life is essential if you want to move forward. And the very first step in rebuilding yourself is learning how to give your body back even the smallest sense of control.

Reclaim Your Body

When something destabilizing happens — a job loss, a rejection, a sudden change, a career collapse, a divorce, a migration, a burnout — your mind doesn't react first. Your body does.

This is why trauma therapists — the people who work with survivors of war, accidents, violence, and displacement — almost always begin in the same place: the body.

As Kristin, one of the reinventors I interviewed, said: *"My whole reinvention started with a 15-minute walk. That's it. Just a walk."* That makes a lot of sense. When your nervous system is overwhelmed, you can't think clearly, dream clearly, or choose clearly. So they help people breathe again, feel their feet on the ground, slow their heart rate. Reclaim the sense that "I am here. I am safe. I exist."

This is why the very first step in reclaiming control — especially during a career transition — is not philosophical. It's physical. Reclaiming control starts as simple as:

- Taking a walk without your phone and letting your senses come back online.
- Unclenching your jaw before you open LinkedIn.
- Noticing the moment your stomach tightens and saying, "I'm safe. This is not a threat."

Once your body feels safe, your mind becomes available again.

And then you can move to the next layer.

Stand on Your Worth

Alfred Adler, one of the early voices in modern psychology, believed that human beings are driven not just by past wounds, but by purpose — by the desire to belong, to contribute, and to move toward a life that feels meaningful. He said that every human life revolves around three core tasks: love, friendship, and work. These tasks shape almost everything we do. They involve other people, but they are not controlled by other people.

Put simply, you can offer your effort, your sincerity, your ideas, your presence while you're performing your tasks — but you can't control whether someone applauds, ignores, misunderstands, or rejects you.

And that's where so much unnecessary suffering begins: we confuse what we *can* influence with what we *wish* we could control.

There are dozens of reasons your message might not land, and most of them have nothing to do with your qualifications or experience. Sometimes the reaction has nothing to do with you at all — it's simply about the match between you and the environment. I see this all the time in public speaking work. The exact same message can feel electric in one room and completely out of place in another.

You can deliver a line that gives one audience goosebumps... and watch another audience blink at you like you've just spoken in a different language.

You don't walk into a group that came to unwind after work and hit them with a fiery "embrace the grind" sermon, or talk about bold risk-taking at a meeting where everyone is literally there to discuss safety procedures.

It's not that the message is wrong.

It's not that you are wrong.

It's that the *room* is wrong.

Easy to say! But what if rejection still hurts?

Of course it hurts. Let's not pretend otherwise. Rejection lands on the part of your identity that dared to hope. When someone doesn't respond the way you wished, it can feel like a tiny heartbreak. Your mind immediately jumps to the most painful interpretation: *"Maybe I'm not good enough. Maybe I misread everything. Maybe I shouldn't have tried."* That's the moment when your nervous system goes into self-protection mode. It tells you to retreat, to shrink, to stop risking anything that might expose you again.

But here's something important I invite you to consider: the pain you feel is not proof that you lack value. It's proof that you cared. It's proof that you were brave enough to imagine a bigger version of yourself. And these are two different things.

Because the pain feels so sharp, your mind will whisper:

"But what if they really didn't like me?"

"What if I'm not ready?"

"What if I embarrass myself?"

"What if this means I should stop?"

These voices feel logical, but they're not. They're emotional echoes of old experiences, old fears, old stories about what it means to be seen.

Rejection becomes terrifying when you believe it reflects your worth. But rejection is not a mirror, it's a filter. Just as beauty is in the eye of the beholder, rejection filters out the people who cannot truly see you, so you can find the ones who can.

Clarify What You Stand For

One of the most powerful ways to reclaim control and reduce the sting of rejection is to become crystal clear about your values — not the abstract ones we list on a CV, but the ones that genuinely guide your decisions, your work, and the kind of impact you want to make.

That's why one of the previous chapters was entirely dedicated to meeting that new version of yourself and her values. You're no longer asking, *"Do they want me?"* You're asking, *"Is this aligned with who I am and what I care about?"* That question puts you back in your power.

From Teaching to a Mentor and Diversity and Inclusion Coordinator — as a Single Mom (Saudi Arabia → Netherlands)

Sarah's story is a story of reinvention through survival, courage, and choosing a different life — from a turbulent childhood in Saudi Arabia to becoming a widowed single mother at 23, to rebuilding her career across continents. Today, she's a teacher, mentor, and diversity advocate who transformed every setback into a new beginning — not just surviving, but redefining who she could become.

I always say I've lived many lifetimes in just 38 years. My story isn't linear. It's a series of battles, reinventions, and leaps — some chosen, some forced. I'm not a businesswoman or

---

an entrepreneur in the traditional sense, but I've walked through enough fire to know exactly who I am today.

I grew up in Saudi Arabia, born to Pakistani parents who moved there for a better life. My childhood was unstable — my parents separated, my mother was depressed, and I never had a role model who showed me what a woman could become. My brothers were all successful businessmen, powerful and respected. My mother was the opposite: selfless to the point of disappearing. She lived entirely for others, and I watched her lose herself piece by piece.

I knew early on that I didn't want that life.

I wasn't a studious kid — I was a rebel. I wanted to study simply because everyone told me not to. In a society where girls were expected to marry, not dream, I insisted on getting a bachelor's degree in English literature. It wasn't easy. Opportunities for women were limited, especially back then. But I pushed through.

At 23, I got married. I had no stable home, no financial security, and no real choices. I worked as a teacher's assistant, then as a teacher, and then I got pregnant. My pregnancy was difficult, and instead of supporting me, the school told me to quit. As an expat woman, I had no protection.

Nine months after giving birth, my husband died in a car accident.

I became a widow at 23, with a baby, no savings, no government support, and no time to mourn. That was the moment my real battle began. I had to survive — not for myself, but for my daughter.

I took a Cambridge CELTA course, and during the training someone noticed my teaching skills. I was hired immediately as an English instructor at King Abdulaziz University — a prestigious place, especially for an expat woman. I worked there for four years, got promoted, and kept studying. I earned another teaching qualification from the University of Sunderland, all while raising my daughter alone.

But even as I built a career, I was fighting battles no one saw.

I was a domestic violence survivor. I had battled depression alone for years. I had fought for my daughter's custody for six years because my late husband's family wanted to take her. The lawyers told me, "You're a woman — just give her to them." I refused. I fought every day, every hour, every minute.

Stress broke my body. I developed autoimmune issues and eczema. But I kept going. I also kept dreaming.

I wanted a different life — one where I wasn't just surviving. And then I fell in love with a Dutch man. I moved to the Netherlands, thinking I would walk into a job at a British International School because of my experience.

Reality hit me hard.

I was an expat again. A foreigner again. A hijabi again. And suddenly, none of my degrees or experience mattered. Schools rejected me because I didn't speak Dutch. Some rejected me because of my hijab. I applied everywhere. Nothing worked.

So I took a job at an optical shop — as a salesperson. With a bachelor's, a master's, a CELTA, and years of university teaching behind me, I was vacuuming floors and selling glasses. My ego hurt.

There were many moments when I felt… I don't want to sound bad or braggy, but I felt like… what if someone comes from my circle and they see me vacuuming? These days I felt ashamed. Most days I felt like I didn't belong.

But I stayed. I needed the income. I needed the integration. I needed the network. I thought, if it helps me integrate, I'll take it.

After a year and a half — and after COVID — I finally got a break. I applied for a maternity cover position at Amsterdam International Community School. I got it. And I stayed. Four years later, I'm still there — now as a teacher, a mentor, and someone deeply involved in diversity and inclusion.

But teaching is only 40% of who I am.

The rest of me is community, leadership, and helping people grow. I became a diversity coordinator. I led projects. I joined the Duke of Edinburgh Award program as a leader. I started tutoring. My Toastmasters experienced helped. I trained teachers in burnout prevention and hope. And I became a mentor at Female Ventures because I wanted to give other women what I never had — support, guidance, someone who says "I see you."

Moving to the Netherlands was also a cultural shock. I came from a place where nightlife starts at 7 p.m., where you have a driver and a maid, where life is buzzing. Here, everything closes early. People dress casually. Life is quiet. Dutch women — especially the older generation — reminded me of Saudi women more than I expected: homely, family-focused, not career-driven. It surprised me. It challenged me. It forced me to redefine what "modern" means.

And then there was my marriage.

After six years of being a single mother, I had built a masculine armor — survival mode. I did everything myself. I trusted no one. I carried all the weight. When I remarried, that armor came with me. I didn't let my husband lead. I didn't let him help. I didn't know how to soften.

It took years — workshops, books, therapy, self-reflection — to reconnect with my feminine energy. To let myself be cared for. To let myself rest. To let myself be vulnerable again.

Today, I'm still reinventing myself. I'm still learning. I'm still healing. But I'm no longer fighting alone.

I'm raising a daughter who speaks fluent Dutch, who is confident, integrated, and growing into a young woman with choices I never had. I'm building a legacy she can be proud of.

And I'm finally at a point where I can say: I didn't just survive. I rebuilt myself. I chose myself. And I'm still choosing myself every day.

I know it might seem like conversations about values are pointless when your current reality is difficult. At the end of the day, when you need money to survive, no amount of reflection feels like it changes that. But I hope Sarah's story showed you that even when life forces you to take a job far from ideal just to stay afloat, it's not a verdict on your worth or your identity. It doesn't mean you stop dreaming or stop moving toward the life you actually want.

Your identity and your values act like a compass in the middle of a rejection storm.. They help you recognize the opportunities that feel right and the ones that drain you. They help you understand why certain environments energize you while others leave you feeling small. And most importantly, they help you stop taking rejection personally, because you can see that not every space is meant for you — and that's a good thing.

Serving a bigger goal is another way to soften the sting of rejection. You can ask yourself: *Who do I care about beyond my immediate circle?* Maybe it's immigrants trying to build a new life. Maybe it's women returning to work after a break. Maybe it's people who feel lost in their careers and need clarity. When you know who you want to help, your focus shifts outward. You stop obsessing over how you're being perceived and start paying attention to the people who genuinely need your voice, and your presence.

When you serve a bigger purpose, you stop shrinking every time someone doesn't choose you. And when you hold that perspective, rejection becomes less of a wound and more of a filter. It simply guides you toward the spaces where you truly belong.

Let Your Voice Be Heard

Having your own voice in the world is one of the most efficient ways you take your power back.

Not because "everyone is a creator now," not because "you need to post," but because it gives you a place where your autonomy is non-negotiable.

When you write, record, share, or build something under your own name, you create a space where you decide what you say, how you show up, and what you care about. You're no longer only a candidate waiting to be evaluated; you're a person with a body of work. You're not just asking, "Will they pick me?"—you're also quietly stating, "This is who I am and what I bring."

We'll discuss this approach more in detail in a later chapter.

Once you reclaim control, the next perspective comes into view.

2. Give Yourself Permission

Do you remember the first story from this book? When you're looking for a job, or looking for customers, and the rejections start coming in, they don't just sting — they feel personal, almost like someone is quietly confirming the fear you've been carrying for years. But what's actually behind that pain? Why does a simple "no" from a stranger land so deeply?

A single rejection is manageable. Most of us can shrug it off. But when the no's keep coming — week after week, month after month — something shifts. It stops being about the opportunity and starts becoming a story about you. It's like getting a paper cut and reopening it every morning. The first cut is annoying. The fiftieth is a wound. And when your mind has a wound, it goes searching for explanations in the darkest corners of your thoughts, pulling out every insecurity it can find and holding it up like evidence. *It's your accent. It's your age. It's your visa. It's who you are.*

But rejection doesn't hurt because of the opportunity itself. It rarely does. The pain usually comes from somewhere deeper, and the only way to see it clearly is to slow down and ask yourself a different kind of question. *What exactly is being touched in you when someone says no? What is the part that tightens, or sinks, or suddenly feels exposed?*

If you sit with it for a moment, you'll notice that the ache isn't about the job description or the company logo or the bullet points you could have written in your sleep. It's about what you hoped this opportunity would give you. And that hope is almost always emotional.

Rejection doesn't hurt because you're too sensitive, it hurts because you're hungry. Hungry for recognition. A sense of being seen. A sense of being valued. A sense of belonging somewhere again. A sense of finally becoming you.

Every application carries a quiet hope that this time, someone will see you and give you what you crave. And when they don't, the hunger sharpens.

So how do you stop this emotional rollercoaster?

1.   Separate Opportunity and Identity

The first step is separating the two things that always get tangled together: the opportunity itself, and the need that you're trying to fulfill.

Opportunities are abundant. Truly. Even when it doesn't feel that way. Even when you've convinced yourself that this one role, this one company, this one moment is your only chance. It isn't. Opportunities come in waves, not single drops. This listing is not the last train leaving the station. There will be another. There always is.

But the deeper layer — the one that actually hurts — is the permission to become the version of yourself you imagined in that opportunity. Someone who's more fulfilled, happy, loved, respected. You saw her so clearly that losing the opportunity feels like losing her.

But here's the truth that changes everything.

You do not need their permission to become that version of you.

The future you pictured is still yours.

It always was.

Rejection only feels like a verdict when you believe the opportunity is the only path to the need you're trying to meet. But it never is. That's when you move to the next step.

2. Recognize Your Deeper Need

There's only one reason why we do what we do in life:

We want to change how we feel.

Imagine someone applying for a role that feels like a step up — a team-lead position she knows she can do. She spends hours on the application, rereads her CV, rehearses answers in the shower. She tells herself it's because she wants the job. But if she pauses for a moment, she'll notice something else underneath: she's tired of feeling that, despite being qualified, no one takes her seriously. She wants to walk into a room without proving herself from zero. She wants her experience to finally count.

So when the rejection email arrives, it's not the job she's mourning. It's the state she hoped the job would unlock — the sense of being respected, the sense of being seen, the sense of finally being allowed to take up space.

If we're not forced into something, we don't chase roles; we chase states. We want the job because we want the feeling behind it — to feel respected, accomplished, chosen, or finally at peace. And the mistake we repeat is believing those feelings will arrive *after* something external happens. After the offer. After the title. After the recognition.

But it doesn't work that way.

I'll say this again because it's important: rejection doesn't hurt because you're overly sensitive. It hurts because you're hungry for something meaningful. There's a deeper need inside you that's still unmet. But you can't wait for the world to hand you the feeling you're starving for. You have to feed yourself first.

So pause and ask: *What am I really pursuing here?* What is the unfulfilled need behind this opportunity? Maybe it's the desire to feel competent again after a long season of uncertainty. Maybe it's the longing to feel seen in a world that has overlooked you. Maybe it's the hope that someone, somewhere, will finally say, "Yes, you belong here."

As you listen to your voice, move to step 3.

3. Find Active Ways to Fulfill Your Need Today

You might think that keeping yourself hungry for recognition, belonging or love keeps you motivated. But staying hungry doesn't make you driven — it just makes you unhappy.

That's why once you uncover the deeper need, the feeling you crave, commit to giving that feeling to yourself in ways you can actually control.

If you want to feel accomplished, finish the thing you've been postponing, send the email you've been avoiding, make progress you can point to and say, *I did that.*

If you want to feel valued, treat your work — even the invisible work — as something that matters. Give it your full attention. Give it dignity. Notice the value in what others are doing too — that's how you train this muscle.

If you want to belong, start with the smallest act of connection. Invite a former colleague or that LinkedIn acquaintance for a coffee. Do something for your community when you can and when you want to. Celebrate someone's milestone — because you'd love others to celebrate yours.

When you meet the need from the inside, you stop approaching opportunities from hunger. You approach them from fullness. And fullness is not afraid of rejection.

This is what giving yourself permission really means. It's not about forcing confidence or pretending you don't care. It's about claiming your identity and deciding to follow through regardless of who says yes or no. It's about becoming the person you imagined, not someday, not after the offer, but now. Because when you live from that place, rejection loses its power. It becomes information, not a verdict. A redirection, not a wound.

The real freedom is not in getting the opportunity.

It's in no longer needing it to feel like yourself.

3. It's Always About Them

Rejection feels personal because our mind makes it personal. It fills the silence with stories about your worth, your talent, your future. But before you accept any of those stories as truth, pause for a moment to consider another perspective.

Value exists independently of reaction. People respond from their own fears, insecurities, timing, and emotional bandwidth. Their reaction is not your responsibility to manage or interpret.

When someone reacts poorly to you — when they dismiss you, misunderstand you, or ignore you — it usually says far more about *their* inner world and their limitations than about yours.

You've been there too. Think of it like a stand-up show. The comedian performs the exact same set twice. Same jokes, same timing, same talent. You laugh during the first show, but during the second you barely react — not because the comedian changed, but because *you* did. You were in a different emotional place.

That's how people respond to you.

None of that is about your worth.

It's always about them.

Rejection is never a reliable measure of value. It reflects timing, context, emotional availability, personal history — everything except your essence.

People's reactions are rarely a mirror of your value. They're a mirror of their inner landscape and timing. Some will meet you at the perfect moment — to them, you feel like fresh air. Others will meet you when they're overwhelmed, distracted, or unavailable. You could be brilliant and they still won't see it. And some will react through the lens of their own history — you might remind them of someone they already know, or trigger an insecurity they haven't dealt with.

Being liked by everyone feels like a dream, but here's something I learned in marketing: some people will resonate with you, and some won't. Some will resonate for a season and then drift away. That's normal. That's human.

So here's the shift. Instead of asking, *"What does their rejection say about me?"* ask, *"What am I going to do next?"*

Try it with a real moment from your life — the last time someone dismissed you or didn't respond. If you knew their full story — their stress, their fears, their insecurities — would you still interpret their reaction as a judgment of your worth?

Next, we'll step into the moment of rejection — not to relive it, but to reclaim it. You'll discover how to turn a "no" into a place where your confidence can grow.

Learning to Listen Beyond Words

Let's say you've shared a video about your career transition. You finally allowed yourself to be visible, and for a moment it feels good. Then a comment appears:

"This is pointless. No one cares about your journey."

Your body reacts instantly. Your mind rushes ahead, filling in the blanks with painful assumptions. But there's a simple five-question routine that can make moments like this stop feeling so threatening — and take their power away.

1. What did they say?

Start with the literal words. Not the meaning your mind attaches to them, not the tone you imagine, just the sentence as it is. This alone slows down the emotional spiral, because it reminds you how quickly your brain tends to add layers that were never spoken.

In this example:

The words are simply: *"This is pointless. No one cares about your journey."* Nothing in that sentence says you're unworthy, incapable, or foolish. Those interpretations come from the inside, not from the text itself.

2. What emotion is underneath?

People rarely speak from a neutral emotional state, especially when they're being harsh. There is almost always something stirring underneath — frustration, envy, disappointment, or a sense of being stuck. You don't need to identify the exact emotion; acknowledging that one exists already softens the impact.

In this example:

A very plausible emotion is disappointment, because it can feel like "no one cares." And if someone lives in a world where no one cares, you're not required to move into that world with them.

3. What part of their identity are they protecting?

Even unpleasant reactions come from a place where someone is defending something important to them. It might be privacy, stability, competence, or a belief about how life "should" work. When you look for the value behind the reaction, the moment becomes less personal and more understandable.

In this example:

They may be protecting a belief that careers should be linear and private. Or they may value stability and feel threatened by people who take risks. They might feel that only famous people or people in power have a voice, and that everyone else doesn't really matter. They feel like your story challenges these values, so instead of examining it, they push you away.

4. Is there any factual basis?

This is where fear often loosens. Ask yourself whether the comment contains anything that can be objectively verified. Most hurtful statements fall apart here, because they are broad, absolute, and impossible to prove.

In this example:

There are **no facts** in the sentence. "No one cares" cannot be measured or confirmed. It's not the truth — it's a projection. They don't know your audience, your intentions, or the people who might find comfort in your story.

5. What's their call to action?

Every message carries an intention, even if it's expressed clumsily. Sometimes the intention is to push you away, sometimes to silence you, sometimes to protect themselves from discomfort. When you identify the call to action, the comment becomes less of a judgment and more of an attempt to influence your behavior.

In this example:

The call to action is clear: **stop**. Stop sharing, stop trying, stop showing up. Your courage makes them uncomfortable, so the easiest way to reduce that discomfort is to convince you to disappear. And here is the real question: should you really stop because someone you don't even know is disappointed in their own life?

Let's take another example. Imagine someone says, *"I don't think your background fits this role."* Your instinct might be to hear something much heavier, like *I'm not capable.* But if you walk through the layers, the moment shifts. The words themselves are just an opinion. The emotion underneath is likely uncertainty or the fear of making a hiring mistake. The value they're protecting is safety — choosing the option that feels familiar. There's no factual basis, because they don't know your full story or your potential. And their call to action is simply self-protection, not a verdict on who you are.

That's all.

You can practice this with small moments: a short email, a cold reply, a dismissive comment, a message left unanswered. Instead of collapsing into the old narrative, try guiding yourself through the layers.

And when you do this consistently, something shifts. You stop assuming that every reaction is a verdict on your worth. You begin to hear people with more nuance, and you begin to hear yourself with more compassion. The world becomes less threatening, not because it changed, but because you're no longer interpreting every interaction as a reflection of your value. This is how fear loosens its grip.

4. Find a Safe Environment

Relatedness is basically our need to feel connected. It's that quiet wish to matter to someone, to feel seen, to feel like you belong — simply because you exist. But in the rush of daily life, we often ignore this need.

And when you ignore it — when there's no one you can talk to, no one you can unwind with, no one who feels like "your person" — something subtle starts to happen. You begin to feel like your sense of being accepted depends entirely on the outside world. On strangers. On likes. On comments. On whether someone replies or not.

But true authentic connections happen in your closest circles — the places where you don't have to perform. When those environments are healthy, there's an ease to everything. People look at you with warmth. They're genuinely interested and enjoy having you around. They support you without needing a reason. You can finally exhale.

And then there are the other kinds of environments — the ones where none of that exists. Places where trust is thin, where respect feels earned only on certain days, where everyone seems to be competing for oxygen. You can't relax. You watch your tone, your words, your posture. You shrink yourself because the space doesn't feel safe enough for the real you.

Let me be honest: I hope your work environment isn't like that. But after years in corporate settings, I know that "friendly," "honest," and "authentic" are rare. Sometimes even "neutral" feels like a win.

If one of your primary environments feels like this, and you lack a sense of connection, your nervous system shifts into protection mode.

And this is the part people often overlook: **you cannot grow in an environment that constantly makes you defend your right to exist.** You need at least one space — one person, one circle, one corner of your life — where you feel safe enough to try, fail, learn, and try again.

So how do you create that kind of space in your own life?

You start by surrounding yourself with people who support you — people who genuinely want to see you win. It may feel idealistic at first, but during transitions this it's essential. It's like choosing the right soil for a plant. You don't blame the plant for struggling in dry sand — you move it somewhere it can take root.

In practical terms, this might mean:

- Spending more time with the friend who listens without judgment.
- Reconnecting with someone who always made you feel understood.
- Joining a community where people share your goals or values.
- Limiting contact with those who drain you or belittle your efforts.

It doesn't require a dramatic overhaul. Even one supportive person can shift your entire emotional landscape. One safe space can give you enough stability to take risks you wouldn't dare take alone.

And yes, it might feel like you're stepping away from "reality" for a moment. But the truth is, you're stepping into a more accurate one — a reality where you're allowed to grow.

5. Look With Loving Eyes

When we talk about rejection, it's worth adding a note about competition — because the two are quietly intertwined. Whatever niche you're moving into, you will always find someone who's doing something similar.

What do you feel when you meet those people?

There are no right or wrong answers. Years ago, when I first got into the entrepreneurial circle, I saw people in "my" niche as competitors who had already taken the space I wanted — proof that I was late, behind, or simply not good enough. Their presence triggered that old familiar fear: *What if there's no room for me? What if they're better — and I really am worse?*

Most of us walk through life evaluating others in relation to ourselves.

Are they better?

Are they ahead?

Are they more confident, more experienced, more talented?

But what if you started noticing what's good about them – without comparing, instead of engaging in downward comparisons?

Let me give you another example. We all have "our" people — the ones we naturally click with. And then there are people who are just… not ours. The ones we wouldn't invite for coffee. Maybe their energy feels off. Maybe something about them rubs us the wrong way.

And then there are people we actively avoid being in the same circle with because they've shown a side of themselves we simply can't tolerate.

You don't need to feel guilty for not liking everyone. Nobody likes everyone.

But here's the biggest favor you can do for yourself: try to find *one* thing about them that you admire or enjoy. It doesn't have to be huge. Just something that makes them more human.

For example, ask yourself:

If I ran the company, what job would I trust them with?

You may not enjoy pushy people in your personal life — but if you needed a lawyer, wouldn't you want someone who fights like a lion? And the person who feels "too meticulous" in daily life is exactly who you'd trust to run a financial audit.

There's a quiet shift that happens when you stop seeing people as competitors or threats and start seeing them as individuals with their own strengths, gifts, and roles in the world. It sounds simple, almost sentimental, but it's one of the most powerful mindset shifts you can make — especially when you're trying to overcome the fear of rejection. Because if you can find grace for someone you didn't naturally like, you'll eventually find grace for the parts of *yourself* you don't naturally like either.

Every person is good at something.

Every person fits somewhere.

And when you start looking at people with curiosity instead of comparison, something subtle — almost magical — happens: you start seeing your own strengths more clearly.

Because once you recognize that others have their place, you begin to understand that you have yours too.

Their strengths don't diminish yours.

Their path doesn't block yours.

Their success doesn't threaten yours.

As Julia, one of the reinventors, put it: *"I used to think that if someone else was doing the same thing as me, it meant fewer clients for everyone. But the truth is, people choose you because they connect with your energy. They don't come to you just for your exercises, information, or tools — they come for how they feel in your presence. No matter how many people exist in your niche, each of you will naturally attract a different crowd."*

This shift doesn't just make you kinder to others — it makes you kinder to yourself.

You stop trying to be everything, forcing yourself into roles that don't fit. You start seeing rejection as a sign of inadequacy and start seeing it as a simple mismatch.

When you look at others with loving eyes, you learn to look at yourself the same way. And that's when fear begins to fade — not because the world becomes easier, but because you finally understand that there is room for everyone, including you.

Embracing Rejection

Rejection hurts — let's not pretend it doesn't. It stings because you cared, because you tried, because some part of you hoped it would go differently. But when you learn that you're always in control of where you're going — that you're not chasing external approval but something deeper inside yourself — everything shifts. And if you can stay with yourself in those moments instead of abandoning yourself, rejection begins to lose its power.

If you can give your body even a tiny sense of safety again, the world stops feeling like a threat.

If you can separate your worth from someone else's reaction, their "no" stops sounding like a verdict.

If you can slow down and listen beyond the surface, you stop spiraling into old stories that were never true.

If you can build even one safe environment, you finally have a place where you can breathe and grow.

And if you can look at others with loving eyes instead of comparison, you'll eventually learn to look at yourself the same way.

When these shifts settle in, rejection stops being a wall and becomes a doorway. It stops feeling like a threat to your identity and becomes just another piece of information — useful, clarifying, sometimes even freeing. It shows you where you don't belong so you can move toward where you do.

And once you're no longer terrified of being dismissed, you're ready for the next part of reinvention. Because the moment you stop hiding from rejection is the moment you can finally turn outward — and start having a real conversation with the world.

That's where we go next.

The Conversation With the World

Now that you've clarified who you are and reconnected with the people closest to you, it's time to take a step outward. At some point — once you've chosen your direction and gathered a small circle that supports you — you reach a moment when you have to own your path and let the wider world see that you've changed.

Reinvention doesn't happen in isolation. You eventually have to step into rooms where no one knows your story yet, into conversations without shared history, into opportunities that only appear when you're willing to be seen — and introduce the new you.

And yes — that part can feel scary.

Talking to strangers isn't hard because we lack social skills. It's hard because it exposes us. It wakes up old questions: *Will they like me? Am I interrupting? Do I sound foolish? Do I belong here?*

In many workplaces, especially corporate ones, you spend years with the same people. That rhythm becomes familiar, and stepping outside it — online or offline — can feel risky. It can create pressure, especially if you've never seen yourself as someone others naturally gravitate toward.

But connecting with new people isn't about charisma or extroversion. It's not about being impressive. It's about showing up as a human being — not a performer, not a job title, not a polished LinkedIn version of yourself. The only two things you need is warmth and curiosity.

Once you understand how to open up, everything becomes lighter. And it helps to remember this: being welcoming and curious is a skill, not a personality type. No one is born knowing how to show their real self. We learn it — slowly, awkwardly, through practice. Openness is simply the ability to let people see a little more of you at a time: your thoughts, your values, your curiosity, your warmth. The more you practice it, the more natural it feels. And with each small step, the world meets you with more ease, more connection, and more opportunities than the polished version ever could.

This chapter is about that shift.

About speaking to new people in a way that feels human, not strategic.

About forming connections that grow naturally, without pressure.

About opening yourself to recognition and opportunities that match who you're becoming.

About letting the world meet the real you — not the edited version, but the one you've worked hard to reclaim.

What Actually Opens Doors

Throughout your career, you had people who knew your character, your work ethic, your integrity. But when you move countries, you lose that context. In your new environment, no one has years of shared history with you. They don't know your reliability, your competence, or your potential. Your qualifications may not be recognized. Your experience might look thin in this market. The people who once knew your value aren't here to vouch for you.

And here's the real secret of career reinvention. The key to switching careers — or building a business — isn't just building skills.

It's building trust.

Trust from potential employers.

Trust from future customers.

Trust from people you might partner with.

Skills matter, of course. But skills alone don't open doors in a new field. Plenty of people have skills. What opens doors is trust — and a bit of luck.

You've seen it in the stories throughout this book: there is always a moment when someone — a manager, a mentor, a colleague, sometimes even a stranger — takes a chance. Someone opens a door, makes an introduction, vouches for them, or simply says, *"I think you can do this."*

Every woman I interviewed could name that person.

That moment didn't happen by accident. Trust doesn't appear out of thin air. It grows through connection — through the small, human moments where someone gets to know you, even briefly. At some point, these women stepped out — prepared to meet opportunities with no guarantee, both offline and online.

Learning how to build real connections is one of the most important skills of reinvention. According to various job market reports, about 70% of jobs are never publicly advertised and are filled through referrals, internal moves, or direct outreach. That's why you need a wide, active network — keep communicating, making introductions, and staying visible so opportunities can find you.

But let's be honest — being "out there" is challenging.

It's vulnerable.

It's awkward.

It can feel like you're walking into a room where everyone already knows each other and you're the only one holding a plate of snacks with no idea where to stand.

So let's make this easier — maybe even enjoyable.

Because here's the wild thing about the time we live in: you can reach out to literally *anyone*. Anyone.

A CEO. A founder. A researcher. A creator. A person whose work you admire. Someone who inspires you. Someone you want to learn from. Someone you want to collaborate with.

And when you learn how to build real connections, all these people — the CEOs, founders, researchers, creators — can become part of your world. Employers, collaborators, mentors, friends. Your circle. Your network. Your net worth.

Instead of treating this as something scary, try noticing the power in it — the simple, human power of being able to reach out and be received.

And if your first instinct is, "No, thank you, I'm an introvert," or even just a quiet swallow, you're not alone. Most of us feel that way.

Connection isn't a personality trait; it's a skill. You can always improve, one small conversation at a time. That's why we'll start with a few simple ways to connect instantly and authentically — approaches that have worked for the supercommunicators I've met, for me, and for clients who once swore they "weren't good at networking."

Let's begin with the three that change everything.

Hack 1: Open Your Mind to Connecting

When you're navigating reinvention — especially in a new country or a new industry — your instinct might be to shrink, to protect yourself, to stay in the familiar corners of your world. Rejection, uncertainty, and feeling like an outsider can trick you into believing that connection is something you'll get to *later*, once you "figure things out."

But connection *is* what helps you figure things out.

Opening your mind to connecting means loosening the grip of your assumptions:

- that people won't understand you;
- that your accent is a barrier;
- that you have nothing valuable to offer yet;
- that you need to be "ready" before you reach out.

People connect to honesty, not perfection. In fact, research shows that perfection often pushes people away. What draws them in is your curiosity and warmth — the version of you who shows up even while you're still unsure, still learning, still rebuilding.

From Banking to A Building a Business Community (United Kingdom → Netherlands)

Julie moved to the Netherlands in her mid-40s, after more than a decade in banking and several intense years as a contractor in the UK. She arrived without a job, without a plan, and without a community. Her husband's new role brought them here; everything else she had to figure out from scratch.
And this is how she tells her story.

I always say my career has two separate chapters: the UK chapter and the Netherlands chapter. They barely resemble each other.

Back home, my background was sales first, then banking. I come from a town where everyone works for the same bank. Truly—everyone. My mum was thrilled when I finally joined. "At last," she said, "you're doing what everyone else does." I resisted it for ages because it felt so predictable, but eventually I went in.

Banking took me from Yorkshire to Scotland. I met my husband through work, moved north, and did all sorts of roles. Relationship management, analytics, customer

---

service—things that don't always live in the same person, but somehow did in me. I liked talking to people, and I liked spreadsheets. I liked keeping promises. I liked saying early when something wasn't going to plan instead of sweeping it under the table.

I also got made redundant. Twice.

The first time was simple: I worked on-site for a contractor, the contract ended, and that was that. The second time was during the banking crisis. The bank I worked for nearly went under. The government had to step in and arrange a rescue. Sixty thousand people worked there. It was only a matter of time before jobs disappeared. I wasn't devastated—I'd moved around a lot, taken opportunities, met people. I even volunteered to join a project that was separating out a part of the bank that would eventually be sold. People said, "But when it's sold, you won't have a job." And I said, "Yes. That's why I'm going."

After that, I became a contractor. Very pressurized environment. You get paid a day rate, no sick pay, no holiday pay, and when the project ends, you're done. You can be finished after a week. I absolutely loved it. I went in for six months and stayed for three years.

Then everything changed at once. My contract ended, and my husband—who had been contracting for a company based in the Netherlands—was offered a permanent role here. Mid-40s. Time for a midlife crisis. I already had the shiny red car, so why not move countries?

We've been here seven and a half years now.

And I had to start again.

I didn't feel like I was starting from scratch—I felt like I was starting from *below* scratch. I had no idea what I wanted to do. I brainstormed everything. I thought about bringing homeware products I loved into the Dutch market. A friend told me, "The Dutch either buy high-end or HEMA. Nothing in the middle." So that idea died.

I even thought about studying, but I'd missed the window to carry over my old university points, and nothing appealed enough to start from zero.

I didn't know the term "trailing spouse" then. Some people hate it. I didn't mind. I thought, I can call it whatever I want—amazing spouse, adventurous spouse. It was a break from everything: career, routine, identity. My husband traveled constantly, so I was alone a lot. I didn't know anyone. I refused to keep flying back to the UK every time I felt lonely. I told myself: do the difficult thing. Build a life here.

One day, someone from a Facebook group invited me out for coffee. I didn't know her. But it was daylight, in a local café, and I thought, "I'll be safe." She turned out to be a business owner who had looked me up on LinkedIn and thought we might partner together.

Completely random. Completely unexpected.

We met a few more times, worked together on one of her clients, and within four months we decided to go into partnership. We ran that business together for about two and a half years. She was more technical; I brought project management and the front-of-house side. We became online business managers—looking at businesses as a whole, fixing processes, improving systems, managing teams, running conferences, traveling. Things I never imagined doing.

It was exciting. And it felt good to be needed again. Starting a business alone can be lonely, but with a partner, there was always someone to figure things out with.

After COVID, the business got a bit rocky. Maybe we'd outgrown each other. I had already joined an online networking group, even though I didn't understand networking at first. Why do I need to go networking? What's the point? But I found I actually enjoyed it. After COVID, I wanted to see people in real life again.

We decided to separate the business. She continued on her own. I started my own thing: networking and events for solo business owners.

I didn't see anything like it here in the Netherlands, so I created it.

The first event had maybe three people. I kept the ticket price low. I asked for feedback. I learned. I also made a hilarious mistake: I structured the meeting beautifully—introductions, learning, sharing—but forgot to include actual networking. Someone said, "I loved it, but there was no networking." I wanted the ground to swallow me. But that's why you need objective eyes. You can miss the most obvious thing.

Still, when that first event ended, I felt drained in a good way. Relieved. Proud. People came. It wasn't nothing.

Running my own business is nothing like corporate life. In banking, time was rigid. Nine to five. Always something to do. Here, I get to choose. If it's a nice day, I might cycle the long way to the shops. I don't take long lunch breaks, but I could. I block time after events so I can stay and talk to people. It's my timetable now. I'm in charge of it. It doesn't bring in bank-level money, but it brings me choice.

I've been doing this for nearly four years. My Facebook group has grown to over 2,300 people. I now have a business coach because the business still needs work. But I feel optimistic. My word of the year is always resilience. It covers everything.

And the stories that come out of my events—they're what keep me going.

I love bringing people together. I had a man driving for 100 kilometers to attend one of the events. A private driver who genuinely cares about making people's journeys easier—car seats for kids, thoughtful service. Another woman helps newcomers relocate. I said, "You two need to talk." And they did. That's the magic.

Two women met at one of my sessions: an introverted illustrator and a cancer survivor. They ended up getting EU funding to create a children's book for kids going through treatment. I only found out because I saw it on LinkedIn. If they hadn't come to my event, they might never have met.

That's why I do this.

People meet collaborators, clients, friends. Sometimes they meet someone who changes their life. I can't promise that, of course—you have to do the work yourself—but it happens.

I'm not from a family of entrepreneurs. No one in my family has ever owned a business. I had no aunt or uncle to call for advice. I had to figure it out myself. Contracting gave me confidence—when you're paid for your expertise, people listen. Being made redundant hurts the first time. The second time, less. The third time, you're ready for it. Eventually you learn to put your hand up for opportunities instead of waiting for things to happen to you.

Women often underestimate themselves. They look at a job description with five requirements and think, "I can do three, so I won't apply." But those three might make you the ideal candidate. You'll grow into the rest. You're already uncomfortable in a new job—why not push a little further?

Don't be afraid to ask for help. Ask for mentors. Compliment people. Support each other. Women are not competition.

If someone wants to change careers or start something new, I always say: if you've already moved countries, you've already proven you can change. Why stop now? If finances allow, try. If they don't, start on the side. But don't let your title define you. Don't get to 70 and think, "I wish I'd tried."

You only get one life.

And if you don't try, you'll always wonder.

When you open your mind to connecting, you stop seeing people as gatekeepers and start seeing them as allies, mirrors, teachers, and companions on the path. You begin to notice how many others feel exactly like you do — uncertain, hopeful, trying. And suddenly, the world feels less intimidating.

Connection doesn't erase the challenges, but it softens them. It gives you perspective, courage, and a sense of belonging that no job title or achievement can replace. It reminds you that reinvention isn't a solo act — it's a shared human experience.

And it begins with one simple shift: being willing to let people in.

Hack 2: Give Before You Ask

Once you step outside your immediate circle, things suddenly feel more complicated. Inside your circle, people know you. They trust you. They've seen you grow, fail, try again. But the moment you log in to LinkedIn, the doubts show up.

How do I connect with people I don't know? Why would anyone help me? What if I look strange or needy? Is it weird to add strangers on LinkedIn?

It's ironic, because you need other people to support your new career — and you live in a world where you can reach almost anyone with a single message. Yet it still feels awkward.

This awkwardness usually comes from one perspective:

You feel like you're taking without giving.

You're reaching out because you need something — clarity, advice, direction, an opportunity — and that makes you feel exposed. Like you're asking for too much.

But there's a way to rewrite this script.

A while ago, I went to a TEDx event. One talk stood out — not because the speaker was famous, but because she was real, funny, and sharp. As someone who admires excellence, I was impressed. After the event, I added her on LinkedIn and sent a short message telling her what I genuinely appreciated about her talk. No agenda. No expectation.

She replied.

We met for coffee.

Now we're friends.

Not because I "networked," it simply happened.

Another time, I had the idea to invite a creator to one of our events. She was practically a celebrity — a YouTuber with 150,000 subscribers. There was no guarantee she would ever respond. But once the idea landed, I couldn't ignore it. So I wrote her a message, told her I'd been a long-time subscriber, and invited her to speak. Again, no expectations.

Imagine my surprise when not only did she reply — she said yes. And then she went even further and promoted the event to her audience.

These stories aren't about luck or charm. They're about something much simpler: a sincere compliment is still the easiest, most natural way to connect with someone you don't know.

Our problem is that we forget to say these things out loud. When someone is brilliant at what they do, we assume they already know. We rarely take the extra step to say, "Hey, that was really good," even when we genuinely feel it. And yes — sometimes it feels almost too intimate to compliment a stranger. In some cultures, praise automatically sounds like an agenda. You say something kind and they immediately wonder, *What do you want from me?*

The secret to a powerful compliment is having no agenda at all. When you appreciate someone's work simply because it moved you — not because you want anything — the pressure disappears. You're not waiting for a reply or hoping for a result. You're just naming something true. And you can try it and watch what unfolds.

Next time you're around people, try seeing what every person is good at. It might feel strange or a bit unnatural at first, especially if you're not used to it. But once you begin, you'll be surprised by what it does to you. You start noticing beauty everywhere — the way someone explains an idea, the way they show up, the way they care about their craft.

And the most unexpected part is how it changes the way you see yourself. Because when you practice giving genuine appreciation, receiving it becomes natural too. You stop tightening up. You stop hiding. Suddenly, accepting compliments doesn't feel threatening. You let them land. You let yourself be seen.

It's a sign that the different parts of you — the confident one, the unsure one, the ambitious one, the quiet one — are finally learning to stand together.

You're no longer fighting yourself.

You're becoming someone who notices the good in others and allows others — and yourself — to notice the good in you.

Hack 3. Be The Opportunity

It's true that you can reach out to anyone nowadays. That's why the first step is simply knowing who you need. Once you have a direction, everything becomes lighter.

But finding people is the easy 10% of the networking journey.

Most of us know how to search on LinkedIn — that's not the real challenge. The hard part — the other 90% — is this question:

How do I connect with someone when I feel like I have nothing to offer?

How do I reach out when their life looks polished and mine feels uncertain?

How do I start a conversation when I'm the one who needs help?

This is where the fear shows up. Not just fear of rejection, but fear of looking out of place, unworthy, or uninteresting. And that's why the most important mindset shift in career reinvention is this:

When you feel like you have nothing to offer, become someone who offers opportunities.

When I first started working on this book, I wanted to talk to people who had switched careers. But reaching out felt strange. They didn't know me, and I kept wondering why they would share something as intimate as their story with a stranger.

But then I shifted my perspective. I realized I could offer something real: my attention, my curiosity, my empathy, and a space where their experiences could be seen. The story I told myself — that I had nothing to offer — simply wasn't true. Giving them a voice mattered just as much as the stories themselves.

So instead of messaging people with, *"Can you help me figure out my career,"* I wrote a post saying I was looking for people to feature in a book. Same intention. Completely different energy.

This is where many people misunderstand online presence. They think it's about selling, promoting, or pushing themselves forward. That's why "personal brand" feels uncomfortable — because the mind frames it as "me, me, me."

But it's never about you.

It's about the people you serve.

The people you give voice to.

The people you listen to.

When you shift from *seeking opportunities* to *creating them*, everything changes.

What Becoming the Opportunity Gives You

When you stop waiting for someone to open a door for you and start creating something of your own, you are rewiring your mind. You're no longer approaching people from a place of need or uncertainty, but from a place of contribution. That shift affects how you feel, how you show up, and how others respond to you.

Becoming the opportunity isn't just a strategy for meeting people — it reshapes your identity, your confidence, and the way you move through your career. Here's what it gives you:

It gives you back a sense of agency.

Most people feel powerless when they're changing careers. They feel like they're waiting to be chosen, waiting for someone to give them a chance. Becoming the opportunity flips that dynamic. Instead of thinking, "I hope someone notices me," you begin to think, "I can create something worth noticing." That shift alone is incredibly motivating.

It removes the emotional cost of rejection.

When you're asking for something, and get rejected, rejection feels personal. When you're offering an opportunity and get rejected, rejection feels neutral. If someone doesn't respond, it's simply because they're busy — not because you're unworthy. This makes reaching out feel lighter, safer, and more sustainable. Well... not everyone recognizes a golden opportunity when it politely knocks on their inbox.

It attracts the right people naturally.

When you create something — a space, a project, a conversation — you don't have to chase people. People who resonate with your topic, your energy, or your curiosity will come toward you. There's no need to spend hours persuading anyone. You'll find yourselves aligning with ease, and sometimes, you'll gain a new friend along the way.

It clarifies your identity faster than anything else.

Creating something forces you to articulate what you care about. You discover your voice, your interests, your direction — not by thinking, but by doing. And during career reinvention, this becomes especially powerful, because taking action in public is often the missing piece.

It makes you memorable.

Most people reach out with something like *Do you have time for a quick chat?"* or *"Can you help me?"*

While there's nothing wrong with reaching out, the first question our brain is asking is *What's in it for me.* So if you change the wording slightly to highlight the opportunity (*"I'd love to feature your story,"* or *"I'm creating something and your perspective would add so much"*), it could become much more appealing for that other person. When you offer an opportunity, you stand out instantly. People remember the person who gave them a platform, not the person who asked for a favor.

It builds confidence through contribution.

When you create something that includes others, you start seeing yourself differently. Not as someone who is "trying to break into a field," but as someone who is already participating in it. Contribution builds confidence faster than competence. And as people respond to what you're building — appreciating it, engaging with it, growing because of it — you gain a new, steadier way of communicating who you are.

It rewires how you see relationships.

Instead of seeing people as gatekeepers, you start seeing them as collaborators. Instead of seeing yourself as an outsider, you start seeing yourself as a contributor. Instead of waiting for permission, you create your own momentum. This shift speaks to your new identity, facilitating the transition.

It feels good.

This is the simplest and most honest reason. Creating opportunities for others feels meaningful. It gives you energy instead of draining it. It builds relationships that are based on generosity, not transaction. People can feel the difference.

Ways to Become Someone Who Creates Opportunities

To become someone who creates opportunities, you don't need a huge audience. You don't need fame. You don't need permission. You only need to build something — even something small — that gives others a place to show up, contribute, be seen and heard.

Here are ways to do that:

- write a book or a blog;
- start a podcast;
- launch a YouTube channel;
- host small events or meetups (even as a volunteer);
- start a LinkedIn newsletter;
- create a small community around a topic you care about;
- organize panel discussions or online conversations;
- curate resources or recommendations in your field;
- start a "spotlight series" where you highlight others' work.

When you give attention instead of asking for it, reaching out stops feeling weird. As I became a TEDx organizer, overnight I went from being a stranger to being someone who could help others fulfill their dream of speaking on a TEDx stage. That's the power of labels — and the power of creating something bigger than yourself.

Take the points above into consideration. Even with a small following, having a blog or a podcast enables you to reach out to people you admire and invite them into a conversation. People love recognition. They love being heard. And it's easier to make them feel heard when you've built even a tiny stage of your own.

When you become the person who sees others — **you become the opportunity.**

Yes, it takes time. Maybe you'll need help or new skills. But isn't that the point — to build a life that feels fuller, richer, more aligned with who you're becoming?

So what does becoming the opportunity look like for you?

Your Networking Plan

Switching careers isn't about "knowing the right people." It's about building the right conversations — slowly, intentionally, and in a way that feels natural.

Here's a plan that works without forcing you to become someone you're not.

1. Start with the people you already know
Before you look outward, look around.

- Make a list of people in your new field — even if you barely know them.
- Reach out gently: "Hey, I'm exploring a transition into this field, and your journey is fascinating. I'd love to hear how you got started."
- People respond much better to curiosity than pressure.

This step alone opens more doors than people expect.

2. Find the communities where your new field hangs out
Every industry has its "watering holes."

- Meetup groups;
- Slack groups;
- Facebook groups;
- Subreddits;
- Online forums;
- Professional associations;
- Niche communities you only discover once you start looking.

Join a few. Observe first. Then slowly participate. You'll start to pick up the language, the trends, the pain points — and you'll meet people naturally, without forcing anything.

3. Build your LinkedIn presence — slowly and intentionally

You don't need to become a "LinkedIn creator." This is about connecting with people, not performing online. Here's how to start showing up in the spaces that matter:

- Follow people in your new field
- Like and comment on their posts — genuinely, not robotically
- Join events they're promoting
- Send a short message after an event: "Loved your point about X — it really clarified something for me."
- Update your profile so it reflects where you're going, not just where you've been

This is how you start appearing in the right circles — naturally, and without becoming someone you're not.

4. Identify the companies you're genuinely interested in
There are always a few that come to mind immediately.

- Make a list of 10–20 companies you admire
- Follow them on LinkedIn
- Look at who works there
- Reach out to people in roles you're curious about

Don't try to impress — try to understand and connect.

5. Show up in real life
Local events matter more than people think.

- Conferences
- Meetups
- Workshops
- Industry breakfasts
- Talks at coworking spaces

If "networking" is challenging, make a commitment to just show up. Start by talking with just one person — one conversation might be enough to change your entire trajectory.

And let's be honest — after each offline event, turning it into a short LinkedIn post is what builds your authority and visibility. It's the simplest way to show you're in the room, learning, growing, and paying attention.

6. Ask for *conversations*, not jobs

This is where most people go wrong. They jump straight to: *"Are you hiring?"* But that question only works in one context — and it's almost never the first one. Here's a better approach:

Online: ask specific questions based on their profile

Let's be real — when you message people on LinkedIn, people rarely allocate their time to answer a generic question from someone they don't know. Yet they respond when you show you've actually looked at their profile and understand their field.

So instead of broad questions, try something like:

- "I saw you transitioned from X to Y — what helped you make that shift?"
- "I saw that you studied Z. What advice would you give someone who's just beginning that path?"
- "Your project on X caught my eye. I would ask you a few questions for my podcast. Would you be open to a conversation?"

These questions work because they're personal, specific, flattering, and easy to answer. You're not asking for a job. You're asking for insight — *from them*, about *them*.

Offline: go deeper

In real conversations — at events, meetups, workshops — people are much more open to reflective questions. That's where you can ask:

- "How did you get into this field?"
- "What surprised you most about working there?"
- "What do you wish you knew earlier?"
- "What's one misconception people have about this industry?"

People love talking about their journey. And these real, human conversations are the ones that naturally lead to opportunities.

Your Personal Brand

Once you've moved past the networking phase, it's time to polish your online presence so opportunities can start finding you. This online presence is often referred to as your *personal brand.*

You might think "personal brand" is a buzzword reserved for coaches and entrepreneurs. But the reality is different: today, even when you apply for a job, you're often asked for a link to your portfolio, your LinkedIn, or your social media. Employers want to see the results you've produced — and they want to get a sense of who you are before they even invite you for an interview.

But let me guess — this idea of being present online doesn't exactly make you jump with excitement.

That's because the term *personal brand* has been flattened into something loud and self-promotional: shouting "me, me, me," sending pushy emails, "warming up" your audience, and generally annoying people. Of course no one wants to do that.

But here's the shift I want to invite you into:

Your personal brand is the alignment between who you are on the inside and how the world experiences you — the version of you that you've been shaping through every chapter of this book. It's also a consequence, not the goal.

un

Kasia has been many things — a teacher, an executive assistant, a decluttering coach — but underneath, all three roles draw from the same core. They are all about bringing clarity into someone else's world. She helps people make sense of things: their thoughts, their tasks, their physical space. She creates order where there was overwhelm, structure where there was chaos, and confidence where there was uncertainty. At the heart of every role she tried is the same instinct: to guide, to support, and to make someone's life feel lighter and more manageable.

You've probably met other people whose careers feel like a natural extension of who they are. You can sense the alignment immediately. They're not boasting, not overselling, not performing. They're simply themselves — and that authenticity is magnetic.

And you've also felt the opposite: when someone claims they created a product "to help others," but everything about their message reveals it's really about themselves. Or when you've introduced yourself and felt that uncomfortable wobble — unsure whether you're presenting the past version of yourself or the future one you're trying to grow into.

This is why personal branding matters.

Not as a performance — but as a tool.

A tool that helps you build trust and meet your next opportunity.

You might wonder: *Why can't I just skip all this marketing fluff and simply be myself? I'd probably be a very aligned person.*

You can. But you'll miss out on opportunities.

Right now, someone is searching for an employee with your exact strengths — but they can't find you. Someone wants to hire a service like yours — but someone else shows up first. It's like living in the early 1900s, when word of mouth was the only marketing tool. If people don't know you exist, they can't choose you.

If no one knows what you care about, what you're learning, or where you're heading, they can't connect the dots. They can't think of you when opportunities arise. They can't associate you with the field you're moving toward. Reinvention becomes harder not because you lack talent, but because you're invisible in the new space.

And invisibility has a cost: you end up investing enormous effort to get the opportunities you want — without getting results. And not getting results quietly drains you.

Developing your reputation story is the process of intentionally building trust with the people and communities you want to belong to — employers in a specific niche, clients in a particular field, collaborators in a new industry — both online and offline. It's a process that asks you to stay curious, grounded, true to yourself, and willing to enjoy the unfolding of who you're becoming.

And here's the good news: after more than ten years in marketing, I can tell you that there are simple, practical steps that dramatically improve your results. You don't need to become loud, or salesy, or someone you're not. You just need clarity — and a way to let others see it.

Without that clarity, you remain a stranger. And strangers rarely get opportunities.

A personal brand is your story told to the world.

And when your story is consistent — when your inner clarity matches the story you send out — people start trusting you. Not because you're louder or more polished, but because you're aligned.

Why Personal Branding Feels Daunting and How to Overcome It

For many people, the idea of "personal branding" lands with a quiet sense of resistance. It can feel fake, self-promotional, or even a little embarrassing. You might think, *I don't want to sell myself. I just want to do good work.* Or, *Who am I to present myself as an expert?* Or simply, *I don't want to be one of those people online.*

And honestly, I understand that feeling deeply.

My work has always revolved around visibility. I've met the fear of being seen again and again, and along the way I've collected tools that can help you navigate it too.

To overcome something, you first have to understand it. So let's look at why personal branding feels so uncomfortable for so many people.

1. Stepping Into the Spotlight

Personal branding asks you to shift from being an observer to being the subject. It's the same discomfort that comes with public speaking — the moment you step away from the group and everyone's eyes turn toward you. Even if you're naturally social, that moment of separation can feel like exposure.

Your body reacts before your mind does. Your pulse quickens. Your breath shortens. Your brain starts scanning for danger. And it makes sense: for most of your life, you were taught to keep your head down, not draw too much attention, and let your work "speak for itself." Personal branding feels like doing the opposite — and psychologically, that can feel unsafe.

The ancient part of your brain still believes that standing out is risky. It whispers, *If they don't like what they see, we're in trouble.* Rejection feels like a threat, not an inconvenience.

And because this reaction is so old, so instinctive, it doesn't respond to logic. It responds to safety. It responds to familiarity. It responds to the stories you've carried since childhood about what it means to be visible.

2. Cognitive Overload

In a large company, product and marketing roles are split. One team builds the product. Another promotes it.

When I worked in B2B SaaS sales, I saw again and again how differently developers and salespeople talked about the same product. Developers saw every flaw, every outdated framework, every piece of duct tape holding things together. Sales saw the potential, the value, the transformation it offered customers.

When you build your personal brand, you don't get those separate departments. You're both the builder and the promoter. You see your flaws up close, and you're also expected to speak confidently about your strengths. That's a lot for one person.

You're no longer just doing the work; you're also explaining it, framing it, giving it meaning. You're inviting people to look at you more closely. And for many women — especially those raised to be modest, agreeable, or "not too much" — this feels like breaking an unspoken rule.

But remember what you've learned in the previous chapters: once you've met the parts of yourself you used to hide, visibility becomes less threatening. You're no longer afraid of being seen, because you're no longer hiding from yourself.

3. Not Living Up to the Promise

Seth Godin, a marketing guru, once said that people don't buy products — they buy stories, relationships, and magic. And he's right. But when you're the one offering the story, it can feel like a trap.

To build a personal brand, you have to make a promise. You have to say, "This is what I do," or "This is what I help people with," or "This is the value I bring." And immediately, another voice inside you panics: *What if I can't deliver every time? What if I disappoint them?*

It's the same fear product teams have when marketing promises something the developers aren't sure they can build. Except in this case, you're both teams. You're the product and the marketer. You're the one doing the work and the one talking about the work. And that dual role can feel like a conflict of interest.

Underneath it all is the fear of rejection — the fear that someone will say, "You're not as good as you claim to be." By now, you can put this fear in its place and reclaim your voice.

4. Collision With Existing Identities

Personal branding also collides with the identities you've carried for years — both the ones you've given yourself and the ones others have assigned to you. Maybe people know you as "the reliable one," "the quiet one," "the safe one." Maybe you've known yourself that way too. So when you start saying things like, "I'm building a coaching practice," or "I'm moving into design," it can feel like you're contradicting the story everyone has about you — including your own.

Your nervous system reads that as risk. Risk of judgment. Risk of rejection. Risk of being called out as "not enough." This taps into something ancient: our need to belong. For most of human history, being excluded from the group meant death. So your brain treats social rejection as a real threat, not a symbolic one.

On top of that, there's the fear of inconsistency. Once you say, "This is who I am," it can feel like you're locking yourself into a box. What if you change your mind? What if you grow? What if you're wrong? The desire to be consistent — normally a strength — becomes a trap.

And then there's the quiet shame that whispers, *Who do you think you are?* You know your own backstage. You know the doubts, the unfinished projects, the days you barely held it together. Presenting a confident version of yourself can feel dishonest.

If you're moving into self-employment, the discomfort intensifies. Suddenly, you're not just doing a job — you *are* the product. Your ideas, your presence, your story become part of what people are buying. That can feel exposing.

5. Visibility is Vulnerability

Many people equate authenticity with staying small, staying quiet, staying unpolished. They fear that if they shape their story or choose their words carefully, they're being fake. But these are not the same. Authenticity isn't staying in the shadows — it's the alignment between what you believe and what you show.

Personal branding feels uncomfortable when it's framed as a performance. It becomes far less so when you see it as an act of translation.

You're not inventing a character. You're translating your inner world — your values, your strengths, your direction — into signals other people can understand. You're making it easier for them to see the real you.

Of course, that doesn't momentarily erase the discomfort. It simply explains it. You're pushing against old rules: don't stand out, don't claim too much, don't risk being seen and then judged. You're challenging your remembered identity — the version of you who stayed safe by staying small. And you're renegotiating your reflected identity — the way others have always known you. No wonder it feels strange.

But remember: it's your task to show up. It's their task to react to how you show up. Feeling uncomfortable doesn't mean you're being inauthentic. It often means you're crossing a threshold — moving from being defined by others to defining yourself, from being passively perceived to being consciously understood.

In the next chapter, we'll explore what a personal brand truly is — and what it absolutely isn't — so you can approach this work with clarity, confidence, and a grounded sense of self-trust.

The Big Secret of Personal Branding

One of the biggest reasons personal branding feels uncomfortable is that it seems like you're making everything about yourself. And for many people — especially those raised to be modest, thoughtful, and competent — this "me-me-me" messaging feels wrong on a very instinctive level. It feels self-absorbed. It feels like bragging. It feels like you're asking for attention you haven't earned. Even the phrase *personal brand* can sound like you're becoming a product, which is the last thing most people want.

The real truth though is this: a personal brand that is built around you is not a personal brand at all. It's just a biography. And biographies rarely move anyone to action. They don't answer the only question every hiring manager, every client, every collaborator is silently asking:

"Can I trust this person with my task?"

Most people approach personal branding the same way they write their CV, cover letter, or LinkedIn profile: by making it about themselves.

- *I graduated from…*
- *I have experience in…*
- *I'm passionate about…*

There's nothing wrong with this. I've done it too. It's our natural instinct: we expect our CV to reflect *our* journey.

However, a hiring manager reading your CV isn't thinking, "Whose passion can I support today?" They're thinking, "Who can fix this?" "Who can take this off my plate?" "Who can make my team stronger without adding work?"

Even when you're switching careers, the decision to hire you is still made by a human being who has deadlines, pressure, and a gap to fill. If you only talk about yourself, you're asking them to do the translation work — to figure out how your story fits their needs. Most won't.

This is why marketers avoid talking only about features. We first translate them into benefits, and then go beyond that connecting it to values and mission. A feature says: "This vacuum has a HEPA filter." A benefit says: "You can finally breathe in your own home without sneezing."

Same truth, but different focus. One is about the product. The other is about the person using it. Apple mastered this. They didn't say, "This iPod has 5GB of storage." They said, "1,000 songs in your pocket."

Make this shift, and people will understand why they need you easily.

Applying This to Your Personal Brand

You're still talking about yourself — you can't avoid that — but you're doing it in a way that answers the only question the other person truly cares about: how does this help me?

For example:

- **Instead of:** "I'm transitioning into UX because I love creativity and problem-solving."
- **Try:** "I help teams understand what their users actually need, so they stop building features no one wants."

- **Instead of:** "I've worked in HR for 12 years."
- **Try:** "I help companies hire people who stay, grow, and actually enjoy being there."

- **Instead of:** "I'm passionate about coaching."
- **Try:** "I help people who feel stuck in their careers find direction."

- Same person. Same skills. Different focus.

What building a personal brand entails?
So what does building a personal brand actually involve?
Below are the core elements you'll eventually create. These are the pieces that make your story coherent, recognizable, and aligned with where you're going next.

1. Your story
2. Your uniqueness statement
3. Your target audience
4. Your 30-second self-presentation
5. Your extended introduction
6. Your portfolio (CV)
7. Your online presence
8. Your visual identity
9. Your testimonials
10. Your emotional signature

Let's get through each of these so that you make notes.

1. Your Story

By now, you've spent time exploring your identities, your strengths, and the parts of your past that shaped who you are today. You've met the voices that held you back and the ones that helped you move forward. You've gathered pieces of your story — some clear, some still forming — and you probably have a sense of the direction you want to grow into.

Now it's time to turn that into a narrative. A story.

If you didn't create your story in one of the previous exercises, now it's time to allocate a few hours to create it. Your story is the foundation of your personal brand. It's the thread that connects where you've been to where you're going, and the piece that helps other people understand how your experience translates into value for them. This is where you stop describing your past as a collection of unrelated pieces and start showing how each chapter taught you something that supports the work you want to do next.

While switching careers, many of us unintentionally tell our story from a place of doubt — explaining why we're not fully qualified yet, why we're still learning, why we're unsure. I want you to try something different. Tell the story of how your life unfolded in a way that prepared you for this next step. Tell the story of the skills you gained, the patterns you noticed, the problems you naturally gravitated toward solving. Tell the story of why you're qualified, not why you're hesitant.

You don't need to be the most qualified person in the room. You just need a story that makes sense — to you first, and then to others.

There is no "correct" length or format. If one page feels right, write one page. If you feel the need to write twenty pages, write twenty. If your story wants to become a book, let it. You can also use any story from this book as an example. The point isn't the length; it's the clarity that comes from putting it on paper.

2. Your Uniqueness Statement

Once you have your story — the thread that connects where you've been to where you're going — on paper the next step is to distill it into something smaller and sharper. Something that helps people understand, in just a few words, what makes you different from the dozens of others who might have a similar background or similar ambitions.

This is your uniqueness statement — a simple, grounded way to express what makes you *you*. When you're switching careers, it's easy to feel like you're the one who must catch up or prove yourself. But you already carry something no one else has: your mix of experiences, superpowers, values, and the way you naturally solve problems. That mix is your uniqueness.

A uniqueness statement isn't about being "the best." It's about being clear on how people benefit from working with you. It's the difference between saying, "I'm good with people," and, "I help people feel safe enough to tell the truth." Or between, "I'm analytical," and, "I see patterns in chaos that help teams make decisions faster." Or, "I'm creative," and, "I turn vague ideas into clear, workable concepts."

For career switchers, this matters even more. In a new field, you don't yet have the familiar labels or job titles. What you *do* have is your perspective — the way your past shapes how you solve problems now. Your uniqueness statement is where you articulate that bridge.

For now, your task is simple: notice the patterns in your story. The strengths that keep showing up. The problems you naturally take on. The way people describe you when they're grateful. Somewhere in that mix is the essence of what makes you, you.

3. Your Target Audience

Once you know your story and what makes you unique, the next step is understanding who all of this is for. A personal brand only becomes meaningful when it connects to the people who benefit from your work. Without that connection, even the strongest story stays abstract.

This is where many career switchers get lost. You focus on explaining your transition or proving your competence and forget the most important part: your work exists to help someone.

Instead of thinking, *How do I present myself?* you begin asking, *In which way their life or work becomes easier when I show up?* That question brings clarity. It also brings humility. You stop trying to appeal to the whole world and start focusing on the people who genuinely need what you bring.

So who do you help and why?

For employees, your target audience might be the team you stabilize, the manager who is overloaded, the projects you bring order to, or the chaos you turn into structure. For self-employed people, it might be clients who share a specific struggle, a stage of growth, or a goal you know how to guide them through.

The "why" matters just as much as the "who." Why these people? Why these problems? Why does this work matter to you? When you understand that, your communication becomes clearer, your decisions easier, and your brand grounded in service rather than self-promotion. You're still talking about yourself — your skills, your experience, your story — but the focus shifts toward the people who benefit from it.

For now, your task is simple: identify the people you genuinely want to help — the ones whose challenges make sense to you, whose struggles you recognize, and whose progress you care about. When you build your brand around them, everything else starts to fall into place.

4. Your 30-Second Self-Presentation

Once you know who you help and why, the next step is learning how to introduce yourself in a way that feels natural, confident, and clear. This is your 30-second self-presentation — a small, portable version of your story you can use in conversations, networking, interviews, or any moment when someone asks, "So, what do you do?"

Think of it not as a way to promote yourself, but as a way to connect with people. Here's a simple structure that helps people understand you quickly at networking events:

- **Who you are** — name and profession you're stepping into now.
- **What you do** — the type of work you focus on.
- **Who you do it for** — the people or organizations you help.
- **How you help** — the problem you solve or the value you bring.
- **What kind of help you're looking for right now** — the opportunity, direction, or task you're exploring.

You main goal is becoming a magnet for opportunities. A clear introduction gives the other person something concrete to work with.

Example 1 — Career switcher into UX design

"I'm Anna. I used to work in marketing, and now I'm transitioning into UX design. I help mid-size product teams understand how people make decisions, so they can build features that actually get used. I'm currently looking for roles in user research or early-stage product discovery at companies that are scaling and need clearer customer insights."

Example 2 — Someone starting their own business

"I'm Sofia, and I've recently started my own brand-strategy studio. I help early-stage founders turn their ideas into clear, compelling stories that attract the right customers. I'm looking to support small startups or solo founders who need help shaping their messaging before they launch. Do you know someone I could help?"

For now, don't worry about perfect wording. Focus on the structure. Start shaping your own version — one that feels honest and grounded.

5. Your Extended Introduction

Your extended introduction is your answer to the classic interview opener: "Tell me about yourself." It's the longer, fuller version of your story — the one that shows who you are now, where you come from, and where you're heading. This extended introduction can include your background, what you do best, your approach, what motivates you, and a few personal details that make you memorable and human.

The hardest part of a longer introduction is deciding what actually belongs in it. Any of us could talk about our lives for hours. The real skill is making it intentional — and clear — for the people listening.

For example:
"I'm Anna, and right now I help teams bring clarity to messy processes and create structure. I work best with teams that are growing fast and need someone who can steady the environment and make things feel manageable again. My background in hospitality taught me to stay calm under pressure, anticipate needs early, and over time, I realized I'm drawn to building systems that make work easier for everyone.

I'm moving toward operations roles where I can support sustainable growth. And on a more personal note, people are always surprised that I can recognize 37 languages just by hearing them — it's my favorite party trick and probably the most unexpected thing about me."

6. Your Portfolio

It's easy to treat a CV like a timeline — a record of everything you've done. But a strong personal brand uses the CV more like a portfolio: a curated selection of experiences that support the story you're telling today.

Your CV isn't just about where you've been. It's about the direction you're choosing now. Here are a few ideas to explore that can help reinforce your new identity.

1. Choose experiences that support your direction

If you look closely at your experience, you'll notice certain moments that support your future direction — the ones that make your transition make sense. A few places to explore:

- Highlight roles where you used the skills you want to use now.
- Bring forward projects that show your strengths in action.
- Downplay or remove experiences that pull your story in the different direction.

For example, if you're moving into project coordination, emphasize moments where you organized, structured, or aligned people — even if your title was something completely different. Think of a system you built for your team, a process you improved, a workshop you led, or a volunteer experience that demonstrates your strengths.

2. Translate your past into the language of your future

Every field has its own vocabulary. Your job is to translate your experience into the language of the field you're entering. That's why it's worth paying close attention to the words you use. When you describe your work in terms that mirror the job descriptions you're targeting — and when you highlight your transferable skills explicitly, not subtly — you make it easier for recruiters, future managers, or clients to connect the dots. What you're really doing is helping people understand how your past fits into their world. The "it's always about them" perspective applies here too.

3. Let your values subtly shape the way you write

Your CV doesn't need to say "I value empathy" or "I value clarity." It's far more powerful to show your values through your actions. If you claim to care about detail but your CV has four errors, the message cancels itself out. Actions speak louder than statements.

- If you value clarity → write clean, simple bullet points;
- If you value people → highlight communication and support;
- If you value impact → emphasize outcomes and improvements.

4. Think of your CV as a living document

Your CV evolves with you and shifts as your direction becomes clearer. It's very normal to change it. So feel free to update it every time you gain a new insight about your strengths, remove things that no longer represent who you are, and add projects that reflect your new path.

7. Your Visual Identity

Your visual identity doesn't need to be fancy. It just needs to be consistent. A single, professional-looking photo — clear, friendly, and true to who you are — is enough to make your presence feel coherent across platforms. One simple strategy most people overlook is using the same avatar photo everywhere. When your

LinkedIn, WhatsApp, email, Slack, Zoom, and website all show the same image, you create instant recognition — and people remember you more easily.

8. Your Online Presence

Once you've clarified your story — your direction, your strengths, your values, your mission — the next step is to let these insights shape your online presence and create a space where your identity feels visible, coherent, and easy for others to understand.

Whether it's a LinkedIn profile or a website, your online presence becomes a mirror of who you're becoming. And now that you have the core pieces — your uniqueness statement, your one-minute introduction, your extended introduction, your curated CV — you can start building these reflections with intention.

- Write a LinkedIn headline that reflects where you're going;
- Use your "About" section to introduce the new you;
- Edit your experience section so it supports the new direction;
- Pin work in your "Featured" section;
- Share what you're learning or building to show you're in motion;
- Make connecting with new people a steady part of your routine;
- Comment regularly so your voice becomes familiar in the spaces you care about.

9. Your Testimonials

We all wish testimonials would just appear, but most of the time you simply have to ask. If you're job-hunting, reach out to a few people from your past and ask them to leave a LinkedIn recommendation — and make it easier by writing one for them first. Some will ask what you'd like highlighted, so be ready to share what supports your new direction.

If you're an entrepreneur, the easiest way to gather testimonials is to offer a free product sample, a workshop, or a trial — and let people know upfront that you'd appreciate feedback or a short testimonial afterward.

In the end, testimonials appear when you create an easy path for people to share their experience — and when you're willing to ask.

10. Your Emotional Signature

You can have the strongest CV, the clearest story, the best proof of work — but people remember one thing above everything else: how you made them feel.

Maya Angelou captured it perfectly: *"People will forget what you said, people will forget what you did, but people will never forget how you made them feel."*

Your emotional signature is the atmosphere you create around you.

It's the energy you bring into a room. It's the tone you set in a conversation. It's the way people feel after interacting with you — calmer, clearer, inspired, supported, energized, understood.

It's good when you're aware of what you bring to the table.

Here are a few ideas to explore:

1. How do people feel after talking to you?

Do they feel safe, or motivated, or tightened? Your emotional imprint becomes part of your brand whether you choose it or not.

2. How do you show up in social settings?

Not the polished version — the everyday one. Do you listen more than you speak? Do you bring calm or intensity? Do you make people feel included?

3. What atmosphere do you naturally create?

Everyone has a "default setting." Is yours structure or warmth? Momentum or ease? Humor or focus?

Opportunities don't come from documents. They come from people.

People trust you because of how you show up. People remember you because of how you made them feel. When you understand the experience you create, you can use that awareness to place yourself in the right rooms.

Final Word

Personal branding isn't about polishing yourself into something artificial. It's about aligning who you are with how you show up so that people can connect with you quicker. Still, it can feel a little staged in the beginning. You want people to meet you as a whole person, not just a carefully selected slice — and choosing which parts of yourself to show can feel unfamiliar at first.

But that's what happens: the number of people who truly know you is limited. Renée, one of the reinventors, described this beautifully in our conversation: *"These days, I see myself more like a tree. It grows in many directions. A tree has many parts — trunk, leaves, branches, fruit. Some people will only be interested in one part, others in another. But my wonderful partner, my children, and my close friends are probably the only ones who see the whole picture. I'm learning how to be strong — how not to be blown over so easily, like I have been in the past."*

People around you only ever see pieces. But in your own life, you hold the whole picture — many parts, many strengths, many stories. None of them are wrong. Most people will only see one of those parts at a time, depending on the moment, the relationship, or the opportunity. That's not inauthentic. It's simply how life works.

What matters is that the right people — and the right opportunities — can find the part of you that speaks to them.

Because that's how opportunity actually moves:

Someone remembers you.

Someone recommends you.

Someone thinks of you when a door opens.

A single interaction leaves a positive impression, and that impression becomes the bridge to your next step. And when connecting with people becomes a regular practice, it always leads somewhere — often in ways you don't expect.

This is Where I Belong

Reinvention begins with making choices that are rooted in who you are. When your identity, beliefs, superpowers, and values become your North Stars, you start moving with intention. Those choices shape a direction that feels like home.

At the beginning of this book, a simple question appeared: What makes you *you*? By now, you've seen that identity isn't one thing. It's a layered, living system shaped by:

- your body
- your cultural and family background
- how you see yourself
- how others see you
- how you connect with people
- the choices you make every single day

And when you rebuild your life — in a new country, a new culture, or a new chapter — you rebuild every one of these layers. What you may not have realized before is that most of these layers are within your control. Your new life and career aren't built from the cards you were handed, but from the choices you make with them.

Throughout this journey, I was lucky to connect with women from all over the world. And I fell in love with each of them — their courage, their contradictions, their doubts, their brilliance. Listening to their stories felt like collecting pieces of myself I didn't know I had lost. Their stories, told with honesty, helped me see myself with more compassion — and I hope they helped you see yourself with more kindness too.

The idea for this book began with a reinvention of my own. I had moved to the Netherlands in 2021, hoping to grow a startup — an extension of my seven-year business reselling and authenticating designer handbags. I wasn't passionate about it anymore, but it paid the bills, and at that moment, that felt like enough.

Then, in 2022, the war began.

And life split into "before" and "after."

Suddenly, war wasn't something happening "somewhere." I had nightmares for weeks — broken houses, people hurt, everything collapsing. I lost half of my business because my inventory was still in Russia. All I needed was a bit of safety, so I desperately wanted to find a job. But the visa I had — issued in a different world — was an entrepreneur's visa. It didn't allow me to be employed.

My background was in product marketing, business development, training, entrepreneurship, leadership — apparently, that was too much. I applied everywhere, hoping some company would sponsor me, but my experience was "too diverse" to justify a visa. Consultants emphasized how "non-standard" my case was and insisted I should focus on a single role to fit into their box. So, they asked, what do you want to be?

What a strange question. In 35 years, the idea of an "ideal role" had never crossed my mind. I simply moved toward the roles where there was a natural fit. Growing up in a home without a toilet inside, the only goal was to escape that insecurity, so hard work became the default. I loved every job I had, but I never gave myself the luxury of pausing to ask what I truly wanted.

And definitely not in a moment like this. At that point, I couldn't even think about giving myself permission to look for purpose. And if someone had taken a snapshot of why, it would look like this.

The war collided with an identity crisis. Every morning I hoped I would wake up to the news that the war had ended, and every morning my heart broke again. It was like the world was going up in flames, and you couldn't do anything about it. All you could do was doomscroll the news every day, shaking from anxiety. I volunteered and helped wherever I could, but nothing touched the deeper sadness underneath.

Being Russian became a burden. The officials represented something completely opposite to who I was. They made sure our group wasn't represented by anyone. Most of the people who tried to speak for democratic forces had been killed or jailed long before. It felt like we, as Russians who wanted peace, hardly existed, as if we had to prove our very existence — and our normality — to ourselves day after day. Back then, the sentiment against Russians was strong, and I didn't have the strength to push back, even inside myself. Staying silent felt safer, as if I didn't deserve a voice. And at the same time, we weren't welcome back either. It wasn't safe anymore. We had lost our home.

On top of that, I was ashamed of not being able to find a job. I had years of international experience, spoke several languages, and built a business. Yet suddenly none of it seemed to matter. With AI rising, even my strongest skill — finding the right words — felt replaceable.

My portfolio was a weird blend of marketing, content creation, communication, training, YouTube, entrepreneurship, sales, leadership, performances, and humor. And every single career option seemed to require erasing another big part of me. If I wanted to become a leader, I had to erase the inner performer. If I wanted to look for a job, I had to erase the entrepreneur. And my Russian background felt like something I had to erase in any scenario.

All of that made me question not only my experience but my values too. Has everything I believed in — hope, humanity, connection, collaboration — been wrong? Maybe it really was as simple as this: might makes right. It didn't feel that people like me were even needed in this world.

At the same time, I was in midlife. After several years of entrepreneurship, I wasn't just searching for a job. I wanted meaning. I wanted something that would define my next 10 years. Something worth committing to.

So where did I even fit?

I was scrolling through YouTube when a video popped up: "Tucker's Masterclass in Journalism." I already knew the context — an American reporting from Moscow — and since it was about journalism, I clicked out of curiosity. A lovely gentleman in his sixties appeared on the screen. It was Jon Stewart and The Daily Show — my first time consciously seeing it.

By the end of the video, I was in complete awe of how sharp every phrase was. Hilarious, incisive, deeply human, well-researched, and full of heart. But what I didn't expect at all was that it made me feel heard. Moreover, the pieces I believed could never coexist were right in front of me — journalism, humor, articulation, and serious topics, all held together by truth, humanity, intelligence, tenacity, and courage.

And under the video, there were hundreds of comments, saying that they needed that voice — a voice that was smart, funny, kind, and human.

That day reminded me of the power of voice. I grew up in a country where people don't have a voice. Where you're expected to stay small and conform. Where they teach how to name certain things, what to make of them, and punish you for not following through. Where being human now means being a "traitor," and a desire to change something means you're dangerous and need to be taken care of. Where you learn very quickly that you can now face jail time for just typing the word "peace."

But I always wanted to find the courage to claim my voice back. That's why I wanted to be a journalist many years ago in the first place.

Slowly, I realized that not only my job is to find the right words, I also care about strengthening my own voice — and helping others strengthen theirs. Through writing. Through videos. Through TEDx. Through public speaking. Through this book. To cultivate communication that brings people together across cultures — helping them listen, collaborate, and build connections that lift each other up.

And yes — you can't always change every single thing in the world just with your voice. But you can start with yourself and see what happens.

So there it was. My transition into being a speaker and communication coach wasn't fast or easy. I started helping people with job interviews and presentations — mostly non-native speakers. And for a long time the voice inside me whispered: *How can you call yourself a communication coach in English when you sometimes mix up tenses or forget words?*

Yet communication was the biggest thing where I could feel meaning, so I walked into it with my eyes closed. And while I was suffocating under my own doubt and self-criticism, people kept trusting me.

Some complimented me when I was raw and vulnerable.

Some offered me speaking gigs.

Some introduced me to others.

Some gave me a chance when I needed it most.

And I am still overwhelmed with gratitude. Because when you're rebuilding your life from scratch in a new country, every small act of kindness can be life-changing. When I wasn't ready to offer myself that kindness, I'm grateful that other people around me could see something in me.

Soon another thing became clear: reinvention happens through people. It's not a solo act. Every woman in this book had someone who stood beside her. They offered advice, opened a door, or simply said, "I see you." Their kindness created ripples. So as much as we admire the courage of reinventors, we should also celebrate the people who made that reinvention possible, and possibly try to spread this kindness further.

My hope is that this book helped you release some of the pressure you've been carrying. That it reminded you that starting a new life — in a new environment, a new culture, a new identity — is one of the hardest things a human being can do. And yet here you are. Trying. Choosing. Becoming.

Despite how lonely immigration can feel, I hope that these stories showed you that you are not alone. In 2024, there were 304 million international migrants — 3.7% of the global population. You're a part of a global community of people who dared to begin again. As you start seeing people around you as mirrors, allies, and sources of strength, I hope you begin to see yourself in a different light — softer, kinder, and far more capable than you've been taught to believe.

Although our cultures and lives are different, across countries and cultures, the reinventors in this book shared the same dreams.

Every person wants to belong.

Every person wants to feel enough.

Every person wants to be recognized.

These aren't women's needs or men's needs. Not Western or Eastern needs.

They are human needs.

And when we recognize them in ourselves, and in one another, the distance between us shrinks.

This book is a love letter to every expat and immigrant — and to anyone who has ever had the courage to begin again. Whether you crossed borders or crossed an invisible threshold inside yourself, you made a choice that required more bravery than most people will ever understand.

As you move forward, remember this: by reinventing yourself, you also reinvent the world around you. Every time you choose compassion over criticism, empathy over judgment, connection over suspicion — including toward yourself — you make the world a little less divided and a little more human. So choose your next story based on the world you'd love to live in, not the one you're living in now.

And, finally, if your story isn't in this book, it's not because it's less. It simply means our paths haven't crossed in the right time. If you'd like to share your story with other reinventors, you're welcome to contact our team at reinventohub@gmail.com.

Many people share similar skills.

Many people share similar experiences.

But no one has your story. And you're writing it throughout life.

So claim it — in your voice.

Further Reading

Primary books and classics referenced in the text

- **Sandberg, Sheryl.** *Lean In: Women, Work, and the Will to Lead.* New York: Alfred A. Knopf, 2013.
- **Csikszentmihalyi, M.** *Flow: The Psychology of Optimal Experience.* New York: Harper & Row, 1990.
- **Tannen, D.** *You Just Don't Understand: Women and Men in Conversation.* New York: William Morrow, 1990.
  Tannen, D. *That's Not What I Meant!: How Conversational Style Makes or Breaks Relationships.* New York: Morrow, 1986/1987.
- **Gilbert, D.** *Stumbling on Happiness.* New York: Alfred A. Knopf, 2006.
- **Goldsmith, M.** *Mojo: How to Get It, How to Keep It, How to Get It Back.* New York: Hyperion, 2007.
- **Rosenthal, R., & Jacobson, L.** *Pygmalion in the Classroom: Teacher Expectation and Pupils' Intellectual Development.* New York: Holt, Rinehart & Winston, 1968.
- **Cialdini, R. B.** *Influence: The Psychology of Persuasion.* New York: Harper Business, 2006.
- **Asch, S. E.** "Effects of group pressure upon the modification and distortion of judgment." In H. Guetzkow (Ed.), *Groups, Leadership and Men.* Pittsburgh: Carnegie Press, 1951.
- **Asch, S. E.** "Opinions and social pressure." *Scientific American,* 193(5), 1955, 31–35.
- **Asch, S. E.** "Studies of independence and conformity: I. A minority of one against a unanimous majority." *Psychological Monographs,* 70(9), 1956, 1–70.
- **Gilovich, T., Medvec, V. H., & Savitsky, K.** "The Spotlight Effect in Social Judgment: An Egocentric Bias in Estimates of the Salience of One's Own Actions and Appearance." *Journal of Personality and Social Psychology,* 78(2), 2000, 211–222. *On how people overestimate how much others notice them.*

- **Pronin, E., & Kruger, J.** "The Introspection Illusion." In *Advances in Experimental Social Psychology,* Vol. 41, Elsevier, 2009 (chapter). *On limits of introspection and self-assessment.*
- **Feldman, J. M.** "Self-presentation and fair treatment: The effect of self-presentational motivation on intentional impression management." *Basic and Applied Social Psychology,* 1(2), 1979, 131–146.
- **Aries, E., & Leet-Pellegrini, H.** "Sex differences in interaction: A reexamination." *Sex Roles,* 9, 1983, 409–429.

Organizational reports, data, and contemporary workplace research

- **U.S. Bureau of Labor Statistics**. Employee Tenure in 2024. U.S. Department of Labor, Bureau of Labor Statistics, 2024.
- **LinkedIn Economic Graph**. Work Change Report: AI Is Coming to Work. LinkedIn, 2025.
- **U.S. Bureau of Labor Statistics**. Number of Jobs, 2014. U.S. Department of Labor, Bureau of Labor Statistics, 2014.
- **World Economic Forum**. The Future of Jobs Report 2023. World Economic Forum, 2023.
- **McKinsey Global Institute**. Jobs Lost, Jobs Gained: Workforce Transitions in a Time of Automation. McKinsey & Company, 2017 (updated 2024).
- **Gallup.** *State of the Global Workplace 2025.* Gallup, 2025. *Annual global employee engagement and workplace trends report.*
- **Pew Research Center.** Fry, R., & Aragão, C. "Gender pay gap in U.S. has narrowed slightly over 2 decades." Short reads, March 4, 2025. *Recent data on the U.S. gender pay gap.*
- **Textio.** *Language Bias in Performance Feedback: 2022 Data Analysis and Survey Results.* Textio, 2022.
- **Harvard Business School Working Knowledge.** Francesca Gino, "How Women Can Learn from Even Biased Feedback," Sept 1, 2021. *Practical guidance on extracting learning from biased feedback.*
- **Harvard Business Review.** Tara Sophia Mohr, "Why Women Don't Apply for Jobs Unless They're 100% Qualified," Aug 25, 2014.
- **World Economic Forum.** *Future of Jobs Report 2023* and related articles on multiple careers and skills (May 2023).
- **World Bank / ICP / Poverty updates.** Foster, Jolliffe, Lakner, et al., *Global poverty revisited using 2021 PPPs* (Policy Research Working Paper No. 11137), 2025; International Comparison Program (ICP) 2023 results; World Bank June 2025 updates. (World Bank publications, 2023–2025.)
- **Gilovich, T., & Savitsky, K.** "The Spotlight Effect and the Illusion of Transparency." *Current Directions in Psychological Science.*

- **Textio press release and Business Wire coverage** summarizing the 2022 report on biased feedback.
- **World Economic Forum** article "Workers set for multiple careers as jobs demand new skills," May 2, 2023.
- **Ministry of Health, Labour and Welfare.** (2025). *Annual Report on the Aging Society: Statistics on Centenarians in Japan.* Government of Japan.
- **U.S. Census Bureau.** (2024). *American Community Survey: Centenarian Population Estimates.* U.S. Department of Commerce.
- **United Nations Department of Economic and Social Affairs.** (2024). *World Population Prospects: Global Centenarian Estimates.* United Nations.
- Waldinger, R., & Schulz, M. (2023). *The Good Life: Lessons from the World's Longest Scientific Study of Happiness.* Simon & Schuster.
- **Burnett, B., & Evans, D.** *Designing Your Life: How to Build a Well-Lives, Joyful Career.* New York: Knopf, 2016. *Practical design thinking applied to career reinvention.*
- **Mohr, T. S.** *Playing Big: Find Your Voice, Your Mission, Your Message.* 2014. *On women's leadership and risk-taking; connects to the "apply only if 100% qualified" theme.*
- **Brynjolfsson, E., & McAfee, A.** *The Second Machine Age: Work, Progress, and Prosperity in a Time of Brilliant Technologies.* New York: W. W. Norton, 2014. *Context for AI and skill displacement discussions.*
- **Susskind, R., & Susskind, D.** *The Future of the Professions.* Oxford University Press, 2015. *On how technology reshapes professional roles.*
- **Diener, E.** "Subjective Well-Being: The Science of Happiness and a Proposal for a National Index." *American Psychologist,* 55, 2000, 34–43. *Used in chapters on meaning, satisfaction, and midlife purpose.*
- **Deci, E. L., & Ryan, R. M.** *Self-Determination Theory: Basic Psychological Needs in Motivation, Development, and Wellness.* New York: Guilford Press, 2017.
- **Deci, E. L., & Ryan, R. M.** *Intrinsic Motivation and Self-Determination in Human Behavior.* New York: Plenum, 1985.